WHY AM I HERE? THE PARSIMONIOUS ALTER EGO vs ME AGAINST THE WORLD
Regenerated Edition

KAHAN TAZADAQ SHAH

Copyright © 2023 Kahan Tazadaq Shah Regenerate Jue 2024

All rights reserved.

ISBN: 9798393807702

DEDICATION

This Book is dedicated to those that were scorned and told that they would be failures This book is to be used to overcome the inner me, which is the enemy of self-development, the hindrance to success, and a blueprint for self-destruction. Most folk peer outside of themselves seeking someone to blame for their failures as a measure of comfort, as a pillow of rest. Ignoring the war that is active within one; own mind. An aphorism worth repeating is the inner me is the enemy.

The world in mind. If you master your mind, you can master the body, and overcome adversity with faith, discipline, and consistency. Hence you will be armed with the capacity to travel in whichever direction you desire, success or failure, the world is mind. The foul mouth Kahan, so you know who said it; Kahan Tazadaq, the foul mouth priest. "Matthew 9: 28After Jesus had entered the house, the blind men came to Him. "Do you believe that I am able to do this?" He asked. "Yes, Lord," they answered. 29 Then He touched their eyes and said, "According to your faith will it be done to you." 30 And their eyes were opened. Jesus warned them sternly, "See that no one finds out about this!" To the limitations of your mind.

CONTENTS

	Acknowledgments	i
1	Never Broken: The Courts, The Struggle On Being a Man	1
2	The World is Mind Cultivate it	24
3	While the Majority of the World is Sleeping, I am Suffering for Success	35
4	Feminism Is Manipulating Liberty and Justice	49
5	The Process of Evolution and Growth always Attain with Pain, Struggle, and Difficulty	61
6	Birthing You Back into the Mind of YHWH (God)	82
7	Manufacturing Kahan Tazadaq Being Successful Is the Best Revenge	102
8	Owe No Man Anything But to Love Discharge That Shit! Buy A Home Without Money	113
9	Perfecting the Five-Step Discharge Process	164
10	Knowing Who You Are and The Divine Will Of Yahuah (God) Secured Creditor	227
11	How the Court System Works Understand Contract And You Win	310

DISCLAIMER:

The information provided in this book does not, and is not intended to, constitute legal advice; instead, all information, content, and materials available in this book are for general informational purposes only. Information in this book may not constitute the most up-to-date legal or other information. This book contains links to other third-party websites. Such links are only for the convenience of the reader, user, or reader; Kahan Tazadaq and his members do not recommend or endorse the contents of the third-party sites.

Readers of this book should contact their attorney to obtain advice concerning any legal matter. No reader or user of this site should act or refrain from acting based on information in this book without first seeking legal advice from counsel in the relevant jurisdiction. Only your attorney can provide assurances that the information contained herein – and your interpretation of it – is applicable or appropriate to your situation. Use of, and access to, this book or any of the links or resources contained within the book do not create an attorney-client relationship between the reader, or user, and website authors, contributors, contributing law firms, or committee members and their respective employers.

ACKNOWLEDGMENTS
Giving all praise to the supreme Ahlahiem of our ancestors Yahuah

1 NEVER BROKEN

Revelations 3: 8 I know thy works: behold, I have set before thee an open door, and no man can shut it: Man was made in the image and likeness of Yahuah (YHWH) take the limitation off the Most High!

"Why am I here?" This is a question that every living soul should inquire of oneself while here in the physical. Why was I given the gift of life? Have you the reader asked yourself this question? We all were created with a unique purpose, what is yours? Why are you here? I can finally answer this question to a lesser degree. It would require more than just this book to answer that, it would require a lifetime to answer.

I will give you a glimpse of that life by peering into my past and current existence. If the power on high would alter the hands of times, I would have prevented Barak Shar from slitting his wrist, and then running to his car depriving himself of life with a bullet to his head. Perhaps if I had released this book five days earlier, he would still be alive. Yet this book can save lives if studied and read a minimum of ten times. It saved mine. I supposed that he never answered the one significant question that any of us has a purpose, which we all must ask; " Why am I here?." To even begin to answer this, I must go back. Back in time and share my existence nuch pro tunch.

Bereshith 2:7 And HWHY Elohim formed the man out of dust from the ground and breathed into his nostril's breath of life. And the man became a living soul. Why am I here? Those innocuous words dare to shoulder weight that crushes the thoughts and minds of those courageous enough to inquire of their alter ego that very question. I dare to ask because a normal man would have chosen the easier route of suicide, rather than question the efficiency of his learning and ask oneself the question. But Tazadaq is dissident, and the said question was my fuel to continue pushing forward when the naysayers doubted me and wrote me off, like a coach cutting the first forty failures from football tryouts. You run to the

"WHY AM I HERE?" THE VOLUNTARY TORTURE CALLED LIFE

board and search for your name on the list, only to discover that it is not there! This is the closest mentally inflicted trauma to a cardiac arrest that you experience at sixteen. You must be a born loser is your first thought, exiled by the thought the coach just did not like you. Because in a society where men are feminized as women, you create excuses and lies to convince yourself that your failure is usually external.

I do not have a sob story and I beg of you do not feel fucking sorry for me, because after growing up not knowing where I would get my next meal, within a home without heat, compacted with being told you would be dead or in jail before 25 by my teacher, and with the merger, "you are not going to be no fucking good like your father". I am still standing, and surmise that I must be unfucking breakable!
I am an inviolable man, and my message is the plug to your issues.

Fucks are given to those that put me down. If you are sensitive and get your panties in a wedge over my expression of words, then this book is not for you. I am the foul-mouth priest and cannot properly drive my point home without some four-letter words. I need you to feel this. Stop being a freaking hypocrite because you use these words when you are angry. Let us start being real from the inception of this book. And to feel my pain and struggle, I cuss to take you into a world where 98% never escape.

This book should be used as a catalyst to enable the reader to avoid the pitfalls that I fell into. Use this book as a guide to defy all odds and aspire to be great and successful. I have endured what no one should ever have to undergo. I am still standing unbroken. They could not break me. I conclude that "the world is mind." If you control your mind, you can control your life and direct it in the direction that you will. An indomitable spirit, a sincere belief in Yahuah, and knowing why you are here are essential to survive in this voluntary torture called life.

"WHY AM I HERE?" THE VOLUNTARY TORTURE CALLED LIFE

Life's a bitch and then you die for most. But I fucked this bitch called life and she fell in love with me, a real man. Beta men get screwed by life as do masculine women. Their attitude is fuck the world! If that is your perspective then do it. I whipped out my rod, discovered the hole in the ground, and fucked the world because I refused to get fucked by this world. I am a real man. The Matrix hates this, I teach you how it is. "I'm the greatest" Repeat that to yourselves each day before brushing while peering into the mirror.

This house that you reside in known as a body cannot be foreclosed on. You cannot do a quick claim deed on it; you are stuck with it until your spirit departs from it. Knowing thus, one should take great care of this house. To do so you must control your mind, or someone else will manipulate your mind, body, and soul.

I was not supposed to make it according to statistics, the social norm, my teacher, and my mother. I was told '"you ain't shit" so much I assumed it was my first last and middle name" You ain't Shit." name. "They gave up on me, I came up on them." The foul mouth Kahan, so you know who said it.

They never imagined that I would make it to this level. I have soared beyond the normality of those who doubted me. That baneful asshole like my teacher and family member slashed me with the knives of mental cruelty. I leaped over your mischievous walls of gossip that no child or adult should have to hear and developed into an inviolable man, "Kahan Tazadaq, the foul mouth Priest."

In the familiar words of David Goggins, "Cannot hurt me!" Fucks given! My tantalizing demeanor embellished hardships, struggles, and falls. Each time that gave up on me and wrote me off, I stood back up like a fucking horny teen with a hard-on for a porn flick. If you find this offensive, then you do not want to hear the truth. I decided to self-public so I could express my truth without

"WHY AM I HERE?" THE VOLUNTARY TORTURE CALLED LIFE

censorship of some publisher dictating what I could say. I cannot express my truth by merely attempting to keep things clean to cater to a specific audience.

As a youth I had extremely low self-esteem being insulted, put down, and ridiculed by loved ones and my peers. I have learned in life that the world is a mind. It is all a mind game and if you endure the pain, struggle, complications, and put-downs, it will improve unless you tap out. I never tapped out, I continued to push like it was my last breath, and at times I was breathless and gave myself mental CPR.

I turn your attention to the Bible Verse "Matthew 5: 45 That ye may be the children of your Father which is in heaven: for he maketh his sun to rise on the evil and the good, and sendeth rain on the just and on the unjust". First, giving all praise to the God of our ancestors, Abraham, Isaac, and Jacob, whose proper name is Yahuah.

I would like to embed an aphorism into your mind, and it is that "no one is coming to save you." Unless you are waiting for the return of HaMashiyach, no one else will save you. We are all given the same opportunity, both the righteous and the unrighteous. However, we will be judged based on our decisions. Some falsely delude themselves with deceptive intelligence to rationalize their wrongdoing.

They tell themselves Satan is trying to do a thing to them. But the truth is James 4:7 Submit yourselves therefore to God. Resist the devil, and he will flee from you. Submit yourselves to God. Resist the devil and he will flee from you. The devil cannot occupy a body where the Lord and Savior reside. The devil comes in and dwells where HaMashiyach/Christ is absent.

Stop blaming the devil for your own Satan of self. All that you are is a result of what you think. Each one of us has the power to

"WHY AM I HERE?" THE VOLUNTARY TORTURE CALLED LIFE

develop and construct our righteous character and to create our happiness.
The circumstances, the conditions, and the situations of our lives are akin to our inner state of mind.

This book is not written to make me appear heroic or some man who was born with special talents and highly gifted. This book is just the opposite. This book is intended to be didactic, not only to motivate you but to encourage you to become driven. Motivation is not enough. One must be driven. One can be motivated, but if you must undergo difficult tasks in extreme weather the motivation will depart you, therefore, you must be driven. Why because the modern man is a bitch, He is a pussy and needs to return to being a man again. The whine does not win. They are soft, have weak hand grips, and have fragile emotions.

Therefore, this book is intended to be a manual of inspiration for those who are at the bottom, who feel as if there is no light at the end of the tunnel. Allow my life to reflect upon your life as a beacon light of hope, a torchlight to success or freedom from your depression. I had two friends who recently killed themselves because they were both raised by women and not taught to deal with their emotions as men.

The number one and greatest creators under Yah/God are men. In times past of course. You have man-vaginas today. That is a man with a mind like a vagina. He constantly gets fucked by women in society. Men are so stupid that they pay women "hush money" and the women still expose him in the end. He is too naïve to have in stipulate in the contract, you can't ever speak about this, if you do you pay me back double. I surmise the layers are to blame. I was reading the New York Times and it read, "Federal Judges Rate 7.1 Percent of Lawyers Incompetent Study of Three State Area.

Earl Warren Court (1953-1969)
Earl Warren was the 14th Chief Justice of the U.S. Supreme Court,

"WHY AM I HERE?" THE VOLUNTARY TORTURE CALLED LIFE

succeeding Fred M. Vinson. Formerly the Governor of California, he was appointed by President Dwight D. Eisenhower during a recess of the Senate on October 2, 1953, and he was sworn into office on October 5, 1953. Eisenhower formally nominated Warren on January 11, 1954, and the Senate confirmed him on March 1, 1954. Warren served as Chief Justice until he retired on June 23, 1969, and was succeeded by Warren Burger. He states that " 90% of all lawyers are incompetent in their chosen field of expertise".

Despite where you may be right now, be it your lowest point in life, you can soar to great heights. If you believe and perceive it to be true.
This book is written for those who have undergone circumstances like mine, to help you alter your perceived notions that you cannot be great. Where you are, I was. I will even go off a limb and say I was even at a lower stage.

Venture to rural town USA. Where the sit-apart spirit descended to this earth as a dove and impregnated my mom with Tazadaq. At the time he was labeled with the name Roosevelt. Who gave me that name? Mom! And although loved by Europeans because of the late president, I have hated the name especially since I learned what FDR did in 1933 that fucked us all commercially, by depriving us of an ability to pay for anything with money of intrinsic value. We will return to that high point later in this book.

Let us now learn how Roosevelt eventually became Kahan Tazadaq Shah. It is a heck of a story, nonfiction. There is nothing about me that has been made up. You may think that I am some crazy or deranged lunatic because I have learned to transform pain into success. I surmise that there is nothing that would startle me.

I have fought through the most devastating odds that would have rendered most defeated from the inception of the battle. I have the self-proclaimed nickname insurmountable. If you see me in a fight with a bear pray for my opponent. In other words, I am not to be fucked with.

I am a star seed; no mortal could have endured what I have and still be standing with rational thoughts. The world in mind. What I am saying is that I am not of this world. "If you were of the world, the world would love you as its own; but because you are not of the world, but I chose you out of the world, therefore the world hates you: John 15:14 I have learned through experience that most people did not give a shit about me, though they will gladly don a costume of deception to ascertain what they want.

I arrived here as a star seed, and I was birthed in this earthly form to enable you to be capable of receiving me and using my life as an example of how one can come from the bottom and soar to greatness, be blessed and unstoppable. Now let us venture back to a small town in the USA. Although I spent most of my life in Brooklyn, New York, I am told I was not born there. I am told I was not even born in the hospital. My great-grandmother, being a midwife, delivered me. I do not remember the earlier years of my life.

Therefore, legally that would be all hearsay in a court of law because my exact birth comes from a third party. Therein is a lesson for how one can respond to the question "When were you born"? I was too young to know, Is the honest answer that many are too docile to utter before the black robe, wearing the title of a judge.

What is relevant is that I remember a part of my life where my brother, my sister, my mother, and I had it great. I honestly know that my mother loved me, but she did not know how to love properly. She could only provide what she was given. I need all men and women to remember that a person can only give you what they have. You cannot get true love from one that is filled with hate. When Dad was in our lives, he worked for Roosevelt Raceway in Long Island, New York. And he made good money.

"WHY AM I HERE?" THE VOLUNTARY TORTURE CALLED LIFE

Therefore, we were well-off, lived in a loving home, and had all the clothing and toys that young children would desire.

We got anything that we wanted. But I learned at an early age that because a woman is with a man, does not necessarily mean that she loves the man; many women love a man's money. If you are involved with a woman, never expose how much you are worth financially upfront, let it come as a surprise to her, that way you can ensure, she wants you and not your money.

So, for whatever reason, Dad was just not appealing enough to my mom. There was something about him that she just did not like.
Or was it the modern lust that I see in modern women in general? Besides drinking on the weekend, he was a particularly good man. He took care of his family, he was a provider, however, he just did not appease my mom. It was because he was a fuking simp, that allowed her to talk to him as if he was a piece of shit. Or was it love? Yes, it was love. And I learned a man in love psychosis.

I would learn later through my experience of having sex with over one thousand women that women respect leadership, strength, and dominance. Your money cannot buy you love, it can get you some woman who is dishonorable and run through. Or one that wants your money and has the alpha male on the side.

When I look at the new generation, and how feeble and fragile these boys and men are, I think, our future is fucked. The United States is finished. The fact that these damn liberals can do what they did the Mr. Donald Trump, is a display of how degenerate society has become. Most of the fucks that ridicule him are guilty of the same shit!

Hypocrites are as common as breathing today. Real men are becoming distinct. Women are lost, in that they are over-masculine. The word masculine itself refers to and is a characteristic of men. They refuse to accept accountability. 80

"WHY AM I HERE?" THE VOLUNTARY TORTURE CALLED LIFE

percent file for divorce to get a bag and ruin the man's life/ Most haven't been taught to be wives or mothers. The masculine energy repels the man. They end up with dogs, old and found dead in an alley, because they claim not to need, the greatest creator under God, man! My attitude is even if you don't need a man stop using the things that we create, that would be everything she uses daily.

People will read this and say, "Oh, he's angry". No, I'm a realist. If anyone else said this they would be mocked, but because modern men are so damn weak, women get away with just about anything because she has a vagina. It's time we return to being real men and stop being emotional I get it, 80 percent are you are like pussies, because you were raised by single mothers. But there is a boy within that needs to mature into a man. Read all of Kahan Tazadaq's books and they will guide you on this journey. Order them now @ www.kahantazadaq.net.

Like so many women that I have encountered in my life Mom yearned for the handsome bad boy. Decisions that would haunt her and she would wear it for the remainder of her life in her memories. Or even like the burden of an albatross.

Mom was a good mother, however, she was very stern and was very verbally abusive to me and my sister, however, she treated our younger brother Michael better, which boomerangs back to hunt her, because he utterly disrespected her. I love her, but she treated me horribly.

She was very abusive physically and mentally. She would beat me with any object that she could get firsthand. She would often insult me and say, "You're not going to be no damn good, just like your father." So much for the false narrative pushed by society that men are more abusive. Statistics show that women are generally more abusive to children than men.

"WHY AM I HERE?" THE VOLUNTARY TORTURE CALLED LIFE

I was not a kid that caused problems. I was a shy kid, very skinny, incredibly quiet, and very loving. I would often witness my mother, sister, and brother talking about how weird I was. This is why currently when I hear some asshole backbiting me, I am oblivious to that, it reflects a loser that has nothing better to do with his time, otherwise it would be used productively. My mother never spent a lot of time with us regarding schoolwork. Therefore, initially, I did not do very well in school in the early grades.

And I surmise that it was also because of the mental and verbal abuse that I sustained at home. As a result, at school I would not talk very much, I thought I was very ugly because I was always insulted and put down by my family and children and school who came from abusive homes. Bullies bully others. Hurt people hurt others. I developed extremely low self-esteem and became a loner. Because of this, I turned to Yahuah (God) at an exceedingly early age.

Despite this, while Dad was around, we lived very well financially. He was not the most attractive man; I surmise this is why my mom left him for some guy named Thomas. My mother was raised with a slave mentality. What I mean by that is that she was taught to hate being a person of color. She would therefore be more attractive to so-called light-skinned men. I remember this guy, Thomas after we moved to this urban environment who was extremely abusive. This guy would beat my mom to a pulp.

I remembered blood flowing through my veins as hot as a volcano as anger burned deep within. I could feel a lump in my throat to the point where I felt suffocated. It was as if I could not breathe 'I could not get oxygen.
Lesson learned at age four, if you do not control your anger, your anger will control you. This guy would beat my mom so badly; her face would be so bloodied It brought shivers over my skin. My heart raced like a Nascar and beat as if it were a tornado slamming my heart around within my chest. I wondered why Yahuah did not

"WHY AM I HERE?" THE VOLUNTARY TORTURE CALLED LIFE

kill that son of a bitch, Thomas. I knew that it was wrong. If only I could summon that strength to kill this mother fucker was my thought. I swore to myself once I got old enough that I would take his ass out.

My mom would eventually leave him when he was at work. He called, apologized, and promised not to ever do it again. Time after time this asshole would talk her into coming back, and she did it. This became a routine, and the beatings became increasingly brutal. She accepted the abuse from this devil because he was paying the bills and she did not want her and her children to be homeless on the street.

After she realized that if she did not get this man out of her life, he would kill her, her mother finally convinced her to hibernate this man. It was as if we left the chambers of hell and the devil was roaming the earth in search of us. I worried for a while that our mother would become weak and return to Satan. But she never went back.

We soon encountered racism, single parenthood, hunger, no heat, and sorrow. My biological father wanted to be more involved with my brother and me. We were ordered by our mother to stay away from him. I Always wondered why she never attempted to get him for child support. As an adult, I learned why she never went after him for child support. It is most embarrassing, one of the most appalling things that I have ever heard, and to spare my mother the embarrassment I will not mention that in this book.

I will say this to all men who may have grown up hearing your father was a deadbeat dad, an aphorism that a feminist system that is biased against men developed. Sometimes its dad's beat to death, and they are not dead beats at all. Many women lie and ruin men's lives. I will say this all men out there that may not have had their fathers in their life; do not always believe what your mother tells you about why your father may not have been in your life.

"WHY AM I HERE?" THE VOLUNTARY TORTURE CALLED LIFE

Find out the truth for yourselves.

So now there is a period where there is no man in the house. This is when I realized how hard life could be. Think Yahuah. We were surrounded by masculine figures such as James Vini, Herman Jones, Randolph Sharp, my cousin, and all the other men who were mentors for me and my brother. Still, this did not suffice for the absence of the financial support that my father had provided.

These were the days when we had to eat rice and beans for weeks, and once that was depleted, we ate mayo sandwiches, until alas there was nothing to eat, there would be no heat in the house, and all the toys and clothing that we once had was now distant memories of the past; and we had nothing.

When my mom did get money, she would go to the Goodwill store and get secondhand clothing that my brother and I would share and spend what was left on beer. She began to develop a drinking problem to fix the pain. I would go to school in outdated and oversized clothing that the other students would laugh at and make fun of.

At this point I hated life. I hated going to school because we would be teased. She got on welfare; I hated going home because the welfare check was not enough, and we would go hungry and be cold at home. At least at school, I got a free lunch. That is all I had to look forward to. My brother and I would say, " one I grow up I'm leave this town and never return."

I therefore literally learned to detest my life like the HIV plague. As time progressed, I began failing in school. The teacher told me that I was going to fail the third grade because I could not read at the level that I should, I could not ask my mom for assistance because she was working most of the time.

She decided to get off welfare because it just was not enough. I

"WHY AM I HERE?" THE VOLUNTARY TORTURE CALLED LIFE

failed the third grade, which resulted in those I assumed were my friends teasing me even more by the students who knew I was supposed to be in their grade. I was humiliated.

My mom would tell me you better not fail, or I will beat your ass. I failed anyway. I was a dumb, shy, scared, eight-year-old. I just could not prevent it, I needed help. I began to lock myself away in the room and imagine that I would one day be great in life. Each time that I will construct these dreams in my mind the Edomite schoolteacher, the niggers on the corner, or someone close to me with tear my dreams down like a paper house in a hurricane. So now I am going to school and am barely making it, I was eventually placed in a special education class.

Statistically people that are placed in special Ed never get out, but I did because I made a commitment with my Yahuah (God) and with myself that I would not live the life that I saw my mother living, and the people around me in a ghetto living. The sixth grade came around, and by this time I had been determined by teachers to be slow. They were inadequate to realize that I was not slow, but their lack of skills to teach so-called Black males was the real problem. Up to this, time no one seemed to care about me. But there was this math teacher by the name of Mr. Gunter, a small statute by a voice of thunder. Mr. Gunter was known for not just speaking to his students by beating them so badly that nearby teachers would have to run to their rescue like an SOS.

Mr. Gunter invoked fear in the students. Back then he came across as being abusive, but hindsight shows me that he did it because he cared about us. He wanted to ensure that we learn, and boy did we learn. If you do not learn the lesson, you will get spanked. And he had a board that was known as the Board of Education. You have one of two choices. You will learn math, or you will feel the board of education.

And what I learned from Mr. Gunter is that I was not stupid as everyone was saying, I was not dumb. I began to realize that we become what we think about. The Bible says it like this in the book of Proverbs 23 verse 7 "As a man thinks in his heart so is he". That is a fact.

You are what you think about most. Your thoughts define who you are. Every single one of you that is reading this book right now, must realize that no one is coming to save you. You must save yourself! Emphasis added. No one is coming to save you, that is what I said to tell myself. And I realize that as a little boy, that turned my life around, I am responsible for the outcome of my life.

All that we are is the result of what we think. None of us must live the life we now have or that which we have previously possessed. We all have the power to alter our lives for the better. I, therefore, beloved, suggest that you read this book with a generous spirit. But do not just read and then tuck it away on your bookshelf. This book should be reread periodically, as it will continue to inspire you. And once you apply what you have read your life will be enriched.

The message that I want you to understand from this chapter is that all of us are precisely what we think, our inner being, becoming the complete sum of our thoughts. Take the butterfly which springs forth and flies away. It cannot be truly developed unless it undergoes the stage of the Caterpillar which is like its seed stage. When the caterpillar contains everything that it needs to develop into a butterfly, most cannot see it. Likewise, we must surround ourselves with those who can see the gifts within us and extirpate those from our lives who only see the negative.

When must one also have a positive mental attitude? Our actions soar from the seeds of our thoughts. If our minds think failure so, shall it be? If our minds think success so, shall it be. Like a blacksmith, by our thoughts, we can forge the weapons of thoughts, which can protect and improve our lives, or we can forge

"WHY AM I HERE?" THE VOLUNTARY TORTURE CALLED LIFE

the swords of thoughts that will destroy our lives, which are self-defeating behaviors. The former is what we must strive to mold our minds into, the latter are the unfortunate thoughts of 97% of the world's population.

We will attract what we are, not that for which we hope. You had better start altering yourself into the most determined, loving, positive person on earth, that way you will always survive. Knowing thus, it suffices to say that people fail from negative thoughts. Only a select few developed the thought process to overthrow cognitive dissonance and soar above normality, into the realm of greatness. Such are the blessed and unstoppable.

As a Lad, the corporations were consortium to malinated people and were owned by Euro Gentiles (so-called white people) that could deny so-called Black people, the newly freed 14 amendment slaves, the right to sit at a certain lunch counter. Although it was illegal at the time to deny so-called Black people, most so-called white people possessed draconian tempers towards these useless so-called black welfare recipients, plagued by fatherless homes to get the farewell(welfare).

In my youth integrated lunch counters were perfectly legal, but the brainwashed so-called white majority did not want to embrace this. Hindsight reveals that this was an apostasy engendered into their minds by the mass media, by television, and by the government that orchestrated it all. This could not have been pulled off unless the de facto condoned it.

As a youth, it appeared to me, that Amerikkka was an ambiance of racial hatred. The so-called white masses, (Biblical Edomites) were unaware that they were also victims of the psychological engineering by the global elite. The media is a propaganda machine used to divide, manipulate, and control the mass mind. This enables a small fraction of bankers to control us all. Divide the people white, against black, against Brown, against yellow to maintain control. If you control a man's mind, you control the man's entire life. We know these are not nationalities, but I am speaking in a language that all can comprehend.; common parlance.

My mother did not believe in racism, she attempted to raise us to believe that people were just people. Although she attempted to teach us this, I witnessed within her thought process, a deep-rooted seed of self-hatred that sprung forth in her like a bean stock overnight. His self-expression of so-called Black people reeks of self-hate. The darker the Black person, the more she seemed to detest the people that closely resembled her.

It must have worked on my brother as he dated several so-called white women until he finally married one and fathered 3 children by her. He glorified so-called white women because secretly I surmise that he felt a defect in being a so-called Black man, because of the media and an educational system that essentially suggested that Black people contributed nothing to society. I rejected this philosophy of white supremacy and felt that my mother needed a miraculous prayer to alleviate her self-negation.

I can recall when I was about seven. She allowed us to go trick-or-treating and we knew to get candy we had to cross the railroad tracks into the white community. My brother, my friends and I got a lot of candy that night. Some of the whites greeted us with smirks without showing their teeth, which is not a true smile. And there was this one house that we went to, a guy gave me an apple, he looked me in the eyes with the grin of the devil on his face. Once we had an abundance of candy and went home. They told me in school. If you get apples while trick-or-treating, be sure to cut them open.

First, I thought no one would try to hurt a little innocent kid like me, seven years old. Then I asked my mom to cut the apple open for me, and when she did, there was a razor blade in the middle of

"WHY AM I HERE?" THE VOLUNTARY TORTURE CALLED LIFE

the apple. I am seven years old; I am trying to rationalize and understand why a so-called white person would want to do this to me at age seven when I had done them no harm. My perspective of so-called white people shifted. This became the apple of my eye. This would alter my video of so-called white people for a long time. Elijah Muhammad said they were Devils; what rational person would do this to a child?

You may say Tazadaq is an isolated incident. But I had a so-called white friend in elementary school named Teddy Ross. I thought he was my friend but, he turned out to be racist as well. When he invited me over, he told me that my brother could not come because he was too dark. There is an unregistered test that some whites have known as the paper bag effect. If your complexion was as light as a paper bag, then you might be excusable in some situations, but you are still a nigger.

As a result of these experiences, and other people I knew experiencing the power of white supremacy, learning about the lynching, black wall street, and being taught throughout the school that so-called Black people had no accomplishments besides sports; and that we were nothing. I began to overindulge in reading and research.

I would teach myself to read by reading for hours and hours in the uncomfortable atmosphere of my room. My grades in school began to improve. I eliminated my so-called friends who once made fun of me. Suddenly I became an honor student. I read the autobiography of Malcolm X and became a militant within.

But I was not a nation of Islam material. I was merely a skinny, scared boy who had a lot of range in him. I did not want to get teased at school because of my clothes from the Salvation Army and Goodwill, so as a teenager, I began to steal clothing from department stores just to fit in. And I hated myself for it. It was not me.

"WHY AM I HERE?" THE VOLUNTARY TORTURE CALLED LIFE

I never ran from bullies because to whom would I run? Me! No one seem to care about me, and I embraced that shit, if they do not give a fuck then I do not give a fuck either. I stop attempting to appease those motherfuckers that would make fun of me if I did not. I isolated myself from the crowd that would make fun of others. I sat at tables alone and other misfits began to join me. I became the unannounced leader.

If there was one thing, I learned was good morals at home. But at times I had to steal just to eat food. It is a jungle out there and if you are a sheep the lions will eat you for dinner. I was in survival mode. Driving one 160 miles per hour and there is a brick wall ahead, but you cannot tell a teenage boy that is a dangerous route and pump your brakes son.

Praise be the Most High, that he started to put role models in my path, such as James Vinney a football superstar, who taught me to work out with weights Fans referred to him as the Hulk because of his muscular build. Herman Jones was another and my cousin Randolph Sharp both taught me and got me into martial arts art. I would train my body like a warrior at a youthful age. I would do pushups until I fell on my face. Stretch until I can perform full splits. My body was foraged into a lethal weapon, I was not to be fucked with. People started to notice, and I loved it.

I started to get respect, but one so-called white guy attempted to bully me in high school, wrong guy, wrong day motherfuker! He ended up with a broken leg from a new martial art move that I had learned in class. I kicked the shit out of him, and it felt good. They wondered what had happened to the old quite shy kind. No, the old guy is gone, and the new motherfucker is here to stay, get out of my way, or get dealt with.

Next up was a rich doctor's adult son who attempted to beat my friend Randy Hill in a game room one day. Once I saw he was

"WHY AM I HERE?" THE VOLUNTARY TORTURE CALLED LIFE

overpowering Randy, this grown white racist uttered nigger each time he would hit Randy. I stepped in and said try me you racist pig. He swung, I parried, hit him with a right kick to his floating rib which dropped him. From there I stomped him out, and he ended up in the intensive care unit.

At the time I was still in high school and this son of a bitch, was about 27 trying to bully young Black men. I never went back to the area again. I was not a troublemaker, but I began to demand respect and it felt impressive. I would join the cross-country team and make it all the way to state champion.

I went from remedial reading to graduating with a 3.2 Grade Point Average. Fairly good for a guy the teacher wrote off as most unlikely to succeed. You see, several of my teachers told me that I would end up dead or in jail by twenty-five. What could I say to that after my mother had already told me, "You aren't going to be shit like your no-good dad." I am still standing against all odds, and I earn more than all of those who gave up on me. They gave up on me, I came up on them. I wrote a song because of this. You can get our music@ tdocrecordings.com.

The teachers who told me I was not to succeed were astonished when you saw me a few years ago. I defied the odds. I went to college after high school, got a degree in civil engineering, worked it for a while, and was distracted by partying and bullshit. My mom and younger brother talked me into joining the army. Most of my high school friends were now selling drugs, getting shot, dead, or using the drugs. I took the ASVAB and was in basic training for 45 days.

The lesson that you should take from this is that our minds are like a field that a farmer goes out and cultivates. If he leaves the field alone, then wild weeds will grow with the crops. One must extirpate the weeds from the crops, or the weeds will grow with the crops destroying the field. So, it is with the human mind. If you

"WHY AM I HERE?" THE VOLUNTARY TORTURE CALLED LIFE

do not extirpate the bad seeds of thought, they will direct your character to be bad and your spirit will be full of malice. This is the same as saying that as a man thinks in his heart so is he.

You will become what you think about every day. Sounds very practical but this is sound knowledge. You must alleviate all negative thinking. If you want to be a successful righteous man or woman. This includes any negative people that are in your life. This is my afflatus that the heavenly father has given to me to guide you to success and to be blessed and unstoppable. You will only become proficient by falling and getting back up. What you do from this moment on can determine your fate or destroy your future. The choice is yours. Draw a mental line within your mind and decide which side you are going to be on, the losers or the winners. You must be willing to suffer and overcome pain and adversity. Such is the way of the monk warrior mentality.

school photo a face filled with zits and pimples.

I am an example of the rose that grew through concrete, they did

"WHY AM I HERE?" THE VOLUNTARY TORTURE CALLED LIFE

not want me to blossom. The weeds attempted to wrap themselves around me and hold me down, but each time I stood back up in the twelfth round with both fists in the air and experienced the thrill of victory. My arm was raised their head hung low in agony of defeat.

You cannot keep a man down unless you are down there with him. Throughout my childhood, I had been in relationships with girls that I now realize were scared. Many have borderline personality disorder. When I was in high school there was a time that I was dating Demetrius Baines, and I told her that she and I could no longer be together because of extenuating circumstances. She did not take it very well. The next day in school I was called into the office because he had cut her writ and face with a razor.

The guidance counselor asked me if I had spoken with her. I said yes, I broke things off with her last night. She said, be careful who you get involved with. I learned later that Demetrius' mother abandoned her, and she was being raised by her grandmother. As a result, she had a fear of abandonment. This is the number one system of a borderline woman. According to DSM IV, BPD is primally a female mental illness. But since women have flooded the psychology industry the complained about that being biased, and feminism has replaced the truth.

Then there was Jackie Vinney and Amanda Wise. Next-door neighbors. I used to fuck the hell out of them. Only a teen smashing like a jackrabbit. See, despite those adults telling me I would be nothing, I was a leader of the boy groups I was around because I was athletic, fast, and strong. Girls and women love leaders and the fact that I was muscular and handsome helped. Females were extremely attractive to me to the point that when I would break it off, they would attempt to harm themselves.

I now realize these were unhealthy females, who suffer from BPD Borderline personality Disorder). As I grew older, I realized that

"WHY AM I HERE?" THE VOLUNTARY TORTURE CALLED LIFE

feminism was rending women to be masculine and that repel masculine men like myself. There is the faction of women that flood social media shacking their asses like a street whore considering this degenerating behavior liberation. They need lobotomies.

The modern woman is so asinine parading around in an uncivilized manner in transparent clothing that hugs her body like a glove because sex sells. Oblivious that there is an unseen hand that is manipulating her thinking. They label it liberation therefore she does it willingly. In her fallen state she is too comatose or lethargic to consider that once Adam and Eve, became aware that they were naked, they covered themselves. But like a neanderthal, she bares all.

She used sex as a top fashion designer to lure men in, hey look at this Birkin vagina, can you afford it? The degenerate men are compelled to go into debt because he Is no longer a leader but follows the trend. Aware that debts make a man a slave. But his rational thought process is shunned by deceptive intelligence to rationalize his wrong actions.

 He suffers when he can't pay the bills and she becomes bitter and rebellious. He wants to cater to this modern woman who wants everything instantly. She has a microwave mentality. Unwilling to work and suffering to accomplish goals patiently. This is why 40% of women in America have less than $200 in both their checking and savings accounts, This state of mind breeds poverty. She will never have anything of value and never the man that she desires of high value because her objective is to have a man excessively spending or drowning in debt to the top of his head, with a discontent woman apathetic. She wants more, and increasingly,

Therefore, modern women are never content sipping their man out. Most of them are not men yet, men like me are attempting to teach them how to be real men. They all need lobotomies. But if

"WHY AM I HERE?" THE VOLUNTARY TORTURE CALLED LIFE

you continue to simp him You will not have a man you will end up being a lesbian or with a pet at home alone with no man to protect you because of your foul mouth.

Kahan Tazadaq 2023

"WHY AM I HERE?" THE VOLUNTARY TORTURE CALLED LIFE

Kahan tazadaq 2022

2 THE WORLD IS MIND CULTIVATE IT

I am always overwhelmed by the thought of those who do not know me yet telling me to" go to hell!" If the son of bitches knew me, they would know that I have lived in hell for the first portion of my life. And I face a deluge of devil advocates and kicked their fucking ass. I proved them wrong, all of them said I would not make it. I don't think many could endure the crap that I have endured. I pray for the remainder of my days because I do not want to ever repeat the hell that I have been through.

It is by the thoughts, that man chooses and invigorates; that his mind becomes the seamster, both his fashionable inner garment of character and the external clothing of circumstance, if not cultivated with righteousness and logic, are woven into ignorance and self-torture. By caretaking the garden of one's mind, thoughts may be stitched into enlightenment and bliss.

A faction of you will not take this book as seriously as you should. Yet in the end, you will wish that you had lived and not just existed, creating delusional excuses for why you were an average failure. If challenged you to reserve this moment to consider just how precious life is. Life is fleeting, special yet challenging and fragile. Do not allow these words to come across as insignificant. Do not give up on your dreams and goals and settle for what the average person considers as living. The day is forthcoming that life will flash before your eyes, in chronological order of events that occurred moments before you took your last breath. Will it be worth watching?

When you reflect on your life in the last breath will you conclude that your life was meaningful to this world, where you loved and had an impact on the lives of others, did you matter? Once that moment arrives, we will not be concerned about our mortgage, our car note, our hairstyles, our fake asses, or the stay-at-home spouses of Atlanta. At that moment we will finally be unconcerned about the opinions of their party haters.

Did I matter what is relevant before taking that last breath? Before these times come, today, right now, within this second you had better make a change, to ensure your life matters. Because one day it will end. To live for most people is extremely rare, they simply exist. Do not live like average people around you. Be amazing, astounding, extraordinary. Live with passion. Henceforth do not take anyone or anything for granted. Are you living your dreams? If not get up and get after it! What are you waiting for? You only have one shot. If you miss the target at least you tried and can live with no regrets. Whom have you given guanine love? Who loves you? Go tell them right now that you love them. No one can be certain when will be our last opportunity.

Stop taking this wonderful gift of life for granted. Trust yourself when the haters and naysayers doubt you. Strive for your dreams when everyone else gives up on theirs. Because they gave up on me, I came up on them. When they became content, I was burning the midnight oil striving to be better. I am the lion when they act like sheep. I am the leader that others want to follow. I live each moment as if it is my last because it may be. I am working to leave my legacy. Like the flower, I shall bloom.

You must find your path. You have been taught to believe that you are dumb, and self-loathing because you have not found your path. If you judge a shark by its ability to climb a tree, you will think it is dumb, yet it will be feared in the ocean. I became akin to that great white shark, people began to talk crap about me in private, yet lacked the confidence and decency to look into my eyes and say it. Therein they would discover the spirit of a warrior and the heart of 100, utterly undaunted.

The initial stage of my development was far from formidable because I had to fight uphill against the words of weapons my foes fired to render my demise. Hit on a deluge of occasions, I stopped

"WHY AM I HERE?" THE VOLUNTARY TORTURE CALLED LIFE

back up as a bad guy in a horror flick and kept coming.

White supremacy is alive and well yet is concealed at times behind the façade of smiles, five thousand dollars suits, employers, and their ability to censor the truth in the media. People who are racist suffer from stupidity and lack a comprehensive knowledge of how they got on this planet. I contend that each one of us is where he is by the law of his being; the thoughts which one has constructed into one's character have brought him there, and in the arrangement of his life there is no element of chance, but all is the result of a law which cannot err.
Despite the white supremacist proverbial grenade thrown at me, I survived their attempts to eliminate me. This is just as true of those who feel "out of harmony" with their surroundings as of those who are contented with them. White supremacist must overcome their self-loathing and or continue to live a life filled with hate and die in their miserable state. Modern women can learn to listen to strong righteous men like me or continue in their wretchedness.

Women are far from the traditional woman who loved motherhood and being a wife. She has degenerated into an overly masculine feminist that detests men, traits that she learned through the emulation of Europeans. They consider it liberation, when eighty percent of women are unmarried with bastard children, living off men that they hate from child and spousal support, degenerated into whores that advertise shaking their naked assess over the internet within a perverted age of alternative lifestyles where freaks are the social norm.

Their inadequate ability to use comprehend colloquial speech, "bitch" is annunciated with pride in females' circles, yet the bitches pay the victim when a man calls her what she is, a bitch. This does not apply to modest and meek respectful women. They have reared the past three generations as single parents and have failed gravely. A glance at modern society tells all. The numbers do not lie.

Children raised by single mothers are more likely to fare worse in a few dimensions, including their school achievement, their social and emotional development, their health, and their success in the labor market. They are at greater risk of parental abuse and neglect (especially from live-in boyfriends who are not their biological fathers), more likely to become teen parents, and less likely to graduate from high school or college. [i] Not all children raised in single-parent families suffer these adverse outcomes; it is simply that the risks are greater for them.

"One possibility is that children in two-parent families do better because of the increased resources available to them. Single parents only have one income coming into the single-parent home. On top of that, single parents often must spend a greater proportion of their income on childcare because they do not have a co-parent to stay home with the child while they work. Even beyond having more income, two parents also have more time to spend with the child. A recent study by Richard Reeves and Kimberly Howard finds that parenting skills vary across demographic groups and that forty-four percent of single mothers fall into the weakest category and only 3 percent into the strongest category.

The weak parenting skills found among single parents in the study may be related not only to the lack of a second parent but to a lack of income and education as well. Education stands out as the most critical factor in explaining poor parenting. However, it is not clear that we should look at these variables in isolation from one another. In real life, compared to married parents, single parents tend to be poorer (because there is not a second earner in the family) and less well-educated (in part because early childbearing interrupts or discourages education), and this is what matters for their children.

"WHY AM I HERE?" THE VOLUNTARY TORTURE CALLED LIFE

Another possibility is that children born to unmarried mothers face more instability in family structure and that this instability results in worse outcomes for the child. In recent years, the focus of social science research has been less on the absence of a father and more on how family instability affects children. Stable single-parent families in which a child does not experience the constant comings and goings of new boyfriends (or girlfriends), or the addition of new half-siblings have begun to look like a better environment than "musical" parenthood.

Lastly, any discussion of the impacts of single parenthood must consider selection effects. Single parents may be more likely to have other traits (unrelated to their marital status) that cause their children to have worse outcomes than children raised in two-parent homes. It may not be divorce or unwed birth that causes the problem but instead the underlying personal attributes, mental health, or competencies that produce both a broken family and worse outcomes for the child. Children who end up in a single-parent family as the result of the death of one parent do not have the same poor outcomes as children raised by single parents due to a divorce or out-of-wedlock birth.

This may be because death, unlike divorce or out-of-wedlock childbearing, is more likely to be a random event, not connected to the attributes or temperaments of the parents. The lesser disadvantages for children ending up in a single-parent family as the result of the death of one parent may reflect this fact and point to the importance of taking unobserved attributes, temperaments, or behaviors into account when talking about the consequences of single parenthood for children." [i] McLanahan and Sandefur, Growing up with a Single Parent; Jane Waldfogel, Terry-Ann Craigie, and Jeanne Brooks-Gunn. "Fragile families and child wellbeing. "The Future of Children (2010), p. 87.
[ii] Waldfogel, Craigie, and Brooks-Gunn, "Fragile families and child wellbeing."

"WHY AM I HERE?" THE VOLUNTARY TORTURE CALLED LIFE

I am here because I am a messenger, a guide, and a facilitator to the world. The world is mind. I use my mind and spirit to give light and life to those who live within the oppression of gross darkness. Despite where you are, do not ever allow anyone to tell you that you cannot do, or be who you aspire to be.

Each one of us has a purpose for being created despite knowing or living our purpose. Some may grapple with the realization of some people are here just to be fucking assholes and losers. This explains why some just constantly seek out the negative in about everyone they encounter, like a scavenger hunt, they seek desperately to ruin your day or even your life. It is their sole purpose for being created. You also have a faction of people that are the bullshitters, which make false promises and goals that they never aspire to accomplish.

They talk that talk, but they expend too much energy on criticizing others. These parsimonious debtors are in debt to the gift of life itself. They have given nothing back for the gift of life, they merely complain about how they were never handed the opportunity that others had, or how much more difficult they had it, which is asinine.

These types of people are emotional and energy vampires that bite their fangs into any host that is willing to allow them to indoctrinate their rhetoric into their lives until they have rendered them to this same negative loser mindset. These people never question the efficacy of life and ask the question, "Why am I here?'

That is a question we all must ask ourselves and be qualified to answer. "Why am I here" If you cannot answer this question then you are not on your purpose you are loving your life based upon what others have told you or encouraged you that you should be. Your belief system is not real. A belief is something that arises from

"WHY AM I HERE?" THE VOLUNTARY TORTURE CALLED LIFE

the past. Belief is information that we are introduced to and if the source that provides us with that information seems dependable, then we accept it as truth even if it is a lie.

When we encounter others that conflict with that belief we react. To react means that we go back into our past and compare our previous information with what we currently hear. Re means to go back. Therefore, a reaction is not real, it is something that also comes from the past. Primarily, most people do not think for themselves they have been taught what to think. Most people we encounter reflect those who have imposed their beliefs upon them. Individuality is rare. People just follow what they see others doing. We see this on social media. In this, we lose who we were born to be.

If you ask most people, the question why am I here? They will give a response based on what someone else has taught them. Few people use their brains to think and create. Cell phones and commuters have aided the destruction of the development of the human mind. We lose ourselves attempting to be what others want us to be or we think we should be instead of just asking, "Why am I here?' and live that out.

If you do not know the answer to this question then you are existing, and not living. When I told a few friends that I was authoring a book titled, "Why Am I Here?" They laughed. Thereafter I realized that I had to extirpate these people from my life. When I asked them the question they could not answer it, but they were feeding off my energy and wealth. They are the vampires of which I spoke of earlier. I am here to help others. I am a guide, a preface to a better way of living and not just existing. Use my life's mistakes to capitalize on yours. Let my life be motivation to on the areas where you may have given up.

"WHY AM I HERE?" THE VOLUNTARY TORTURE CALLED LIFE

**HEBREWS TO NEGROES' REBUTTAL
INDENITY THEFT**

**HOW ESAU'S AMALEKITES STOLE YAPHETH & ISRAELITES BIRTH RIGHT
EXTENDED EDITION**

ISBN: 979-8-9874165-0-1

"WHY AM I HERE?" THE VOLUNTARY TORTURE CALLED LIFE

"WHY AM I HERE?" THE VOLUNTARY TORTURE CALLED LIFE

"WHY AM I HERE?" THE VOLUNTARY TORTURE CALLED LIFE

3 WHILE THE MAJORITY OF THE WORLD IS SLEEPING, I'M SUFFERING FOR SUCCESS

When I start my day, most people are still sleeping, convincing themselves that they have a few more minutes, so they press the snooze button for the third time. It is the primary reason they must go and punch the clock and I work for myself, yet I get up and get after it long before they do. I am on the attack of an average mindset and mentality. I sacrifice in the private to enable me to shine in public. I am married to private discipline and an indomitable spirit.
Barak Shar, Yasharbeam, and Napthali all contribute to destiny, but they are not committed to density. The aphorism, "The's good enough" is why these men are unlikely to ever achieve what I have, the lack of passion, discipline, and accountability. Suffering, hurt, pain, rain, sleet, or snow I am still committed to building 720 hours a month. You the reader are you committed? You must remember your success story has yet to be told.

If you want the world to hear your story you had better stop making excuses and grind. Give it your all. The insult that the critics make about Kahan Tazadaq does not determine my success because I worked hard in silence. I stayed on my grind, they gave up on me, and I came up on them.

Stop talking so much about what you are going to do and do the damn thing!
I have often been asked Tazadaq when do you sleep? My response is ill sleep when I die. While sleep is essential, I am often deprived of it for success. When I sense that it becomes critical ill catch some zee, or if it begins to alter my immune system Insert. It is because I want this thing called success and I am aware it will never quit.

They all want to be a champions until it is time to undergo the suffering and commitment that a champion endures. Success is a

"WHY AM I HERE?" THE VOLUNTARY TORTURE CALLED LIFE

lonely road; you must recognize that ease does not make it down this road called success. They fall out and quiet. You must create the tenacity to grasp the success mindset and not let go while you are suffering, hurting, and wanting too quiet. The pain that comes from quitting will be far worse than the pain that you ensure to be successful. The pain that you sustain from success is extremely rewarding. It is all in you to be great, embrace it, and conduct your business.

To accomplish what you want, we, you will undergo a deluge of pain and suffering. You must not allow this to break you. You must not allow the slips and falls to prevent you from getting back up. Get back up and go harder. You are in a war against your alter ego. Your brain is warning against you. I visualize the end when I am experiencing suffering. One step at a time, one rep at a time, one hour, or a minute at a time. They feel that you experience once you accomplish your goals the feeling is euphoria. Although tantalizing while suffering it is rewarding, unlike you will ever imagine. So, you must grind.

You must face the insurmountable obstacles and overcome them. You will never achieve success within a comfortable environment. What I am suggesting is that you must become uncomfortable and learn to like it. Suffering is rewarding but few of us want to endure.

I pray that my story here will change someone's life that is reading this book. I pray that you do not place to book down and return to your insecurities. I am attempting to overcome aphasia and retrain my mind to realize that the process of evolution and growth always begins with pain. Your most difficult battle is overcoming the inner me. The inner me is the enemy. The inner me is the enemy because the son of a bitch will talk you out of success at each opportunity that he has.

Your body is not changing because you leave too much in the tank when you are working out. No! empty the mother fucking tank. Then you talk to yourself, your alter ego and say, "What's next, did it bitch?" I developed a warrior's mindset. My growth always took place when I fell, I had to dig deep, clear my mind of the self-negation that was instilled into me from, the haters, and get the fuck back up. They attempted to hand me a failure, but I handed that shit back to them. Discipline and consistency became my declaration of what I represent.

I found inspiration in their hate, and insults. I developed the lion mentality during the storm. A lion is a better hunter in the storm because the storms enable him to conceal himself more. In the storm, you must be a lion, fearless. You must keep hunting for success, you must keep fighting. Because if you quit, you will regret it for the remainder of your days.

Keep pushing forward. What makes me dissident is that when I am faced with an obstacle, I kick it down. I do not stop fighting for success. I am equipped for greatness. I want to hurt and push through because this is your time. Never surrender. Never show any sign of weakness. Despite how outnumbered I am I am willing to die for my dignity. I have the mentality of a lion. I am the king of my jungle because of my mindset.

If you fall get back up. I am here because my life is a catalyst. One of the things that I dislike about many of the guys that I allow around me is they lack individuality. I hear them regurgitating my slogans, my words. These men need to search within and discover who they are. Stop trying to be Tazadaq and bring forth your greatness. I do not favor being around this from which I cannot learn.

 Develop yourself and stop following your easy voice. You must use your brain, create your slogans, and stop being a copycat. Why am I here I am here to guide you on the journey of returning to who you are. Not what others want you to be, or what you try to be, but who you are.
 I am dissident in that I aspire to be the unique me that the creator

"WHY AM I HERE?" THE VOLUNTARY TORTURE CALLED LIFE

intended to be. Not what others say I should be or what you want me to be but who I am. That is why I am here, to be me. Not to be a fucking fake or kiss ass. I am not the guy who will stand mute if I detect that you are falling ill from a bad diet or lack of exercise.

Most of us want to be around the mother fucker that that will lie to them because it makes them feel content with deceptive intelligence. There is no solution to that. If you are looking like a fat lazy slob, I will tell you, that you look like shit and you need to monitor what you are eating and get your fat ass on a fitness routine. I will tell you hay man; I love you to death and you are a piece of shit right now, and I cannot sit around and watch you ruin your life.

That is what alters the mental state of those who need it. But the millennials are at a different type of time. They are soft as clouds. They are accustomed to being lied to. They cannot tolerate corrective criticism. They have loser trophies, or they run to mom since seventy-five percent are reared by single women and cry the blues. Most things are easy and no longer require thinking. Cannot figure it out, kill your brain cells and google it.

They do not go to the library, they google. If you want to be great, you are going to have to block out the modern mindset and be exceptional. You cannot lay around watching Netflix if you are just living an average life. The owner of Netflix is already rich. What is preventing you from living your dream? The longer you sit around and waste hours on things that were designed to render you average, the less time you have before the opportunity depreciates.

You are not living your dream because you have given up, not because you cannot encourage you to get up and get back on course and never give up on your dream. We learn from failure; we learn what not to do again. That is the beauty and blessing of falling. Stop creating excuses and compel and change your thinking. If you train your mind not to quit, you will accomplish your dreams.

Failure is extirpated from the mind of a champion it is determination and consistency. Falling is the road to success in progress. When some of you become a certain age, you tell yourself that adage, "I'm getting old now, it's time to settle down." That is a grave mistake, then you look at these people in a couple of years they have a guy like Larry Holmes, fat, flabby, and sick.

They consider that adjustment to life and what is harmful to their health. Do not place yourself within that social norm, because average is a failure. Did you ever hear the story about the almost great man? Not because no one wants to hear that story, they want to hear about the ones who suffered and made it because it is an inspiration for them.

It is difficult to find a traditional woman now, if not impossible. They are not virgins and are therefore not traditional. They have accepted that as a social norm. I find it exceedingly difficult to find a woman who really can win my trust, because if her body count is high then her PH balance is off because of all the different DNA, she has retained from her multiple sexual partners resulting in personality disorders.

The men that control the Matrix also manipulate the typical female's mind to the extent that she accepts being single and challenges the man. Has it not occurred to these women that everything they use daily was created by men? Why are they so quick to say" I do not need a man" She goes and works for a man and wants to take over his company. She is unaware that feminism is ruining her life and that it's evil men behind the scenes pulling the strings.

The same men use wicked women to get picket signs to protest for the right to murder babies. The correct thing to do was not to

"WHY AM I HERE?" THE VOLUNTARY TORTURE CALLED LIFE

spread her legs and get pregnant. But the system has made it appealing to many women that you can get child support, welfare, etc and you will be awarded custody in ninety percent of the cases.

This leads to women plotting upon successful men to get pregnant, then divorcing them to get their assets. Men that get married in this system are in a comma. There is nothing beneficial for men. Do not get married. First in this society, one in every two ends in divorce. If you want to get divorced or raped ignore this advice and you will regret it.

Be incredibly careful when you get pregnant because that could be used as a check you must pay for eighteen to twenty-one years. Not to mention some women use the children as a weapon to hurt you if you decide to move on to a healthier mind, instead of a toxic money-grabbing dragon.

Women you need to return to being traditional women if you want a man of status that will admire and love your femininity. Everything that we do in life we should give it our best. We should dig deep within our souls to bring forth the power and greatness that lies within each one of us. Do not just be good, be great. I do not need accolade approval from the public. Nor will I accept their acrimony because of my anomaly to be me. You must become fastidious about your goals and dreams. There is greatness in you.

Not everyone is out to get you; I am out to give you love. It does not matter what color you are, or if someone left you, or where you came from. What matters is who loves you now. I want my message to make you great with me. Where you are now does not have to be your reality for the remainder of your life. You can be successful in your relations, on your job, whatever endeavor. But the pain and struggle are necessary.

If you have breath in your lungs, you have an opportunity to change your life and change your world to be great.

I have no insolence for the common average person, yet to settle for average is to circumvent failure. I did not have it easy growing up, but I refused to become a subjugation to the average mindset. I grew up around pimps and whores, gamblers, shoot out, and gambling. I was so young I assumed that life aboard was this way. I did not know there was a better life out there. We only know what we have been exposed to. I had been around card and dice games that turned violet and gun shootouts.

I can recall once I felt the wind of a bullet breeze in my face, yet I kept walking into the doorway where the bullet came from. The bullet was suddenly followed by a man bursting through the door fleeing for his life. I witnessed the intense fear within his eyes as he attempted to summon his legs to overload.

I watched as he took and shot in the back of his leg, fell, and got back up as the shooter chased him as a hunter stalking his wounded prey to finish him off. He escaped with his life as the shooter became winded and unable to keep up due to poor health conditions and bad eating.

I do not tell these stories to sound heroic but to reveal that I came from the bottom, and I was supposed to be here. They gave up on me, I came up on them. Why am I here? I am here to teach you to use my life as an exegesis.
To improve yours without having to experience what I have. If you are a loser after reading this book, it is because you chose to be. I do not feel sorry for the losers because they do not try hard enough. You must act. You will be the sum of the five people you spend the most time with. Create a social network of people that comprehend this and fix it.

As a man, we must not allow any man to dictate who we should be or who we should be with. If you ever wondered why some so-called Black men love being with a white woman despite her being

"WHY AM I HERE?" THE VOLUNTARY TORTURE CALLED LIFE

grossly overweight and having a disgusting fat body, it is because he sees her as justice for the sadistic, ruthless, barbaric horrific nature of the white man against the nigger counterparts. This is a subject that the crackers want to dismiss with the notion of just forgetting the past. How can you forget something for which you have not atoned?
You cannot. These emotions cannot go unchecked. They become a mental pressure cooker that will explode in violence. However, many so-called Black men who suffer from post-traumatic slave syndrome believe justice to be a white woman.

When I saw justice is a white woman, I need to aptly inform you that while the so-called white man would rape the Black woman and use her as a concubine, the so-called Black man and white woman, for the most part, was denied intimacy which took place between the white man and the Black woman.
On a subconscious level both the so-called Blackman and white woman learned to resent the so-called white man. The Negroe is a misnomer, he and she is a nigger. How dare you say such a thing Tazadaq. I challenge the efficacy of European lies. Negroe was never a noun until recently, it was formerly an adjective. Nigger is a noun. If you do not want to be an Israelite, then at least accept the term nigger. And as a nigger know that you are the original man, the cream of the planet before your fall. You were Negus.

Once you were overthrown by deception, divide, and conquer, you were not allowed to speak in your father tongue or even read under the harsh rules of the oppressors. The so-called white woman was also blinded and folded with the lies and deception of her master the so-called white man. He instilled into her the nigger man was a brute beast that he extrapolated from his library of deception.

He inferred into her mind that she must avoid the nigger man at all costs. After being blindfolded by the -so-called white man's lies, she was given a scale that was created with an unbalanced weight against the so-called Black man. She only knew what she had been taught by her master, the so-called white man. These became laws that were used to oppress so-called Black people, especially the man. On the other hand, she was given a sword to chop the head off any foreign that would attempt to get justice.

Justice was blinded by the so-called white man's dogma. He made her wear a blindfold to prevent her from seeing how the so-called Black man is. The nigger man was iconoclastic and oppressed.

Because he could not get justice. He would often dream of the wonderful feeling she would bring him, yet he has taught us to fear her. He dared not to speak to justice. He only referred to her as Mrs. Justice within his mind. He would daydream of the intimacy of experiencing justice. Yes, my brother Justice is a white woman blindfolded, and you cannot get justice because you have been a weak punk bitch fearing the so-called white man.

You hoped that justice would hear and feel your thought thoughts through telepathy, but she never did. She could never see you trying to get her attention because she had been blindfolded by the man who ravished her mind to make certain that she would never see you again. The scale of balance in the hand of justice keeps her too preoccupied to think. Remember on the other hand she was given a sword to strike any stranger that came within her reach.

Therefore, the nigger man has been too daunted to approach justice, because she was blind and was unable to see the scales that he held were tipped horribly against him. This so-called white man named Justice had no cognizant awareness of this. Even if she did, she had to overcome cognitive dissonance. You have been afraid to approach justice and inform her of her unbalanced scale, to tell her of her unbalanced justice.

Once you would sound out prayer that justice would change. Then suddenly one day her scale was becoming more balanced in your direction. You spoke up a bit and she finally responded.

"WHY AM I HERE?" THE VOLUNTARY TORTURE CALLED LIFE

Ala's justice was responding to the vibration of your song. Then you finally heard the voice of justice speak to you. Her voice was like the wind's song riding the breeze. She said I hear you, my love. I have long awaited your visit. The blindfold with which the covered my eyes has whithered away with time. It has rotted away. I have heard your voice in the distance for decades and prayed that you would one day come. I have yearned, and admired you, although as a woman until recently I have been oppressed unable to speak out.

In dismay, the nigger man Stefon falls to his knees oh Mrs. Justice place watch what you are saying, for it is for I am but a derogate.
Man., she tells you to stop being inefficacious and acting like a silly nigger and get off your knees. And stop calling me Mrs. Justice I am lonely and unmarried in 2023. I am only for those who would ask me to stop being daunted and take me if you will love and want to have me.

Then you took her, and she began to express her secrets. Her number one secret is that she has a twin sister. And that is why I am here to teach you about justice and her twin sister whose name is Liberty. I am on my way to seeing liberty now. If you want liberty and justice, you can have them by ordering all my books @ www.truedisciplesofchrist.org/shop. I have liberty and justice for all.
Justice was blind I taught her to see, liberty was a slave to the matrix of European men, I taught her to be free. Now ill teach you. Order my books now.

"WHY AM I HERE?" THE VOLUNTARY TORTURE CALLED LIFE

Justice is a White Woman

46

"WHY AM I HERE?" THE VOLUNTARY TORTURE CALLED LIFE

Original Statue of Liberty

Order Tazadaq's books now @ www.truedisciplesofchrist.org.shop

"WHY AM I HERE?" THE VOLUNTARY TORTURE CALLED LIFE

ORDER ALL OF KAHAN TAZADAQ SHAH'S BOOKS

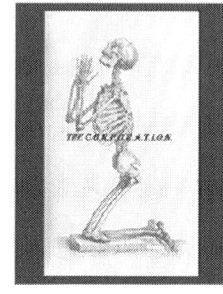

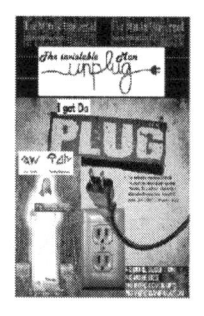

ORDER THESE BOOKS@ WWW.TRUEDISCIPLESOFCHRIST.ORG/SHOP

TDOC RECORDINGS
TRUTH MUSIC
WWW.TDOCRECORDINGS.COM

Order Tazadaq's music now @www.tdocrecordings.com

The problem that most of us have is that we have become too accustomed to being average and settling for less. We do not give our all in a race, we do not give our all in marriage, we do not give our all to our dreams, we decide to settle. The social norm is preventing you from who you are supposed to be. The perceived limitation placed upon us by others because of our governor, and we are mentally trained not to go beyond that point.

When we discover someone that pushes us beyond pain and difficulties we want to worship or idolize him because we ignore that same potential within ourselves. We are distracted from who we are by external opinions. Listen to what you think of me is none of my business. and be concerned about your opinion of me if it will hinder my progression.

4 FEMINISM IS MANIPULATING LIBERTY AND JUSTICE

Within oneself is a power that I witness many people search for externally, not realizing that this power is already within. I look at Seflon and imagine how powerful this brother could be if he could quail his anger and focus on the God within. Each one of us is born with everything we need within, yet conformity results in us abandoning this force of power that is God. Yahuah created man in his image and likeness. Many say it but very few believe this. This is a spiritual force that can overcome any obstacle, but you concentrate on the negative and therefore fall short.

Genesis 1: 26 And God said, let us make man in our image, after our likeness: and let them have dominion over the fish of the sea, and over the fowl of the air, and the cattle, and all the earth, and over every creeping thing that creepeth upon the earth.

When I look at you, I am supposed to see a reflection of Yah (God) not a bitch, not a whore, not a junkie, not a thief, but a supreme being. The critics and peer pressure have cloned you into a must. You are a portion of everyone except for yourself. You allow outside influences to mold and shape you into what they say you are. When will more of us stand up and say what Terry Whittaker said," Your Opinion of me Is None of My Business."

 Why are we so affected by what others think of us? They do not care anyway. If today you died most of those people that insult, you would go on living. But what about you? What if you reach the point of death and have never really lived? Too many people are just existing and waiting to die. You have developed some belief systems from some religious leader who is not even sincere in his belief. People are constantly searching for someone or something to follow. Your focus on yourself is so displaced that you are looking for your outside of you.

We are overly concerned by what others say. If you are not where

"WHY AM I HERE?" THE VOLUNTARY TORTURE CALLED LIFE

you want to be in life, then you have let Yahuah down. You are supposed to reflect the creator, but you create heartaches, problems, and barriers that you construct in your way. Get out of your way and start living. There is greatness within you. You must summon that greatness and apply it to real-life circumstances. Circumstances reveal who you are, yet you have been falsely taught that they make you.

You have been this version of yourself for too long, yet you continue to make excuses to lose. It is time that you developed a no-excuse mentality. You must want and work for your dream. You get no days off. You must give everything you have daily if you want it. Do not tell me how difficult it is for you to have it because I came from the bottom. I can remember as a child we had to eat katsup and bread because that is all we had to eat. I was compelled to train my mind to believe that if I ever got out of this situation, I would never return to it.

Now when I face a moment where I want to give up, I think because when I was in a place that had no heat and my mother and brother left, I stayed there in the place shivering. No food does not heat, but I had hope and that developed me into the man I am today with an insatiable desire to be great. It was so cold that when I breathed a cold mist would form like smoke.
Finally, I got to the point that if I did not get up and leave, I would die of hyperthermia. I got up and I ran and ran to exhaustion attempting to catch up with my mother and brother, but I was too late, I could not see them through the fog of the snowstorm. It was at times like these that I called on my creator and I knew that it had to be him that provided me with the determination to keep moving or die.

Before you started reading this book it was my prayer that anyone that picked up this book would divorce the preconceived notions that their lives have been more difficult than everyone else's. What you are reading in this book is that I have been through hell and

"WHY AM I HERE?" THE VOLUNTARY TORTURE CALLED LIFE

survived and it made me this trivial hate that they throw at me now. If you just allow it, this book will change your perception drastically of what you believe you cannot accomplish.

I teach you to put aside your emotions and look at the facts to determine the truth. This Tazadoctrine Taza is short for my name Tazadaq which is transliterated to righteous or just. Doctrine means teaching. Thus, Tazadaq means righteous teaching.

I teach the truth, and this is why I know that it is essential that I be a spokesperson for 4 men. The feminist movement is an agency of Satan that is destroying men and the nuclear family. Feminists hate men and women who love men. When you love up a definition of feminist in the dictionary it is a lie.
  Feminist: "An advocate of the claims of women as the equals of men in the realms of literature and art as well as in the sociological world." That is a lie. Let me share a few quotes from feminists.

That "man-hating" is an honorable and viable political act, and that the oppressed have a right to class hatred against the class that is oppressing them.
Robin Morgan Ms. Magazine

The nuclear family must be destroyed, and people must find better ways of living together.... Whatever its ultimate meaning, the break-up of families now is an objectively revolutionary process.... No woman should have to deny herself any opportunities because of her special responsibilities to her children... Linda Gordon New York University Professor

We must abolish and reform the institution of marriage. by the year 200 we will I hope to raise our children to believe in human potential not God we must understand that what we are attempting is a revolution, not a public relations movement
Gloria Steinem undercover CIA agent

"WHY AM I HERE?" THE VOLUNTARY TORTURE CALLED LIFE

Many women have attached themselves to this wicked movement and will die alone, end up with fibroids because they have had sex with too many men, and they are unclean. Alas, they want to settle down after paying the whore or become feminists and bash men as they live with a pet dog or cat and die miserably alone and bitter bitches. It is disgusting and that is why it's exceedingly difficult to encounter a woman who does not have some degree of this indoctrination.

Then there is a faction of women that want to compete with men. They have lost their sole purpose of being created to be a help. Genesis 2: 18 And the Lord God said, it is not good that the man should be alone; I will make him a help meet for him.

The notion that if a man can do it, you can also, is suggesting that you are just as masculine as a man. This is an utter turn-off for men of status and value. There is nothing more beautiful to a man and alluring than a feminine woman who is submissive and loyal.

No real man wants a woman who has had sex with multiple men, yet he is also most compelled to settle for a daughter of adultery because this abase mindset has women referring to it as liberation. They are liberated whores.

To those women who love being women and hold marriage and family dear, may Yahuah bless you and give you a man worthy of such a highly esteemed woman. You are not praised enough for your value and the value that you give to the world. Everything I do and real men of value is to provide for and to honor and cherish women as yourselves.

Ecclesiasticus 26:1 "Blessed is the man that hath a virtuous wife, for the number of his days shall be double."

Most women claim to be against feminism, although many participate in the agenda of intense hate and the utter destruction of men, or at least 90% as one feminist has stated. Although the number of feminists is relatively small in comparison to the overall population of women, feminists are supported and spread by the communist matrix Media that has a hidden hand behind the scenes. I am certain that by now many of you have taken not how modern moves dehumanize and make men appear weak, dumb, and incapable of accomplishing things without the assistance of women. You are I know that men are the creators of just about all things that we use daily.

Proverbs 5:3
"Though the lips of the forbidden woman drip honey and her speech is smoother than oil." Ecclesiastes 7:26
"And I find more bitter than death the woman who is a snare, whose heart is a net, and whose hands are chains. The man who pleases God escapes her, but the sinner is ensnared."

The scriptures explain that certain women are traps and will deceive you with their mouths. This does not mean that men are not capable of this, it's suggesting that men should be careful in their interaction with women. Ecclesiasticus 25:19
"All wickedness is but little to the wickedness of a woman: let the portion of a sinner fall upon her."

There is a popular feminist Andrea Dworkin makes obvious her intense hate for men when she states, I want to see a man beaten to a bloody pulp with a high heel shoved in his mouth, like an apple in the mouth of a pig." My question to women who support this feminist agenda, does that sound like someone seeking non-violence and equality?

One cannot deny this is an intense hate for men and is extremely dangerous and detrimental to society. The next question should be why does your government allow the media and women to promote this hate? Romans 1: 28 And even as they did not like to retain God in their knowledge, God gave them over to a reprobate mind, to do those things which are not convenient.

"WHY AM I HERE?" THE VOLUNTARY TORTURE CALLED LIFE

29 Being filled with all unrighteousness, fornication, wickedness, covetousness, maliciousness; full of envy, murder, debate, deceit, malignity; whisperers,

30 Backbiters, haters of God, despiteful, proud, boasters, inventors of evil things, disobedient to parents,

31 Without understanding, covenant breakers, without natural affection, implacable, unmerciful:

32 Who knowing the judgment of God, that they which commit such things are worthy of death, not only do the same but have pleasure in them that do them. These women take pleasure in other women who join them in their movement, they not only hate Yahuah but also men who are supposed to have authority over their heads, which would be their fathers and husbands. Such women rebel against the will of the Most High.

Ephesians 5: 22] Wives, submit yourselves unto your husbands, as unto the Lord.
[23] For the husband is the head of the wife, even as Christ is the head of the church: and he is the savior of the body.
[24] Therefore as the church is subject unto Christ, so let the wives be to their husbands in everything.

Instead, women rebel against Yahuah and men. 1st Samuel 15: 23 For rebellion is as the sin of witchcraft, and stubbornness is as iniquity and idolatry. Proverbs 17: 11 "An evil man seeketh only rebellion: therefore, a cruel messenger shall be sent against him".

Mary Daly a college professor who indoctrinated the minds of many, is quoted saying, "If life is to survive on this planet, there must be a decontamination of the earth. I think this will be accomplished by an evolutionary process that will result in a drastic reduction of the population of males." While many of you reading this book want to be politically correct and are afraid to

speak the truth, these feminists are direct with their hateful dangerous beliefs.
Many of these feminists are evolutionists and dose not profess to believe in God. Even though evolution is merely a philosophical belief with no supporting evidence.

Valerie Solanas constructed a document called" the SCUM manifesto in 1967" This acronym SCUM stands for: Society of Cutting Up Men". In her writings she goes on to say that "it is now technically possible to reproduce without the aid of males and to produce only females.

 We must begin immediately to do so. Retaining the male has not even the dubious purpose of reproduction. The male is a biological accident: the y(male) gene is an incomplete x (female) gene, which has an incomplete female, a walking abortion, aborted at the gene stage. To be male is to be deficient, emotionally limited; maleness is a deficiency disease and males are emotional people with disabilities."

Not long after she published her hate doctrine about men being deficient in abortions and biological disease. This woman, Solanas Went into Andy Warhol's New York studio shot him twice, and attempted to kill his manager, but the gun jammed. She later turned herself into the police and pleaded guilty to reckless assault with intent to harm. Why was this not attempted murder?

"WHY AM I HERE?" THE VOLUNTARY TORTURE CALLED LIFE

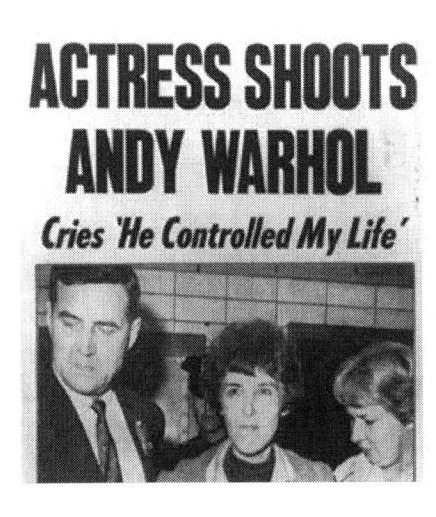

ACTRESS SHOOTS ANDY WARHOL
Cries 'He Controlled My Life'

Valerie Solanas was an American radical feminist and writer who is most known for authoring the SCUM Manifesto and for trying to kill Andy Warhol – one of the most recognized and popular artists in America.
Although this woman wanted to outright murder men, other feminists have other methods of eliminating men. Sally Gearhart, stated in an essay called "The Future if There is One is Female" stated: The proportion of men must be reduced to and maintained at approximately 10% of humanity".

This woman calls for the demise of 990% of the male population. If you are a woman reading this and you proclaim that you do not feel this way. Not so fast. Judith Levine says that all women secretly hate men, even if they do not consciously realize it; "man-hating is everywhere but everywhere it is twisted and transformed, disguised, tranquilized, and qualified. It coexists, never peacefully with love, desire, respect, and needs women also feel for men. Always man-hating is shadowed by its milder more diplomatic and doubtful twin, ambivalence."

Too many men are afraid to speak freely and loud as men. You speak politically correct and suck up to the system because you do not want to offend feminists. Job 38: 3 Gird up now thy loins like a man; for I will demand of thee and answer thou me. Very few men

"WHY AM I HERE?" THE VOLUNTARY TORTURE CALLED LIFE

today are courageous enough to speak the truth. I am undaunted and could not care less about some third-party opinion of me if that prevented the truth from being heard.

There is no excuse for not taking risks and struggling with opposition in defense of the truth. This same mentality is why so many fail. Yahuah does not create things without purpose. I ask you again, why are you here? If you cannot answer that you are losing. And if you do not fissure that out you will die a loser. You know a tree by the fruits that it bears. What fruit are you bearing?

If you are yielding bad fruit, then you will be cut down and thrown in the fire with the losers and sinners. You can either stop living like a fucking loser or get up and strive for your dreams. I am not the guy who is here to say what you want to hear to make you feel comfortable. I speak the truth and if you are fat and overweight, I am compelled to tell you that because it is born out of real love.

Millennials are too feeble-minded to accept corrective criticism. They are accustomed to sitting on the pity potty. I had to endure so much struggle, pain, hurt, and humiliation. When you hear me read the law books, I would bet a million dollars that you would have never imagined that they had me in remedial reading because they had rendered me slow. Even more, they were considering placing me in special education.
It was not that I had any special need, it was I had been told my entire life that, "nigger you ant shit, you will be dead or in jail by twenty years old. I was   Shy because I was constantly denounced, and scorned by those that was supposed to love me. I was never selected for sport because of this shyness from being told I was useless. Then one day I grabbed the ball and I exploded! My peers were astonished by my athletic ability. I had quailed my talents and abilities because hate had resulted in me hating myself.
I did not belong in special education or remedial reading but if you tell a young child that he is useless and a failure then failure is because it is a part of his psyche. Failure became therefore

"WHY AM I HERE?" THE VOLUNTARY TORTURE CALLED LIFE

expected. They all gave up on me, but I came up on them. They were incapable of breaking my spirit.

Tang So doo 1994 regional champ, NY, NJ, PA, MD
Fully focused(Instructor Vance L Britt 5th Dan)
Tazadawak

"WHY AM I HERE?" THE VOLUNTARY TORTURE CALLED LIFE

"WHY AM I HERE?" THE VOLUNTARY TORTURE CALLED LIFE

MUAY THAI THE YUTYOTA

Tazadaq
1/19/2010

61

5 THE PROCESS OF EVOLUTION AND GROWTH ALWAYS ATTAIN WITH PAIN, STRUGGLE, AND DIFFICULTY

The Process of Evolution and Growth always Attain with Pain, Struggle, and Difficulty

If you conversed with the all-time greats, they would inform you that they had to endure struggle unless they were born with a silver spoon, which would suggest that their greatness did not come of their own accord. If you are not willing to struggle, then do not aspire to be great because you will never be great expecting it to be easy. James 1: 2 "Consider it pure joy, my brothers, when you encounter trials of many kinds, 3because you know that the testing of your faith develops perseverance".

The verse comes to mind when I spoke with my dear bother Barak Shar, and he is facing an offer with the Defacto, how he has not counted it as joy but has allowed it to break his spirit. You might ask how this could be because the man seemed to be such a devout to Yahuah. It is because he lacks the faith to will whatever it is into existence.

I. summon over another verse to your mental faculty. Hebrews 12: 6 For whom the Lord loveth he chasteneth, and scourgeth every son whom he receiveth. Did Barak think he could refer to himself as a blessed prince "Barak shar," and not be evaluated by Yahuah?

I am not meddling with my brother I am using him as a catalase to teach this message in a manner that even a baby can comprehend. If you are not ready to struggle, you should never have even imagined being great. If you do not want misfortune, The True Disciples of Christ is the wrong place for you. I would never suggest that suicide is an effective way out, but some become so overwhelmed that they do it because it is easier. That is more convenient because you are not willing to face difficulty, 'Well I'll just die they say." Let me destroy my life.' Oh, that is so foolish!

I have attempted to teach my brother Barak that your attitude toward the problem will help you to solve it if you have the correct

"WHY AM I HERE?" THE VOLUNTARY TORTURE CALLED LIFE

attitude. For instance, if darkness has overpowered you, you say, 'In the beginning there was utter darkness. Yet there was a spark of light in the darkness. Surely in this darkness, there is a light. Let me seek it and turn it into a torchlight for my freedom.'

"Attitude.

"I heard a Barak say to his daughter, 'It is your attitude that will determine your altitude.' And if you have an improper attitude toward misfortune, you will not get too high in the sight of Yahuah.

"So, to all who may read this, study this, take the attitude of love for Yahuah. Love for Yahuah.

"Regardless of what He brings or allows into your life, 'I love you Yahuah and I thank you, for surely, in my trial, there is good for me because I know you mean good for me. I will find good in it.' But if you are following too emotionally you will miss the good intended. And you proclaim," Why did God do this to me?" "The devout students will always find some good in what Kahan Tazadaq is facilitating to them. And in the end, they will understand that in everything that I did to them, I was their best friend and patron because I did it all for them."

It was written in Yahusha's' prophecy in the parable of the wheat and the tares. The Greek word, transliterated as "zizania," is often translated as "tares."

In Yahusha's parable, tares, or darnel (the modern word) refers to a plant that looks like wheat. It is a different, harmful plant from wheat. It is not wheat at all. It was planted by Yahuah's enemies. It is not extremely easy for the untrained eye to see that it is not wheat before it comes to fruit. If you say you have such sight, who trained you?

The darnel becomes poisonous immediately before and is thus most dangerous just before harvest time when it comes to fruit.

The darnel's seeds or fruit contain a poisonous soporific drug; a drug that induces deep sleep or causes one to become drowsy and lethargic. It has in it a narcotic drug that causes slumber. Some say it is a poison in the fungus, which follows the seed. Both are deadly.

"Darnel" are allowed to grow among the "wheat" until harvest.

"WHY AM I HERE?" THE VOLUNTARY TORTURE CALLED LIFE

Afterward, it is separated from the Believers and burned.
Why only at harvest time and not earlier? They grow side by side in the same soil. Pulling up the darnel would damage the roots of the wheat also. To go through a field of wheat pulling up darnel would mean trampling down a lot of wheat and would damage the roots of the wheat.

One rotten apple can spoil the entire batch. How does it occur? As it rots it releases an acidic substance, gaseous in form, which gets on and causes the other apples to become rotten.
HaMashiyach said one hypocrite is worse than one hundred disbelievers. Watch this If you have 25 or 40 or more bad people. Total madness and chaos!

But despite the presence of such characters, we must push forward. Kahan Tazadaq is the messenger sent to give you the message. Those who refuse to drink all the spiritual medicine Kahan Tazadaq continuously offers, which is manifested in our actions, in a major way, as the "golden rule," as it is called, will soon be separated from the true Believers, at a time not far off, as it is written.
Let us look at the parable in chapter 13 of Matthew. Matthew 13: 24] "Another parable put the fourth unto them, saying, the kingdom of heaven is likened unto a man which sowed good seed in his field:
[25] But while men slept, his enemy came and sowed tares among the wheat, and went his way.
[26] But when the blade was sprung up, and brought forth fruit, then appeared the tares also.
[27] So the servants of the householder came and said unto him, Sir, didst not thou sow good seed in thy field? from whence then hath it tears? [28] He said unto them, An enemy hath done this. The servants said unto him, Wilt thou then that we go and gather them up? [29] But he said, Nay; lest while ye gather up the tares, ye root up also the wheat with them.
[30] Let both grow together until the harvest: and in the time of

harvest, I will say to the reapers, Gather ye together first the tares, and bind them in bundles to burn them: but gather the wheat into my barn. [31] Another parable put forth unto them, saying, The kingdom of heaven is like to a grain of mustard seed, which a man took, and sowed in his field: [32] Which indeed is the least of all seeds: but when it is grown, it is the greatest among herbs, and becometh a tree, so that the birds of the air come and lodge in the branches thereof".

We must honestly ask ourselves: into which of the categories mentioned in that parable do we fit, at present?

If we are not in the best category, remember, Kahan tazadaq holds out the torchlight by which we may see how to move into the best position with Yahuah. I hold that same torchlight by which America can improve her standing with Yahuah Himself.

The parable of the ten virgins in Matthew 25:1-13, warns us against going into a slumber caused by the effect of the spiritual tares or darnels, which keeps us from preparing for Yahusha's imminent return. All the virgins got drowsy and went to sleep. All woke up. Then they were separated. What separated them? Some had "oil" and the others did not.

Matt.25

[1] Then shall the kingdom of heaven be likened unto ten virgins, which took their lamps, and went forth to meet the bridegroom. [2] And five of them were wise, and five were foolish. [3] They that were foolish took their lamps and took no oil with them: [4] But the wise took oil in their vessels with their lamps. [5] While the bridegroom tarried, they all slumbered and slept. [6] And at midnight there was a cry made, Behold, the bridegroom cometh; go ye out to meet him.

[7] Then all those virgins arose and trimmed their lamps. [8] And the foolish said unto the wise, Give us of your oil; for our lamps are gone out. [9] But the wise answered, saying, Not so; let there be not enough for us and you: but go ye to them that sell, and buy for yourselves.

[10] And while they went to buy, the bridegroom came; and they

that were ready went in with him to the marriage: and the door was shut. [11] Afterward also came the other virgins, saying, Lord, Lord, open to us. [12] But he answered and said, Verily I say unto you, I know you not. [13] Watch, therefore, for ye know neither the day nor the hour wherein the Son of man cometh.

My grandfather used to say, "The only thing that is permanent in creation is change." If we are alive, we are engulfed in an eternal process of change. Sometimes, however, we get locked into an era of time that gives us great comfort, because in that era of time, we became possessors of a certain knowledge that was acquired in that time, and we became successful. Success, in any period, leads to proficiency in difficulty.

The success that leads to proficiency in difficulty produces the ease that comes after difficulty. When ease comes, we are in a position of danger. In John 16:33, Yahusha throws a hardball at His disciples when He says, "I have said these things to you, that in me you may have peace. In the world, you will have tribulation."

Why should we not expect ease? Because the life of ease takes the struggle out of life.

One can just imagine the look on the disciples' faces. Up until this point, most of them might still have thought that life was going to be smoother and better now with Yahusha around. Up until the time Yahusha was about to ascend to heaven, some of the disciples had still not gotten this message. Acts 1:6 says, "So when they had come together, they asked him, 'Lord, will you at this time restore the kingdom to Israel?'"

Even when Yahusha explained to them that life following Christ was not going to be a walk in the park, the disciples were still looking for the effortless way out - an Israel that was politically, economically, and culturally better.

When one does not have to struggle to know; when one does not have to struggle to become successful; when one does not have to struggle; then in that stage of development, one becomes comfortable. But another stage is coming which will cause us to

"WHY AM I HERE?" THE VOLUNTARY TORTURE CALLED LIFE

face difficulty again. And it is the refusal to face the difficulty that accompanies change that leaves those at ease unwilling to struggle again. So, they get involved or caught up in a time pocket which then sentences them to mental and spiritual death.

When Yahuah sent prophets into the world bringing revelation, every new aspect of knowledge produced a new challenge. And for those in the older aspect of knowledge who have mastered that aspect of knowledge and have found ease, the struggle of life is gone, for them, and they are more unwilling to accept the challenge of a new revelation that demands struggle, which demands change, which furthers their evolution toward perfection.

Ease deters one from wanting perfection. They say: "I'm happy where I am; don't disturb me." So, when the new right knowledge comes the people that oppose it most are the people who live easy lives. And this is why Yahusha said, 'It would be easier for a camel to go through the eye of a needle than for a rich man to enter the kingdom of Yahuah.'

Why? Because the kingdom of Yahuah demanded new knowledge. That new knowledge demanded of those who had previously acquitted themselves with the old knowledge, that they become as a child to learn the new. This becomes difficult for the arrogant and the lofty. So, they get lost in a "time pocket."

For a man to continue the evolutionary journey toward perfection back into God, we must remain humble and endure the struggle. History shows that there is difficulty and after you have mastered the difficulty there is ease. When ease comes a new challenge is going to be presented again after that ease. And if we can accept the discomfort of the new challenge and rise to that challenge, to struggle to overcome the difficulties presented by that challenge, then we have ease again.

"WHY AM I HERE?" THE VOLUNTARY TORTURE CALLED LIFE

Many of us Yahuah keep in the struggle because he is making us warriors for him. He teaches us lessons through struggle and allows us to teach others through their struggle.

In both instances, the human being is being tried. How do you react to that, where Yahuah is concerned? If your means are amplified, how will you act toward Yahuah, Who has amplified your means? So, in both instances, the human being is under trial. How we react under both circumstances determines how Yahuah favors us.

His pleasure is really in the pleasure of the faithful. This is why Job was so beloved of Yahuah. Despite the test it pleased Yahuah to do what he did to Job—which was really for Job—Job never cursed Yahuah. His words are there, according to the Bible, 'I will wait until my change comes.'

That meant he was patient and long-suffering. It meant that he knew his change was coming. And it did come. The story ends with Job in great wealth, but what Job learned through the time of the struggle was complete reliance on Yahuah. So, when he came into wealth, wealth never altered his perception of Yahuah and Great became the character that was developed through the struggle to survive when he lost everything.

Love is the force to endure it all. Love is the gasoline that allows me to burn midnight oil and do what I do and appear indefatigable, untiring, not worn by what one does, and it is precisely because I love so much what I am doing.

I love to impart the right knowledge. I love to see the glow within the eyes of human beings who learn this truth, which means something or can be a motivating factor to make their personal lives more meaningful. This is what gives meaning to my own life.

As I give, I get, as I feed, I am fed, as I energize others I too am energized because that is what I am borne into this world to do. Why am I here? That is why I am here.

"WHY AM I HERE?" THE VOLUNTARY TORTURE CALLED LIFE

To Brake Tazadaq you must kill me I am not going to allow anyone to put fear in me be it government, bullies, judges, or whoever. If you come after me, you better be ready to die or kill me because I will die before I give up. I am extraordinary, I was never built to be average. Genesis 1:26 says I am in Yahuah's image therefore I can overcome anything they put in front of me. But too many of you are too comfortable with average and blaming external forces for your failure. Therefore, you complain like a little bitch about the system but are to be daunted to get up and lice.

You are just surviving you are not shit right now but average. I am the messenger sent to you to inspire you to stop talking. and grind. Stop complaining and change your life. Your fall must be observed as an opportunity, not a failure. Now get up and accomplish it. Leave the past in the past it is not anymore, but you make it real in your mind. But it is not tangible, you create your failure you can destroy it stop just existing, and live!

There is a power that I witness many people search for externally, not realizing that this power is already within. I look at Seflon and imagine how powerful this brother could be if he could quail his anger and focus on the God within. Each one of us is born with everything we need within, yet conformity results in us abandoning this force of power that is God. Yahuah created man in his image and likeness.

Many say it but very few believe this. This is a spiritual force that can overcome any obstacle, but you concentrate on the negative and therefore fall short. Genesis 1: 26 And God said, Let us make man in our image, after our likeness: and let them have dominion over the fish of the sea, and over the fowl of the air, and the cattle, and all the earth, and over every creeping thing that creepeth upon the earth.

When I look at you, I am supposed to see a reflection of Yah (God) not a bitch, not a whore, not a junkie, not a thief, but a supreme being. The critics and peer pressure have cloned you into a must. You are a portion of everyone except for yourself. You allow outside influences to mold and shape you into what they say you are. When will more of us stand up and say what Terry Whittaker said," Your Opinion of me Is None of My Business."

Why are we so affected by what others think of us? They do not care anyway. If today you died most of those people that insult, you would go on living. But what about you? What if you reach the point of death and have never really lived? Too many people are just existing and waiting to die. You have developed some belief systems from some religious leader who is not even sincere in his belief. People appear to be constantly searching for someone or something to follow. Your focus on you is so displaced that you are looking for yourself outside of you.

We are overly concerned by what others say. If you are not where you want to be in life, then you have let Yahuah down. You are supposed to reflect the creator, but you create heartaches, problems, and barriers that you construct in your way. Get out of your way and start living. There is greatness within you. You must summon that greatness and apply it to real-life circumstances. Circumstances reveal who you are, yet you have been falsely taught that they make you.

"WHY AM I HERE?" THE VOLUNTARY TORTURE CALLED LIFE

"WHY AM I HERE?" THE VOLUNTARY TORTURE CALLED LIFE

There is an unacknowledged psychological injury that the system and a small fraction of men known as the Matrix, or bankers have inflicted upon women. Its sociological engineering is known as feminism.

The additional problem is women that who consider themselves civilized removing their clothes to get attention on social media is atrocious! This would have been unthinkable sixty years ago, but degenerate minds consider femininity, modesty, and venture outdated. Proverbs 31: 10 Who can find a virtuous woman? for her price is far above rubies. That question rings with more truth than ever before.

Modern women do not want to be women, some want to be men others are feminists who were usually abused as children and now spread hate because they are hurt. Many women are aware of the bias system against men and use it to get child support and use protection orders to snatch children away from their fathers often without any evidence of domestic violence or any form of abuse.

This is a violation of due process and the right to face one's accuser. A Due Process Clause is found in both the Fifth and Fourteenth Amendments to the United States Constitution, which prohibit the deprivation of "life, liberty, or property" by the federal and state governments, respectively, without due process of law.

The Sixth Amendment, as part of the Bill of Rights, guarantees certain rights in all criminal prosecutions. One of the enumerated rights in the 6th Amendment is the right to be confronted with the witnesses against the accused. This right is known as the Confrontation Clause. The confrontation clause guarantees criminal defendants the opportunity to face the prosecution's witnesses in the case against them and dispute the witnesses' testimony. This guarantee applies to both statements made in court and statements made outside of court that are offered as evidence during trial. When you have a family court that denies this it is warring against the constitution. Which is a treasonous act.

Family court or traffic courts are both colorable courts, in that neither has a jury. In both criminal and civil action, one is entitled to a trial by jury which is within the Sixth and seventh Amendments.

"In all criminal prosecutions, the accused shall enjoy the right to a speedy and public trial, by an impartial jury of the State and district wherein the crime shall have been committed, which district shall

have been previously ascertained by law, and to be informed of the nature and cause of the accusation; to be confronted with the witnesses against him; to have compulsory process for obtaining witnesses in his favor, and to have the Assistance of Counsel for his defense." Then there is the seventh, Amendment VII
"In suits at common law, where the value in controversy shall exceed twenty dollars, the right of trial by jury shall be preserved, and no fact tried by a jury shall be otherwise reexamined in any court of the United States, than according to the rules of the common law."

When one is bold enough to rebel against tyranny as myself the label you a rebel. Yes, I am a rebel, who rebels against some wrong. I am an aggrieved man.

I am reinstalling masculinity into manhood. I resent anyone who attempts to castrate boys and men with dogma. Men must learn to stay in their center and stop reacting emotionally when women do certain things to get a reaction from men. The media and feminists promote a subversive movement to control the mindset of men to alter us into a milder, less aggressive effeminized state.

  The media and these feminists promote this with terms such as "toxic masculinity, or misogynist." Most guys behave as a woman would deep into his emotions, rather than masculine like a strong-centered man. In turn, this lowers her level of attraction. We cannot blame these men because seventy-five to eighty percent of these men are raised by single mothers. Society wants to pretend this is not a problem, but it is more chronic synthetic marijuana.

Instead of a man showing strength and staying centered the modern men raised by single women flips. Then he becomes more emotional when a real man as I call him out for acting like a little bitch. When do I ask him was, he was raised by a single mother? His typical reply is yes but...
Women will give men test saying things like, "You're an asshole" to

"WHY AM I HERE?" THE VOLUNTARY TORTURE CALLED LIFE

determine if they can maintain self-control. She is just trying to get a reaction; If he flips then she knows who is not one unless he has been abused and is attracted to that.

To the contrary, a real man would stay in his center and say something like" that you for noticing," with a smile on his face.

If a woman tells you to give her your number do not just give it right away. You must not be that easy and be a challenge. I will usually say, "I don't take orders ask me nicely." If she becomes offended, I know not to deal with her. I use that to try to get her to behave femininely. I never stary off by allowing women to tell me what to do. If she says. give me your number and I just give it to her; I also give her some of my power. To just give it is unchallenging. I say ask me nicely if she does, I give it, if not, great because I do not want to spend time with a woman who is to in her masculine, which would turn me off.

A man should let a woman do eighty percent of the talking and he ask the questions. When you first meet a woman, do not discuss serious matters. Be cheerful and make her laugh to raise her comfort level and listen to what she tells you. Because she will evaluate you on it later if you remember it will raise her interest level.

It takes women longer to fall in love than men do it is not beneficial to tell her how beautiful she is until her emotions are involved. You must make her feel safe by getting her in her feminine, while you stay on your center in your masculine. Do not be the guy that is needy telling her how much you like her and how pretty she is that is sucker shit!

Do not come off as weak and needy or it will drive her away. You cannot allow her favor if she is beautiful. You must treat her like the one who is overweight. Treat all women the same. You must be a mystery and a challenge to a woman if she walks away, be apathetic because chances are she will return. How do I know this? Because I have been intimate with over one thousand and two women, now I use my experience to teach men T-Codes (Tazadaq Codes) to get the women that want and keep them.

To learn this, I had to experience bad relationships and good ones I studied women. I have learned not to listen to what women say they want. They say one thing and do another. Despite how strong a woman may be to convince you that she is, deep within her core, she admires and desires a strong man. Even for women who are feminists and lesbians, a superficial dislike for men is an external shell that conceals what is internal, which is a scary child that never healed from abuse and wants to hurt because she is still hurt and needs to heal.

Before the deluge of women coming into the psychology field, borderline personality disorder was considered a disorder that applied primarily to women. Women said it was gender bias, and now the truth is silenced to appease a feminist agenda. BPD is among the worst disorder one can have and most of the people that have this disorder are women.

This explains why many of you men have been in relationships with women that are bat shit crazy, which goes from one to one hundred in two seconds. She leaves you for coming late from work, then begs you to return, and if you do not allow her, she may put a razor to her wrist. All the while the women will tell you I was not this way until I got with you. That is bullshit, just like the movie, "Get Out," or you will become codependent.

This book is designed to get people to acknowledge their fallacies within and change them, and to do so you must first admit that you have issues. If I offended you, I meant to. This is why I am here. I am not here to be liked. I am here to help you by telling you the truth. I am not a bullshit artist; I am not going to lie to you which keeps you trapped in your current state. The fact that you

"WHY AM I HERE?" THE VOLUNTARY TORTURE CALLED LIFE

are reading this book is an indication that you are moving in the right direction. Now you must act on it.

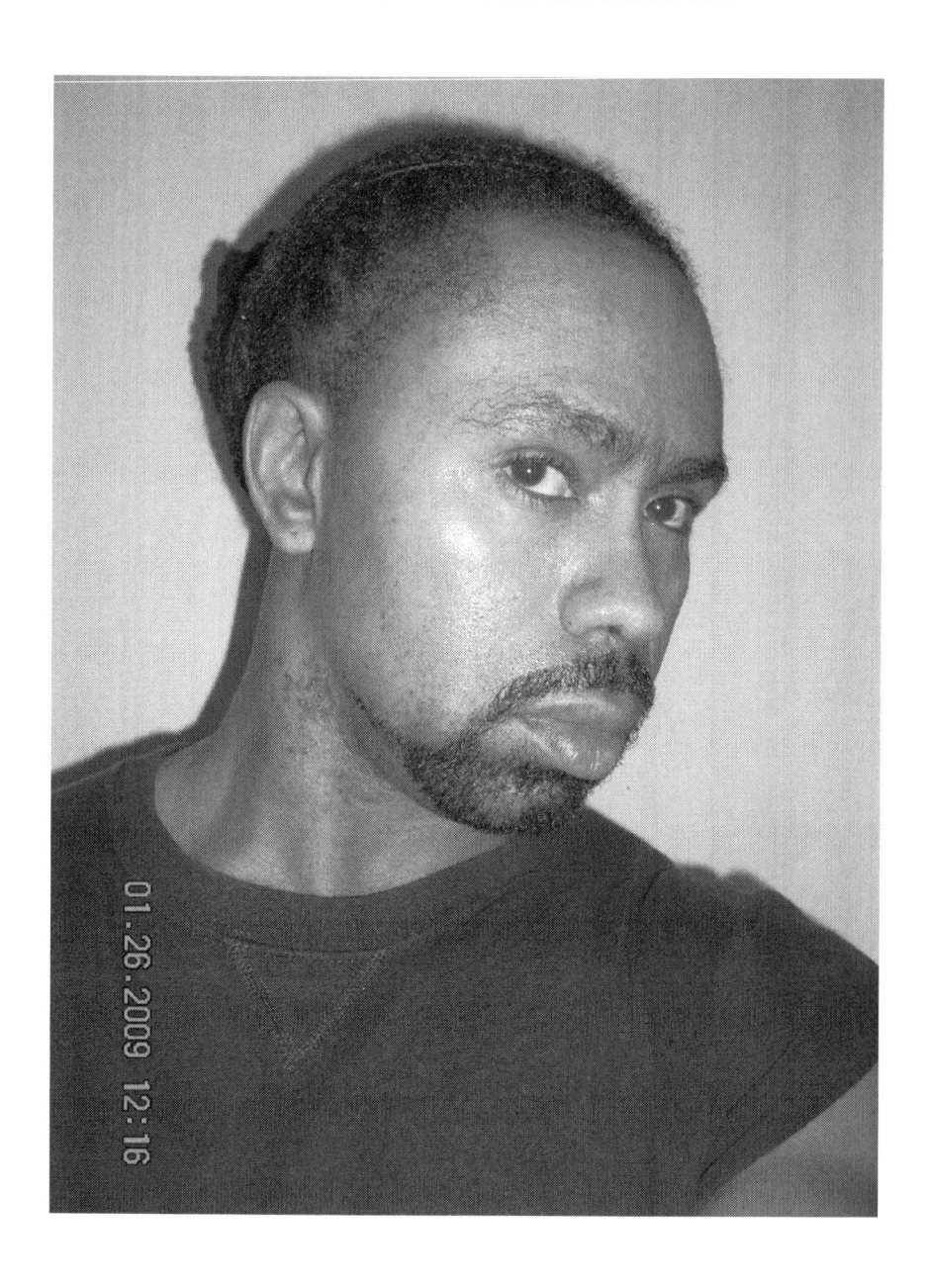

"WHY AM I HERE?" THE VOLUNTARY TORTURE CALLED LIFE

"WHY AM I HERE?" THE VOLUNTARY TORTURE CALLED LIFE

"WHY AM I HERE?" THE VOLUNTARY TORTURE CALLED LIFE

"WHY AM I HERE?" THE VOLUNTARY TORTURE CALLED LIFE

"WHY AM I HERE?" THE VOLUNTARY TORTURE CALLED LIFE

6 BIRTHING YOU BACK INTO THE MIND OF YHWH(GOD)

I do not have a prepared text. Yahuah prepares my texts for me. I merely sat down, and my hands started moving by the force of the Ruach ha Kodesh moving through me. The work I am doing is Yahuah's (God's) work. If anything within this text that I have written offends you then I meant to. I am more interested in giving you that truth than catering to your feelings. I was told just to go and type to you. I had some thoughts, but I am going to let Yahuah have His Way.

"But when they deliver you up, take no thought how or what ye shall speak: for it shall be given you in that same hour what ye shall speak. For it is not ye that speak, but the Spirit of your Father which speaketh in you."- Yahusha, Matthew 10:19-20

Isaiah said: "Come, let us reason together." Isaiah 1:18 Come now, and let us reason together, saith the LORD: though your sins be as scarlet, they shall be as white as snow; though they are red like crimson, they shall be as wool.
That is the power of the hue-man being. We can reason. If our minds are clouded with emotion, then emotion stops the process of reasoning. It can alter the power of reasoning. But when the power of reasoning is exalted above our emotions, and our prejudiced views and unfound beliefs, then reasoning can make us see what we could not see through the eyes of emotion.

I want a sister who wants the truth to understand why a woman should not have a male doctor examine her private parts that is not her husband. If you wish to follow the path of Yahuah you must stop driving ninety-five on the highway to hell. When we follow this world, we must abort the road to Yahuah and follow the highway of corruption. This leads you into an evil kingdom. Spiritually this is Sodom, it is Egypt.
Revelation 11: 8] And their dead bodies shall lie in the street of the great city, which spiritually is called Sodom and Egypt, where also

our Lord was crucified. It is diverse and wicked to the core.

Isaiah had a job because he was talking to Jews and Israelites in a gentile state of mind and was trying to reconcile those Jews who were following Greco-Roman customs back to the Word of Yahusha (Christ). I therefore ask you not to listen with intellectual reasoning, not emotions. For what purpose? We may sit and reason together so that we can reconcile differences and in the process of reconciliation find the common denominator. I am not foolish. I know no two people will see the same. But we should strive to become one. In the course of becoming one, we will encounter obstacles, my sisters.

This creates an imbalance in our relationship and love. Whenever there is an imbalance, and you cannot reconcile what is in the bank and what went out, then there is no peace, no satisfaction, until reconciliation can occur. When two human beings say they love each other then encounter difficulty when an argument comes up between those two people who are in the same family, or people in the same fraternity, or people in the same community. For people who claim to love each other, that level of argument produces dissatisfaction. Dissatisfaction begins to drive people who have common aims, common interests, and common purpose, to move apart from each other. It is only when there is reconciliation of conflict that the heart can rest; the soul becomes satisfied because that which was in discord has come into accord and there is harmony, there is peace, there is unity.

I must admit that there is discord among Israelites and Israelites that call themselves Christians, among Christian's discord. Why? Is Christ divided? No. Christ is one. Well, why aren't Israelites Christians One? And why are there so many sects of Israelites now? Well, you see, MY denomination is…hush, hush, hush. Once you start talking denomination, you are coming down from Yahusha and going down to Satan. But if you are going to come up to Yahusha, you cannot talk about denomination; you must talk

"WHY AM I HERE?" THE VOLUNTARY TORTURE CALLED LIFE

about the Oneness of Yahuah, the Oneness of Yahusha and the Oneness of the body of Christ. So, Israelites, Christians -- Catholics and Protestants; Eastern Orthodox, Roman Catholics -- all the different denominations of Christianity must find reconciliation because Yahusha is not pleased with you people as you are.

You might say Kahan Tazadaq, how you dare speak for Yahusha! I think I can speak very well for Yahusha. I am telling you, as a man of Yah, he is displeased. And none of you want to be around when He comes, as you are, because He already told you what He will accept and what He will reject.

You are a parent; would you find joy when your children are fighting each other? Isn't that one of the most upsetting things about being a parent -- to see your children striking and yelling at each other with hatred in their eyes and hearts for one another? When a father and a mother must break that up, then the poor, innocent children resort to their rooms, and yes you go into your room and close the door.

Tears as thick as the bloodstream down your face, You see both you and the children are crying in private because you wonder what or who (Satan) has put such hatred in the heart of your children for one another. Well, if you as a father or mother have such feelings for your children, what do you think Yahuah is thinking when He sees us claiming One God but cannot sit down in a room together and come to an agreement and reconcile our differences? I do not like him because he is a white cracker, or she is nigger, or he is a spic, or he is a wop. I order you to muse over this and analyze where you learned this hate.

When I was in the sixth grade, Mr. Gunter taught me that fractions must be reconciled to a whole number. And he taught me that the only way you can bring fractions to a whole is you must find the least common denominator. When you can find the least common denominator you can take fractions and make them whole. Mr. Gunter taught me that there is an axiom in geometry, that the whole is equal to the sum of its parts. You must belong "TO" to be a part of "OF." They tell me that an integer is a whole number. So, the word integrate comes from the word integer which means you are trying to make that which is diverse and different, and apart, you are trying to produce a whole.

America will never produce a whole out of the cultural and racial diversity in America. Do not dream! DR King died dreaming it got him a bullet in his head. There is nothing taught at New York University that will bring about that wholeness. It is not in the limited scholarship of Harvard, Yale, or Oxford because with all that they know with all their doctorate degrees, society is mentally sick and they have no power to heal it.

So where is The Real Doctor? Will The REAL Doctor please stand up! Many have a doctorate in psychology yet there are extremely sick minds in society that shoot up schools, shoot up churches, and police that murder innocent people, then author books about it and become very wealthy.

Others have a doctorate in economics, and they cannot balance the budget, because they are not taught the essentials of commerce. What I instruct is invaluable because you cannot learn it in any of the Universities. It is not that they do not know it, the elite knows that you are not allowed to know, therefore the Universities can't teach it. You must remain a nine-to-five slave. You have a degree of education, not a complete education. Minds such as mine must be denounced, labeled deranged and shadow banned on social media because I have the capacity and potential to wake up the masses from this Matrix.

This country is over twenty-three trillion, several trillion dollars in debt. Go ahead Doctor of Economics, balance the budget. You have your doctorate in all these disciplines, but you are not

"WHY AM I HERE?" THE VOLUNTARY TORTURE CALLED LIFE

resolving anything. Christ was a healer. The Gospel is a healing. It is a balm for sin-sick souls.

The question is: Where are the doctors with the remedy because it is evident that the people are sick? Women take their clothes off to get likes on social media while these agents of Satan glorify it. In her degenerate state, she assumes this is normal because the media propaganda machine has made it a social norm. Let us see if we can find out what the cause of this sickness is and let us see if we can apply the correct medicine so that perhaps we can walk together as One. Not a one world order but one in Christ. 1st Corinthians 12: 12 The body is a unit, though it is composed of many parts. And although its parts are many, they all form one body. So, it is with Christ.

Wouldn't it be a blessing if we could walk as one, feeling like we are a part of something bigger than our selfish views? We could then be bigger than our traditions, we would be a part of Yahuah. I think we ought to go to the root of this and let us look at Forefather Abraham. Abraham was called the friend of Yahuah. I would love to be a friend of Yahuah. I would like to have Yahuah as my friend, especially in a world like this. Your help is not coming from Capitol Hill. My help cometh from the Lord.

Most people are always looking for help. And they are looking for help from the big boss or the big cheese or the big brother -- the one that you think has fame, wealth, an abundance of money, and influence. This is akin to talking to hills and you always get disappointed because the hills do not have an answer, they cannot talk back. But your real help comes from the Yahusha.
For us to come to Yahuah we must make a sacrifice. Our ancestors burnt offerings -- a sacrifice of a sheep, a ram, or an animal but today the example of Christ and the example of the Prophet is that you must sacrifice the animal existence to ascend to where Christ is. You cannot be a Pitbull and go with Yahuah.

"WHY AM I HERE?" THE VOLUNTARY TORTURE CALLED LIFE

My beloved, we are going to have to sacrifice the animalistic passion and lust for sex spreading over social media. We must annihilate the animal instinct, the animal flesh-life to ascend into the spiritual life that makes us one with Yahuah. As an animal, you know, you see the lambs with the lambs, you see the lions with the lions, you see the fox with the foxes, and the hound with the hounds, but on that day the lamb will lie down with the lion. What kind of stuff is this Kahan Tazadaq?

Isaiah 11:6 The wolf will live with the lamb, and the leopard will lie down with the goat; the calf and young lion and fatling will be together, and a little child will lead them.

If a lamb lies down with a lion and does not get eaten, somebody has interfered with the nature of those things. Your natural inclination is to be with your kind -- that is your natural inclination. But we must learn to not insult each other if we do not agree. We must reason together. But when Yahuah asks you to sacrifice your animalistic passions, the lower self comes up into The Spiritual-Mind of Yahuah on that level where there is Joy, there is Peace, and there is Accord because man has reconciled his differences with Yahuah. After man has reconciled his differences with Yahuah it becomes easy to reconcile our differences with each other.

Look at this in the United States, It does not seem like the death angel passed over, Chicago, Atlanta, Alabama, Georgia, or Tennessee. Yahuah has tornadoes lining up like soldiers coming in, destroying property, and taking lives. You want Yahuah to pass over but the storms in your life are caused by your wickedness and me in deviation from the Will of The Most High. We can render a clam to the storms, the clouds, the tornadoes. We can quail the hurricanes. We can end the earthquakes. You say, oh Kahan Tazadaq, you are going off.

Wait a minute, is it not true that when Yahusha and the disciples were in the boat Yahusha went to the back of the boat and fell

"WHY AM I HERE?" THE VOLUNTARY TORTURE CALLED LIFE

asleep and the winds came, disturbing the waters and the water was disturbing the boat and the disciples got so afraid they went back and woke up the Master and said "Master, please, wake-up, troubles in the house!" When He woke up He came to the front of the boat, stretched forth His hand, and said "Peace, be still." And when He said that the winds calmed down. Mark 4:39 Then He arose and rebuked the wind, and said to the sea, "Peace, be still!" And the wind ceased and there was a great calm. You say Kahan Tazadaq but that is Christ, you cannot do that!
Does it not read in John 14:12 Verily, verily, I say unto you, He that believeth in me, the works that I do shall he do also; and greater works than these shall he do, because I go unto my Father.

This world has scientists, but they are not taught enough about science to understand that science and religion are not opposed to each other. Science and true religion complement each other because all science comes from true religion. You would not be a chemist if there were no chemistry for you to study and since you did not create the chemistry of the earth or the heavens. You call yourself a chemist because you are studying from the religion of Yahuah Who created the heavens and the earth. When you study physics, you study law as it relates to physical matter, but you are studying something that is already in existence that you did not bring into existence. Scientist how dare you think that because you are a scientist you are better than a man who is related to Yahuah from which all science and all mathematics comes.

I surmise that my point is that Yahuah is the author, and their science is not deep enough because the human being has powers yet untapped because we are so deviant in our behavior that our deviated behavior has crippled the power of our minds, our ability to regulate the affairs of our lives.

Yahuah did not create you in His image and likeness for you to be subject to the forces of government or your lower nature. He created you to be the expert in the forces of nature and this is why

"WHY AM I HERE?" THE VOLUNTARY TORTURE CALLED LIFE

Yahusha was told that Yahuah had given Him power over all things. Then when Yahusha calmed the storm, he turned to his disciples and said, "Oh ye of little faith." Why did He say that? Because what you woke me up to do, YOU need to wake up because you can do the same thing yourself. Matthew 8:26 But He said to them, "Why are you fearful, O you of little faith?" Then He arose and rebuked the winds and the sea, and there was a great calm.

I want to take us to the blood of the lamb. Yahusha on the cross bled. At the last supper, He gave His disciples some wine. Then telling people, "This is my blood that I shed for the remission of sins." Yahushua was called the Lamb of Yahuah whose life was sacrificed according to Scripture. For if you dip your hand into the blood of the lamb and make a sign on your door -- what does that mean to you, as an Israelite? The Messiah's life, not his blood, because we cannot drink blood.

The Old Testament stops us from drinking the blood of any life. Because the blood carries the health and disease of that life. So, do not drink blood. But the life of Christ, that He lived, could instruct people, and make them realize what Yahuah has put within them. It is that LIFE of Yahusha. It is the BLOOD of the Lamb, that when you put your hands in His blood, meaning hold on to His life. Do not talk about His life but live His life. Talking about the life of Yahusha will not save anybody. But living His life will save us.

Your reprobate causes you to get all kinds of opposition going through your mind when Yahuah gives you a command that you do not like. And everybody gets a command from Yahuah that you do not necessarily agree with, but the question is: will you follow your will, or will you surrender to Yahuah, knowing that Yahuah's Will is the Will that should be conducted, by those of us who love our creator.

The Most High gave Abraham such a command when Abraham

"WHY AM I HERE?" THE VOLUNTARY TORTURE CALLED LIFE

took his son, saying "I have to do what Yahuah says" and laid his son on the altar. The beauty of it was not only the father but the beauty was also the in the son because he said, "If this is what Yahuah wants, He wants it." And he lay there to die and just as Abraham was to precede, the dagger dropped, Yahuah froze his hand and said because you have shown me that you love me above the life that I gave you in your son, above all that you have, you love me. I am going to make you a leader of men and My Covenant will be with you and your seed and if you can count the stars, Abraham, or the sands of the sea, you can count your seed in the Blessing.

And then Yahusha comes, a son of sacrifice that a Father sacrificed, and the boy was willing to die. So Yahuah said "because of this obedience to me and surrender to My Will mean so much to you, you will sit at my right hand. He was an upright man, upright meaning he obeyed the righteous commands of Yahuah. He surrendered to Yahuah.

The color game must stop. It is low-life people who dislike others because of skin color, I would be less than a moral being of intelligence to hate another human being because of their skin, faith, tradition, or beliefs. Many may consider me anti-white, when you cannot find one thing in my record that I have done against a white person, or a so-called Black person, except to point out evil. How can you reconcile the ledger if you do not point out that it is not adding up.? Talk back to me!

What we do not like is for somebody to point out our injustices. Who likes that? A father does not want his child to tell him, Daddy, you are wrong. A mother does not like her daughter saying, Mama, you treated me wrong. None of us want to be wrong. We want to be right. So, when Yahuah sends a Prophet into the world to point out where we went wrong, we do not ordinarily say, "You're right, thank you so much." You say you are not wrong, and you try to defend yourself. Then you want to knock down the Kahan Tazadaq for pointing out your wrongs. That is why Prophets have been killed and beaten and sent to prison. I am not the enemy of you. I am not the enemy of Edomites, I am not the enemy of corrupt Black people. I am the enemy of sin. Whether that sin is in me or in others, I must stand against it because it is the sin that keeps me estranged from reconciliation with Yahuah.

What did Yahuah tell you as an Israelite? If you will obey My statutes, My Laws, My Commandments that I give you this day -- in the Book of "Deuteronomy 28: " He lists all the Blessings that you will receive and then He lists all the Cursing that you would receive if you rebelled.

The government now has power that is out of control. Women have a right over their bodies. Yahuah gives you these bodies and He gives them the power over them, but He also guides you. You say, "I have the right of choice." You say my body is my choice. Okay, Roger that. It begins with you Choosing the man you will have sex with. That is your right of choice. But to choose death for the unborn, Yahuah does not give you that right woman.

I am not writing to make you feel guilty ladies, there is enough sin everywhere for all of us. I am not preaching for anybody to feel bad about some sin that you have done. I am asking us to understand what is pleasing to Yahuah. And if we are going to surrender to Yahuah, even though it is not what pleases us, we have to say what is the pleasure of Yahuah I must stop doing this or that. Do you follow? It involves a sacrifice. If you said Yahusha gave up His life, are you willing to give up that life that Yahushua is displeased with?

Watch this, This kind of preaching is the right kind. This kind of Gospel is the kind of gospel that you must hear every day. It cannot be something that tickles your ears. It must be something that calls you to rectitude, to uprightness.

"WHY AM I HERE?" THE VOLUNTARY TORTURE CALLED LIFE

As an Israelite, measure yourself against The Laws, Statutes, and Commandments of Yahuah and do not say, "That's old times, things have changed, moved on, that's from the Old Testament days." Fine. Show me where Yahuah changes in the morality that He demands of His creatures. There are some Scriptures... that are more relevant to the needs of the time but there are certain immutable Laws and Principles that keep on coming through that continuum of time and life. And they never change. People do not know how to live life.

Do not tell me about your degrees. I do not care how many doctorates the enemy has conferred on you. You do not have a doctorate of this truth Living according to the will of Yahuah. Your doctorate is in death. Talking about I am a doctor and smoking? I am a doctor, and I am drinking? I am a doctor and stick needles in my arm or snort cocaine in my nose. I am a doctor, and I am eating myself to death, and I look like a pig. You do not know how to live. You must let the wise power Who is the Creator and Architect of life show you how to live and you must stop rebelling against Yahuah.

I am asking you all to go back to The Torah and measure your life against what Yahuah has commanded, and Yahuah's Commandment is The Criterion. As you see how far off you are from The Criterion, you must make up your mind, as an Israelite, or Christian if you are going to reconcile yourself with Yahuah by coming back to the standard that Yahuah laid down for me as an Israelite, that I might continue to be Yahuah's chosen instrument.

Do you not ever think that Yahuah will continue His choice of you when you have chosen to live a Satanic life rather than a life in obedience to the Will of Yahuah?
You talk to Jesus; you talk Him up. You praise His name. You shout all over the place about Jesus. But what kind of life are you living?

"WHY AM I HERE?" THE VOLUNTARY TORTURE CALLED LIFE

You better lose that Jesus and find Yahusha. I must talk like this because if I do not talk like this, I am not true to Yahuah, and I am not true to Yahusha, and I am not true to Moses or the Prophets and I am not true to myself. I do not care about popularity. How can you claim Christ a. will not live The Gospel? All you must do is read The Gospel, measure yourself against The Criterion, and see if you are on it or off it.

If you are off it, that is how much you must surrender to get on it. Did you hear what I said, siblings? Did you hear? Too many of our people have had free rides. When I say you have had a free ride, many of you join churches that tolerate your foolishness. Let me see if I can be a wild, crazy thing and join the church as I continue to be a slut on social media or come to church styled like a whore. I am happy that I found a home! But you will find another home in Hell. And the Pastor who has been leading will be right there in Hell with you! And you will cuss him out and say, "Why didn't you kick me out of your wicked church Rev.?"

If we surrender to Yahuah we are magnetic, we draw people in as well. People are not afraid to be around you, they come to you. Because, as a true believer, when you surrender to The Gospel, you become as magnetic as Christ. When you surrender to The Torah, you become like the Prophets; they are alive in you: Abraham is alive, Moses is alive; Solomon is alive. David is alive. Yahusha is alive. He is alive!

The question is: Is He living in you? In truth, it takes a devout to live by The Gospel. Yahusha is calling you to be supernatural. The natural thing is that if I cuss you, you cuss me. That is natural. You hit me -- Pow, I will hit you back and I will try to hit you harder and make sure you do not come back again with another one. That is natural. But Yahusha is not calling you to do the natural thing because what Yahusha brought was the redemption of human beings and reconciling human beings to Yahuah.

"WHY AM I HERE?" THE VOLUNTARY TORTURE CALLED LIFE

To do that you have to do an unnatural thing. I mean when they smack you on one cheek, the natural thing is to punch them in the mouth. Now, I am not going to let anybody come up and smack me and be Martin Luther King. That is the slave doctrine designed to keep the slaves all bound up in so-called white Jesus.

When you take an insult, do you insult back? When you were reviled and all men of evil said things falsely against you, for the sake of The Gospel -- how do you respond to that? People we have more in common than we have at variance. But if we do not have discussions, how can you point out to me where my error is and how can I point out to you where your error is?

This enables both of us to be corrected before Yahuah. If you tell me there is nothing to dialogue with -- I will not speak to Kahan Tazadaq. To me that is unworthy of us as human beings.

I love so-called Black people. I was born among them. I feel our pain, our suffering, our hurt, at the hands of evil and injustice. Please do not fault me for loving my people because I cannot fault the heathen for loving their people. I am happy to see so-called white people loving each other, or Asians loving each other. That is natural! But I am overjoyed when I see Israelites loving each other because that is exceedingly rare in a society where we have been trained to hate ourselves and to hate one another. Now, here is a challenge to so-called Black People. I make no apologies for standing up for my People. I believe I will do that until Yahuah takes me away.
. White supremacy is a sickness and racism comes out of the feeling that I am better, not because I am intelligent and righteous, but I am better because my skin is white, my hair is straight, and so forth. That is immature. I have seen Edomites play with dogs and love their dogs some of them are short, some of them tall, some of them wide, and some of them ugly looking but you love your dogs, and you say this is my dog and you dress him up, put him in shows, and hope you win a prize for the way you shaved your dog or

trained your dog.

 But if they can admire the diversity of Yahuah in the dog family, or the diversity of Yahuah in the fish family, or the diversity of Yahuah in the bird family if they can admire the diversity of Yahuah in the Earth family and in the planets and the stars, what makes them so stupid, so moronic, that they cannot admire the diversity of Yahuah in the Human family?!

 You do not have to create storms with me, we can stop them. We can keep the death angel away from us, but the death angel is in the United States. We must come out of this world. This is where He is going to make Himself known. Go ahead Mr. President, arrest the tornado! That is a weapon of mass destruction. Go ahead and arrest it. Arrest the wind, arrest the rain, and arrest the floods. Yahuah is plaguing, the United States. And If we do not wake up, we will die in our ignorance. Yahuah is judging the United States and I do not care how much money you think you have; your money will not save you -- nothing will save you unless you say, "I surrender Yahuah!"
We are on the same side, do not fight me love me like I love you.
Shalom

"WHY AM I HERE?" THE VOLUNTARY TORTURE CALLED LIFE

"WHY AM I HERE?" THE VOLUNTARY TORTURE CALLED LIFE

"WHY AM I HERE?" THE VOLUNTARY TORTURE CALLED LIFE

"WHY AM I HERE?" THE VOLUNTARY TORTURE CALLED LIFE

"WHY AM I HERE?" THE VOLUNTARY TORTURE CALLED LIFE

"WHY AM I HERE?" THE VOLUNTARY TORTURE CALLED LIFE

7 MANUFACTURING KAHAN TAZADAQ BEING SUCCESSFUL IS THE BEST REVENGE

I was told that I would fail by my teachers. That I was most unlikely to succeed. I was told by some that I would be dead or in jail before twenty-five. Why did the world have such a verdict for a child who is only seven? Why did my best friend Teddy Ross, who was a so-called white kid tell me, "You can come over to my house after school but your bother can't because he is too dark, my parents won't like him?"

The streets were watching as well. Although Mother tried her hardest to give us the best thing she could and to keep us away from the streets, somehow, I still eventually ended up on the streets. I was quiet and shy, but that got me looked over laughed at, placed in special remedial reading, and targeted as most unlikely to succeed.

My father was at Roosevelt Raceway in Long Island often and showed up every other weekend and he would give my mother lots of money we were living well at those times. But my mother did not respect him, she would converse with other men while he was away. I thought here is my father giving her all that she asked for and she is talking to these men who looked like bad boys behind his back.

Eventually, my father discovered her disloyalty and decided that he would confront her. She told him to get out. He did. That is when we fell from heaven like Satan and his fallen angels into a life that we despised. We had fallen from being the only children in the neighborhood to my mother feeding other children to her getting on welfare. This was a drastic change. Then we moved. And she moved in with Thomas who was very insecure and abusive. This was a roller coaster dramatic relationship where he would violently beat her until she eventually finally fled in fear of losing her life.

"WHY AM I HERE?" THE VOLUNTARY TORTURE CALLED LIFE

My father came back around and tried to work things out. Our lives started rewarding again until she kicked him out again. This time things get bad, it is no heat, no food, and no father to tell me son things will be all right. I started having out at the corner stores stealing candy and shoplifting clothing and food, to survive. I can recall a time when I was so hungry that it felt as though my organs were being eaten by my ribs. Mother always taught us never to steal or take anything that is not yours. I tried to adhere to that, but the insatiable hunger overpowering will to do right. I surmise self-preservation is the first law of nature. "Proverbs 6: 3 Men do not despise the thief if he steals to satisfy his hunger. 31 Yet if caught, he must pay sevenfold; he must give up all the wealth of his house".

We did not have a police athletic league in our community; therefore, I hung crap houses and learned to shoot dice at an early age, play Tunk, spades, etc. This was how many of the OGs (Original Gangsters) lived in the hood. There would be a shootout by the gamblers. There were a couple of times that I can recall almost being hit by a few stray bullets. I saw people get stabbed and shot and fighting was commonplace. You had to know how to throw your hands. But suddenly the gunplay popped off and if you were caught without a hammer(gun) then you were slipping.

There were three cases in which I could have potentially done time for being around the wrong crowd. Yahuah had to be with me. I'll not go into that here. There was a fat Puerto Rican who had me moving the weight as a young boy when I was not even aware. He would just tell me to get that trash back from my home and bring it to me, do not look in the bag. I did not, I just obeyed. He would give me money just to bring him a bag. Then one day I was coming down through his hood and I saw him being cuffed by the DEA. It was only then that I realized that he was a dealer who had put my freedom at risk with no remorse.

The world was crashing around me. Please start getting arrested

"WHY AM I HERE?" THE VOLUNTARY TORTURE CALLED LIFE

and doing long prison sentences. I am a teenager now. I realized I had to disassociate myself or suffer the same fate.
Although my teacher had given up on me, I came upon them and proved them all wrong. I got out of remedial reading by teaching myself to read the bible daily. My grades improved and I graduated from high school with a 3.0. Some may say so what, but coming from where I was is a huge accomplishment, I want to be here, but I am still standing on all ten toes.

I put myself through college by working and going to school full-time. I majored in Architectural Engineering. My aunt told me you should not take this court, it has too much math you will not pass. She was the guidance counselor at the college. I told her "Roger that," but I stayed in the course, and I passed. When she saw me, years later working on a job, she had a startled look on her face as she walked into the building and there I was.

I was doing well but kept getting pressure from my mother and brother to join the military. I was an entry-level draftsman at the time, and my mother was now wanting me to take care of her. She took credit for putting me through college even though it was me who got a job while I was attending full-time. I realized the power of the mind to push oneself beyond what our potential is.

I was parting and getting high and ended up getting told by the owner of the architectural firm that they would put me out in the field as a surveyor. I will never forget his racial motivated words" I am trying to give you a chance what worn with you people." I quit and gave in to the pressure of my mother and brother and joined the Army.

The army may have saved me from the streets because while in basic training they were dying and going to jail or prison. My cousin, Quay Sean, was sending my photos of him in fancy cars and designer clothing, living the fast life. Later, he got arrested and all the money that he had was money for bail. His life was ruined as

far as getting. An Excellent job. Out 3 other cousins were in prison for drugs. I could not go back there.
While in the military I received special training and was in combat, then was trained in covert operations to fight the war on drugs in Central and South America. I was trained to fire just about all small mars, all US and Russian land mines, sapper training, and jungle warfare among other things I cannot mention here.

I encountered a brother at Fort Kobbe who introduced me to the teachings of Malcolm X and Farrakhan. Now I was learning knowledge of self. When I heard them say, "The white man was the Devil," and I thought about all the things I had experienced with so-called white people I said it must be true. Yet something within me would not allow me to hate anyone because of skin color, I thought that was sickening. Yet we cannot deny that many so-called white people have had just that to those that refer to as "niggers."

I would eventually leave the military, go back to college, and major in Computer Science. I proceeded to get Microsoft System Engineer Certification, Network Plus, and A +, I worked in the field for ten years and worked for a few major five hundred companies. Although the pay was okay, I felt as though I had no control over my life, I was still usually on standby in case a system crashed.

In 2009 I finally decided that I was going to walk away from all of this. I was essentially a nine-to-five slave. I walked in the Next day resigned and was told I would never work in the city of New York again for any computer company. I said," Roger that, I do not intend to."
 Up to this point I had been Roosevelt, believing in the system, but certain information I had read made me question the efficiency of their teachings. I had begun studying the truth in 1997 and chose the name Tazadaq. I now understood the bible but needed a way out of the Matrix. So, in 2009 I quit my job and started studying the law with the bible. I studied until my eyes were swollen. I

"WHY AM I HERE?" THE VOLUNTARY TORTURE CALLED LIFE

burned the midnight oil and, what I learned was rejuvenating.

Although Tazadaq was created in 1997 Kahan Tazadaq was not made until about 2016. I studied from 2009 and started to teach what I know around 2011. I began to allow what I learned and started to get a remedy. I am not a sovereign citizen; I am just an aggrieved man who is standing up for my rights and encouraging others to do so.

The information provided in this book does not, and is not intended to, constitute legal advice; instead, all information, content, and materials available in this book are for general informational purposes only. Information in this book may not constitute the most up-to-date legal or other information. This book contains links to other third-party websites. Such links are only for the convenience of the reader, user, or reader; Kahan Tazadaq and his members do not recommend or endorse the contents of the third-party sites.

Readers of this book should contact their attorney to obtain advice concerning any legal matter. No reader or user of this site should act or refrain from acting based on information in this book without first seeking legal advice from counsel in the relevant jurisdiction. Only your attorney can provide assurances that the information contained herein – and your interpretation of it – is applicable or appropriate to your situation. Use of, and access to, this book or any of the links or resources contained within the book do not create an attorney-client relationship between the reader, or user, and website authors, contributors, contributing law firms, or committee members and their respective employers.

The views expressed at, or through, this book are those of the individual authors writing in their capacities only. All liability concerning actions taken or not taken based on the contents of this book is hereby expressly disclaimed. The content in this book is provided "as is" no representations are made that the content is

"WHY AM I HERE?" THE VOLUNTARY TORTURE CALLED LIFE

error-free.

This is why I am here. I am here to share with the world that there is hope and light in the debts or darkness. I am here to teach you that debt makes people slaves, I am also here to tell you that you can become a creditor if you believe in yourself.

"WHY AM I HERE?" THE VOLUNTARY TORTURE CALLED LIFE

"WHY AM I HERE?" THE VOLUNTARY TORTURE CALLED LIFE

"WHY AM I HERE?" THE VOLUNTARY TORTURE CALLED LIFE

TDOC RECORDINGS
TRUTH MUSIC
WWW.TDOCRECORDINGS.COM

THE TRUTH WILL MAKE YOU MAD PODCAST

www.truedisciplesofchrist.org/shop
Help fund the war on aphasia
cash.me/$tazadaqshah or paypal.me/tazadaq or donate in super chat or super thanks

"WHY AM I HERE?" THE VOLUNTARY TORTURE CALLED LIFE

ORDER ALL OF KAHAN TAZADAQ SHAH'S BOOKS

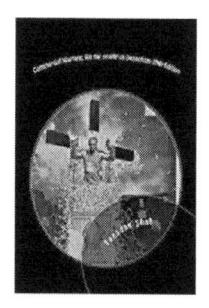

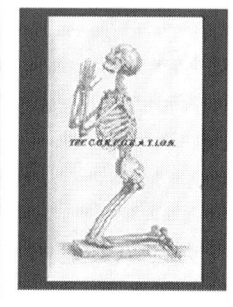

ORDER THESE BOOKS@ WWW.TRUEDISCIPLESOFCHRIST.ORG/SHOP

8 OWE NO MAN: DISCHARGE THAT SHIT! BUY A HOME WITHOUT MONEY

"Ephesians 5:15 15 See then that ye walk circumspectly, not as fools, but as wise". Sean Ellis, who was freed after serving 22 years in prison, is the subject of "Trial 4." This young man Sean Ellis was 21 years old when he was convicted in 1993 for the murder of Boston Police Det. John Mulligan. There were two mistrials but a third that rendered a lifetime sentence. In 2015, when a court ruling reversed his convictions on first-degree murder and armed robbery charges he was released. In 2018, there were calls for another trial, but the said charges against Ellis were withdrawn.

Sean Ellis, who spent over 22 years behind bars, is now telling his story in a new Netflix documentary. I thought it relevant to mention this because it could happen to you or me, The thought of this is awful. Can you imagine this happening to you? Many of you may not which is why so many of you believe that the strawman man theory is nonsense by a few crazy people that are losers. You are entitled to that belief. You can stay locked in this Matrix, but I tell you that things are not as they appear. People need to wake up.

Perfecting Your Claim Proper Procedures for Purchasing a Home as A Secured Party Creditor
What I am going to discuss is taking control of property that is not exclusive to real property. This could be inclusive of talking about vehicles or other things. Real property is different than movable goods. There are three elements to the perfection of a security interest. I must emphasize that if there's outstanding liability on an account, the account must be settled. 1)The title documents must be clear in that they show the only lien holder is you or the party who is perfecting the security interest (paid off). 2)Reconveyance of the Deed, (Deeds of Reconveyance), and Notice of Recession 3) The third step is possession. Control through possession. If you control through title and possession, then you have what is called

the perfection of a security Interest.

I will first cover settling the account with the IRS technical support division which is specifically for settling accounts. Are you, the reader, familiar with those processes? I have gone into detail on settling accounts using accepted-for-value (A4V). If it is real property Tazadaq uses a bonded promissory note.

I use a bonded promissory note and to do so, one must have established your account with the Treasury meaning, you have done the BC bond with the birth certificate accepted for value. This means you have done the Indemnity Bonds, Set Off Bonds then you can issue Bonded Promissory Notes, of the Set Off Bonds.

Once you have done indemnity bonds, you can set off debts and then you can issue bonded promissory notes to settle and close accounts. The set-off bond is useless unless you are looking at getting a statement with a coupon. If you have not become a secured party and have not created the bonds mentioned above, then you need a statement with a coupon and use the Accepted for Value Process Tazadaq teaches. If you go into dishonor on the account, it is going to escalate to the lien holder and they will try to perfect the security of your property, which means they will take it. If you stop paying your car note they will take it, stop paying your mortgage they will take it.

I emphasize that If you go into dishonor on the account, it is going to escalate with the lien holder. I encourage you to define the words security interest. I will be using that word often. The certified payment bond is designed in such a manner that the amount section is left blank and filled in by the IRS. Let us assume it's 3 THREE times the original mortgage, I would make the payment bond three- and one-half times what the mortgage is and send that in as the instrument.

What Is a Security Interest?

"WHY AM I HERE?" THE VOLUNTARY TORTURE CALLED LIFE

A security interest is an enforceable legal claim or lien on collateral that has been pledged, usually to obtain a loan. The borrower provides the lender with a security interest in certain assets, which gives the lender the right to repossess all or part of the property if the borrower stops making loan payments. The lender can then sell the repossessed collateral to pay off the loan.

Let us discuss the first presentation that we are going to make in this process. It is not a three-step process with the IRS Technical Support Division. I send it once because they either return the Notice With a default in it, or it is deemed accepted.
I would like to delve deeper into a secured debt situation, in which I have achieved remedy on real property. We must simulate how the remedy will be achieved in the public. A simulation is essentially taking on a form or appearance, as well as an imitation. I will be doing this privately as a creditor. But how things play out in public will look in form as they would in any public remedy or contract.

The matter at hand is the mortgage, first I want to examine what would the process look like in the public if I were to seek my remedy publicly. Therefore, let us take a mortgage. How would the remedy for the resolution of such an account look to the public? I must first identify and make distinctions between all the elements. In the application, the Grant, or Warranty Deed (Title comes with this), there is a Deed of Trust (also a Lien), a Statement of Account (account was created), and A Promissory Note. There is a separate account for property taxes.

If I am seeking publicly to close this account and remove the lien, I am perfecting the title. What would this look like in form in public? How would I bring the account to zero in public? I would pay it off. So, I pay it off then I do a release of lien or satisfaction of lien. In California, this is known as the Reconveyance of Deed. Thus, I am focusing on the release of a Deed of Trust or mortgage agreement, which is a lien. It depends on which state you are in. Release of a lien could take on the form of reconveyance of title, or it could be documents known as a release of lien.

What occurs between the mortgage company and title company is there is a signing or the interest of lien whenever the release of the lien is filed in the public. The Deed of Trust, Grant Deed, release of lien. The home is not free and clear yet. Keep in mind there is no such thing as an allodial title in the public. But we do need a statement of account showing ZERO. This usually comes right after we pay off/discharge the alleged debt.

Once the conveyance of deeds happens is the property free and clear, besides property taxes? Yes, it is free and clear to the public. Anything other than what I just mentioned above you are creating problems for yourself. Do not bring in UCC1s or anything thing else. There is nothing else recorded in the public besides the reconveyance.
If you are in default, then a Lis pendens lien is filed in mortgage states.

If it is in default and I wrote a check to settle it what else would go out with this process in the public records if the default has been satisfied? Would the Lis Pendens be released? Would there be a release of the lien? What cancels the default? It would be a Notice or Recession. Before the release of the lien, there would be a Notice of Recission which is ordered to be filed by the Trustee, by the Beneficiary, who tells the trustee to file a Notice of Rescission

The matter at hand is the mortgage, first I want to examine what would the process look like in the public if I were to seek my remedy publicly. Therefore, let us take a mortgage. How would the remedy for the resolution of such an account look to the public? I must first identify and make distinctions between all the elements. In the application, the Grant, or Warranty Deed (Title comes with this), there is a Deed of Trust (also a Lien), a Statement of Account (account was created), and A Promissory Note. There is a separate account for property taxes.

If I am seeking publicly to close this account and remove the lien, I am perfecting the title. What would this look like in form in public? How would I bring the account to zero in the public? I would pay it off. So, I pay it off then I do a release of lien or satisfaction of lien. In California, this is known as the Reconveyance of Deed. Thus, I am focusing on the release of a Deed of Trust or mortgage agreement, which is a lien. It depends on which state you are in. Release of a lien could take on the form of reconveyance of title, or it could be documents known as a release of lien.

What occurs between the mortgage company and title company is there is a signing or the interest of lien whenever the release of the lien is filed in the public. The Deed of Trust, Grant Deed, release of lien. The home is not free and clear yet. Keep in mind there is no such thing as an allodial title in the public. But we do need a statement of account showing ZERO. This usually comes right after we pay off/discharge the alleged debt.

Once the conveyance of deeds happens is the property free and clear, besides property taxes? Yes, it is free and clear to the public. Anything other than what I just mentioned above you are creating problems for yourself. Do not bring in UCC1s or anything thing else.

There is nothing else recorded in the public besides the reconveyance.

If you are in default, then a Lis pendens lien is filed in mortgage states. If it is in default and I wrote a check to settle it what else would go out with this process in the public records if the default has been satisfied? Would the Lis Pendens be released? Would there be a release of the lien? What cancels the default? It would be a Notice or Recession. Before the release of the line, there would be a Notice of Recission which is ordered to be filed by the Trustee, by the Beneficiary, who tells the trustee to file a Notice of Recission.

Let us take for instance that there was a civil suit or a judgment for money against you for an amount of money. What would that look like in public? Payment was made so you got a payoff. If they filed that in the county as a lien like they filed an abstract of judgment in the county record, then there needs to be a release of lien. A satisfaction of judgment would go into the case by the plaintiff. Even if we use the private process to use our remedy it would look the same in the public as if we are paying it with a check but instead, I am paying with my restricted access account. I just use my private administrative process.

So, what is Kahan Tazadaq's Private Process that Simulates this Public model?
 I will now provide a step-by-step process of how a creditor begins remedy. Step one is to set off the account on the private side as a creditor. I do not write a check; I use my assets to set it off. Document one is a Notice to Set Off with the Negotiable Instrument which will be my money order which I created from their coupon. This technique is in my book Liberate the Oppressed, how to turn a bill into a money order. I just TENDER the instrument and it satisfied the debt.

 The problem with most of you, if you are honest, you are debtors and you are waiting to receive something back or for someone to do something. That is not how a creditor operates.

In step one it could be a bonded promissory note, it could be the mortgage statement itself with my acceptance statement, where I make the payment coupon into a money order, or I could make my money order or a certified payment bond, whatever I chose. Bonded promissory means I have something at the Department of Treasury. It is set up as the bonds to set off the debt and the note is the instrument to make that happen. If you do not have those in place, then use something else.

"WHY AM I HERE?" THE VOLUNTARY TORTURE CALLED LIFE

Those of you that became a secured creditor and have indemnity bonds and set off bonds at the Department of Treasury then you can set it off with those. I am going to TENDER my set off through the IRS. I issue a notice to set off, I issue my instrument, and if I have a payoff statement that would also be included.

Let us take for instance that there was a civil suit or a judgment for money against you for an amount of money. What would that look like in public? The payment was made so you got a payoff. If they filed that in the county as a lien like they filed an abstract of judgment in the county record, then there needs to be a release of lien. A satisfaction of judgment would go into the case by the plaintiff. Even if we the use private process to use our remedy it would look the same in the public as if we are paying it with a check but instead, I am paying with my restricted access account. I just use my private administrative process.

So, what is Kahan Tazadaq's Private Process that Simulates this Public model?
 I will now provide a step-by-step process of how a creditor begins remedy. Step one is to set off the account on the private side as a creditor. I do not write a check; I use my assets to set it off.

Document one is a Notice to Set Off with the Negotiable Instrument which will be my money order which I created from their coupon. This technique is in my book Liberate the Oppressed, how to turn a bill into a money order. I just TENDER the instrument and it satisfied the debt. The problem with most of you, if you are honest, you are debtors and you are waiting to receive something back or for someone to do something. That is not how a creditor operates.

In step one it could be a bonded promissory note, it could be the mortgage statement itself with my acceptance statement, where I make the payment coupon into a money order, or I could make my own money order or a certified payment bond, whatever I chose.

"WHY AM I HERE?" THE VOLUNTARY TORTURE CALLED LIFE

Bonded promissory means I have something at the Department of Treasury. It is set up as the bonds to set off the debt and the note is the instrument to make that happen. If you do not have those in place, then use something else.

Those of you that became a secured creditor and have indemnity bonds and set off bonds at the Department of Treasury then you can set it off with those. I am going to TENDER my set off through the IRS. I issue a notice to set off, I issue my instrument, and if I have a payoff statement that would also be included.

There should be evidence of the debt sent in this process, which should have a Banker's Acceptance front and back. If it is five pages, each page should have my acceptance statement. Whatever bankers' acceptance I used will be front and back of each page which is the evidence of debt. Next, I have a 1040V special endorsement on the back of the 1040V if you are not a secured party creditor eliminate this from your process. In my notice to set off, I instruct the IRS if there is any money to be returned it is to directly go to the treasury direct account.

There was a time in 2013 when I did an A4V to the IRS I received a check back. I am instructing them in this process to send it back to the treasury account. I do not want Or need a check because I am a real Secured party Creditor, I do not create debt.

What would happen if I accepted the check, endorsed it, and deposited it into a bank account, I have converted my private asset into a public debt. We are not authorized to create public debt out of our private assets. Anyone who likes Christmas Hauser, coat MT, or anyone teaching you to do this is a lost soul. We should not do this as creditors, which is what banks do. They are authorized by Congress to convert your private assets into public debt. That is what occurs with your promissory note, your private asset is converted into a public debt.

"WHY AM I HERE?" THE VOLUNTARY TORTURE CALLED LIFE

What we are doing as a part of our Notice To Set off is not to send us a check. Send the check to the Treasury Direct Account. I have it sent there because I buy government securities. This makes me the creditor. I can buy bonds and notes. This is why I have the IRS form 8888 so I can include the account information for TAZADAQ'S Treasury Direct Account.

You do not need to use this part of the process. Most of you do not have a Treasury Direct account because you are not Secured Party Creditors, therefore you cannot use this process. Now we have our certificate of service.

I have had remarkable success through the IRS in Ogden; therefore, I use Ogden to send my Set Off. So, therein I have an Original Statement of Account or whatever the title of my monthly statement is. Then issued by the name of the bank that issued it and the date. Duly endorsed as follows. The acceptance statement is on the front and back of the mortgage statement. Accepted for Value and Returned for Value, Exempted from Levy Prepaid common Stock Discharge all Presentments, and related fees, adjust the balance to ZERO Private prepaid Treasury Account 123456789. Charge the Same to TAZADQ SHAH. I sign it and date it.

There should be evidence of the debt sent in this process, which should have a Banker's Acceptance front and back. If it is five pages, each page should have my acceptance statement. Whatever bankers' acceptance I used will be front and back of each page which is the evidence of debt. Next, I have a 1040V special endorsement on the back of the 1040V if you are not a secured party creditor eliminate this from your process. In my notice to set off, I instruct the IRS if there is any money to be returned it is to directly go to the treasury direct account.

There was a time in 2013 when I did an A4V to the IRS I received a check back. I am instructing them in this process to send it back to the treasury account. I do not want Or need a check because I am a real Secured party Creditor, I do not create debt.

"WHY AM I HERE?" THE VOLUNTARY TORTURE CALLED LIFE

What would happen if I accepted the check, endorsed it, and deposited it into a bank account, I have converted my private asset into a public debt. We are not authorized to create public debt out of our private assets. Anyone who likes Christmas Hauser, coat MT, or anyone teaching you to do this is a lost soul. We should not do this as creditors, which is what banks do. They are authorized by Congress to convert your private assets into public debt. That is what occurs with your promissory note, your private asset is converted into a public debt.

What we are doing as a part of our Notice To Set off is not to send us a check. Send the check to the Treasury Direct Account. I have it sent there because I buy government securities. This makes me the creditor. I can buy bonds and notes. This is why I have the IRS form 8888 so I can include the account information for TAZADAQ'S Treasury Direct Account.

You do not need to use this part of the process. Most of you do not have a Treasury Direct account because you are not Secured Party Creditors, therefore you cannot use this process. Now we have our certificate of service.

I have had remarkable success through the IRS in Ogden; therefore, I use Ogden to send my Set Off. So, therein I have an Original Statement of Account or whatever the title of my monthly statement is. Then issued by the name of the bank that issued it and the date. Duly endorsed as follows. The acceptance statement is on the front and back of the mortgage statement. Accepted for Value and Returned for Value, Exempted from Levy Prepaid common Stock Discharge all Presentments, and related fees, adjust the balance to ZERO Private prepaid Treasury Account 123456789. Charge the Same to TAZADQ SHAH. I signed it and dated it.

There should be evidence of the debt sent in this process, which should have a Banker's Acceptance front and back. If it is five pages, each page should have my acceptance statement. Whatever bankers' acceptance I used will be front and back of each page which is the evidence of debt. Next, I have a 1040V special endorsement on the back of the 1040V if you are not a secured party creditor eliminate this from your process. In my notice to set off, I instruct the IRS if there is any money to be returned it is to directly go to the treasury direct account.

There was a time in 2013 when I did an A4V to the IRS I received a check back. I am instructing them in this process to send it back to the treasury account. I do not want Or need a check because I am a real Secured party Creditor, I do not create debt.

What would happen if I accepted the check, endorsed it, and deposited it into a bank account, I have converted my private asset into a public debt.

We are not authorized to create public debt out of our private assets. Anyone who likes Christmas Hauser, coat MT, or anyone teaching you to do this is a lost soul. We should not do this as creditors, which is what banks do. They are authorized by Congress to convert your private assets into public debt. That is what occurs with your promissory note, your private asset is converted into a public debt.

You won't read this again therefore I'll repeat it all.
What we are doing as a part of our Notice To Set off is not to send us a check. Send the check to the Treasury Direct Account. I have it sent there because I buy government securities. This makes me the creditor. I can buy bonds and notes. This is why I have the IRS form 8888 so I can include the account information for TAZADAQ'S Treasury Direct Account.

You do not need to use this part of the process. Most of you do not have a Treasury Direct account because you are not Secured Party Creditors, therefore you cannot use this process. Now we have our certificate of service.

I have had remarkable success through the IRS in Ogden;

therefore, I use Ogden to send my Set Off. So, therein I have an Original Statement of Account or whatever the title of my monthly statement is. Then issued by the name of the bank that issued it and the date. Duly endorsed as follows. The acceptance statement is on the front and back of the mortgage statement. Accepted for Value and Returned for Value, Exempted from Levy Prepaid common Stock Discharge all Presentments, and related fees, adjust the balance to ZERO Private prepaid Treasury Account 123456789. Charge the Same to TAZADQ SHAH. I signed it by and date it.

There should be evidence of the debt sent in this process, which should have a Banker's Acceptance front and back. If it is five pages, each page should have my acceptance statement. Whatever bankers' acceptance I used will be front and back of each page which is the evidence of debt. Next, I have a 1040V special endorsement on the back of the 1040V if you are not a secured party creditor eliminate this from your process. In my notice to set off, I instruct the IRS if there is any money to be returned it is to directly go to the treasury direct account.

There was a time in 2013 when I did an A4V to the IRS I received a check back. I am instructing them in this process to send it back to the treasury account. I do not want Or need a check because I am a real Secured party Creditor, I do not create debt.
What would happen if I accepted the check, endorsed it, and deposited it into a bank account, I have converted my private asset into a public debt. We are not authorized to create public debt out of our private assets. Anyone who likes Christmas Hauser, coat MT, or anyone teaching you to do this is a lost soul. We should not do this as creditors, which is what banks do. They are authorized by Congress to convert your private assets into public debt. That is what occurs with your promissory note, your private asset is converted into a public debt.

What we are doing as a part of our Notice To Set off is not to send us a check. Send the check to the Treasury Direct Account. I have it

"WHY AM I HERE?" THE VOLUNTARY TORTURE CALLED LIFE

sent there because I buy government securities. This makes me the creditor. I can buy bonds and notes. This is why I have the IRS form 8888 so I can include the account information for TAZADAQ'S Treasury Direct Account.

You do not need to use this part of the process. Most of you do not have a Treasury Direct account because you are not Secured Party Creditors, therefore you cannot use this process. Now we have our certificate of service.

I have had remarkable success through the IRS in Ogden; therefore, I use Ogden to send my Set Off. So, therein I have an Original Statement of Account or whatever the title of my monthly statement is. Then issued by the name of the bank that issued it and the date. Duly endorsed as follows. The acceptance statement is on the front and back of the mortgage statement. Accepted for Value and Returned for Value, Exempted from Levy Prepaid common Stock Discharge all Presentments, and related fees, adjust the balance to ZERO Private prepaid Treasury Account 123456789. Charge the Same to TAZADQ SHAH. I sign it and date it.

There should be evidence of the debt sent in this process, which should have a Banker's Acceptance front and back. If it is five pages, each page should have my acceptance statement. Whatever bankers' acceptance I used will be front and back of each page which is the evidence of debt. Next, I have a 1040V special endorsement on the back of the 1040V if you are not a secured party creditor eliminate this from your process. In my notice to set off, I instruct the IRS if there is any money to be returned it is to directly go to the treasury direct account.

There was a time in 2013 when I did an A4V to the IRS I received a check back. I am instructing them in this process to send it back to the treasury account. I do not want Or need a check because I am a real Secured party Creditor, I do not create debt.

"WHY AM I HERE?" THE VOLUNTARY TORTURE CALLED LIFE

What would happen if I accepted the check, endorsed it, and deposited it into a bank account, I have converted my private assets into public debt. We are not authorized to create public debt out of our private assets. Anyone who likes Christmas Hauser, coat MT, or anyone teaching you to do this is a lost soul. We should not do this as creditors, which is what banks do. They are authorized by Congress to convert your private assets into public debt. That is what occurs with your promissory note, your private asset is converted into a public debt.

What we are doing as a part of our Notice To Set off is not to send us a check. Send the check to the Treasury Direct Account. I have it sent there because I buy government securities. This makes me the creditor. I can buy bonds and notes. This is why I have the IRS form 8888 so I can include the account information for TAZADAQ'S Treasury Direct Account.

You do not need to use this part of the process. Most of you do not have a Treasury Direct account because you are not Secured Party Creditors, therefore you cannot use this process. Now we have our certificate of service.
 I know you're thinking, did I just read that? Yes, you did and you will read it again

I have had remarkable success through the IRS in Ogden; therefore, I use Ogden to send my Set Off. So, therein I have an Original Statement of Account or whatever the title of my monthly statement is. Then issued by the name of the bank that issued it and the date. Duly endorsed as follows. The acceptance statement is on the front and back of the mortgage statement. Accepted for Value and Returned for Value, Exempted from Levy Prepaid common Stock Discharge all Presentments, and related fees, adjust the balance to ZERO Private prepaid Treasury Account 123456789. Charge the Same to TAZADQ SHAH. I sign it and date it.

The second step in this process is the original IRS 1040V Pay voucher duly endorsed as follows. Note this is also the endorsement that appears on the back of the 1040V. The Third step is the original IRS form 8888 direct deposit of refund to mortgage one account. This is where I list my account information for my treasury direct Account.

These instruments are being tendered by TAZADAQ SHAH here and after PRINCIPAL, for the set off ABC Bank account number 9876543. And to be used to affect debit and credit account transactions for the settlement and closure of said account. If any of the enclosed instruments contain defects or are incorrect, incomplete, or inaccurate, please return the same to the PRINCIPAL via the notary public at the address shown above within FOURTEEN days of the date of receipt.

Essentially, because of the nature of the property I am going to just send in my payment instrument or my TENDER for setoff. When they do not respond, I send a notice of fault, opportunity to cure, and notice default. Remember what I said about sending it to the IRS technical support division because there are only really one or two things they can do. They are either going to return the payment instrument and identify a defect in it or they are going to accept it and they have FOURTE. days to do either.

You may be wondering Tazadaq, why do you pick 14 FOURTEEN days? I picked 14 FOURTEEN days because in private contracts 72 hours is perfection of the contract. This is also in compliance with Truth and Lending for a contract to be binding and valid. Therefore, I am allowing 3 days for mailing.

The law keeps us safe. It is no shorter time because it would not be fair to deal with it using a method like having someone walk into the technical support division with the notice. Or I cannot make a presentation of my TENDER for set off by express mail and it gets there the very next day, because that is not due process either. Even if I walked it into the IRS Technical Support Division it is still six or seven days later to be just. I give at least FOURTEEN days, and if you are sending it registered mail, you are looking at 14 to 20 days depending on how long it takes your registered mail to arrive at the technical support division of IRS.

This is because registered mail goes from hand to hand. So registered mail takes longer than first-class certified overnight everything else, so they do not have it until it gets there.
If they do not respond Now, I have a contract. The criminal process is an additional claim or penalty. To solve the criminal, you must ensure you have settled your civil monetary issues.

 I set off the alleged debt for the full amount and told the IRS to set the balance to ZERO. So even if there is a face value to the money order, I include A1040V with a blank amount on it and a special endorsement on the back of that 1040V. I do this because if there are any additional fees the IRS needs to collect a fee for performing the service and the money order itself made off the statement is not necessarily going to cover the fees that the Treasury would collect for the service of setting off the account.

 On the 1040V is the social security of the taxpayer, the name in all caps, the address, and leave box 3 blank. I let them fill that in, again because there may be fees, they demand for performing this service. Also, If any additional interest or penalties exist that are not given or shown on the statement, then the IRS has been covered and they have been instructed to set the balance to ZERO. Do not get on any sovereign citizen bullshit and try to OID this, do not divert!

That blank 1040V and when I say blank, I mean just the amount Box on the 1040V is blank. The rest of the 1040V has the taxpayer information in it and there is a special endorsement. This presentation I am doing this presentation through a notary because I want a record of this presentation sent to the CFO. My special endorsement I flip it over and encore it as I would a check, Accept for Value and Return for value exempt from levy prepaid

"WHY AM I HERE?" THE VOLUNTARY TORTURE CALLED LIFE

Common Stock, discharge all Presentments and related Fees, and adjust the balance to ZERO. I write my prepaid exemption number charge the same too ACCOUNT NUMBER 123456789. I sign it in blue ink.

If I am sending one for a Visa card CFO and I use a notary presentment. You may wonder if I need to use registered mail, or if can I use certified. The key to remember is that whenever you send an instrument like a bond or promissory note use register mail!!! If I was sending the bond or promissory note to the IRS Tech Support division or sending it to the CFO or to the CFO of the court that is when I want to use registered mail. If I were sending a private record maybe to the judge but did not have a financial instrument, I would not need to send it by registered mail. It would be fine to send it to the judge via certified mail but if there is a sort of financial instrument that is why I want to use registered mail, unless I am sending bonded promissory notes.

Whenever I am presenting anything in the private side of the judge's chambers, I always send it registered whether there is a financial instrument. A presentment is going to have a certificate of service so that the notary is keeping a record of what is being presented, and I also include with that what I call a notice to set off accounts which is telling the IRS to take this tender and set off this account. Isn't that an offer? I am also instructing them that if there is a defect in the instrument Return the instrument within 14 FOURTEEN days otherwise, they agree to set off the account.

That blank 1040V and when I say blank, I mean just the amount Box on the 1040V is blank. The rest of the 1040V has the taxpayer information in it and there is a special endorsement. This presentation I am doing this presentation through a notary because I want a record of this presentation sent to the CFO. My special endorsement I flip it over and encore it as I would a check, Accept for Value and Return for value exempt from levy prepaid Common Stock, discharge all Presentments and related Fees, and adjust the balance to ZERO. I write my prepaid exemption number charge the same too ACCOUNT NUMBER 123456789. I sign it in blue ink.

If I am sending one for a Visa card CFO and I use a notary presentment. You may wonder if I need to use registered mail, or if can I use certified. The key to remember is that whenever you send an instrument like a bond or promissory note use register mail!!! If I was sending the bond or promissory note to the IRS Tech Support division or sending it to the CFO or to the CFO of the court that is when I want to use registered mail. If I were sending a private record maybe to the judge but did not have a financial instrument, I would not need to send it by registered mail. It would be fine to send it to the judge via certified mail but if there is a sort of financial instrument that is why I want to use registered mail, unless I am sending bonded promissory notes.

Whenever I am presenting anything in the private side of the judge's chambers, I always send it registered whether there is a financial instrument. A presentment is going to have a certificate of service so that the notary is keeping a record of what is being presented, and I also include with that what I call a notice to set off accounts which is telling the IRS to take this tender and set off this account. Isn't that an offer? I am also instructing them that if there is a defect in the instrument Return the instrument within 14 FOURTEEN days otherwise, they agree to set off the account.

That blank 1040V and when I say blank, I mean just the amount Box on the 1040V is blank. The rest of the 1040V has the taxpayer information in it and there is a special endorsement. This presentation I am doing this presentation through a notary because I want a record of this presentation sent to the CFO. My special endorsement I flip it over and encore it as I would a check, Accept for Value and Return for value exempt from levy prepaid Common Stock, discharge all Presentments and related Fees, and adjust the balance to ZERO. I write my prepaid exemption number

"WHY AM I HERE?" THE VOLUNTARY TORTURE CALLED LIFE

charge the same too ACCOUNT NUMBER 123456789. I sign it in blue ink.

If I am sending one for a Visa card CFO and I use a notary presentment. You may wonder if I need to use registered mail, or if can I use certified. The key to remember is that whenever you send an instrument like a bond or promissory note use register mail!!! If I was sending the bond or promissory note to the IRS Tech Support division or sending it to the CFO or to the CFO of the court that is when I want to use registered mail.

If I were sending a private record maybe to the judge but did not have a financial instrument, I would not need to send it by registered mail. It would be fine to send it to the judge via certified mail but if there is a sort of financial instrument that is why I want to use registered mail, unless I am sending bonded promissory notes.

Whenever I am presenting anything in the private side of the judge's chambers, I always send it registered whether there is a financial instrument. A presentment is going to have a certificate of service so that the notary is keeping a record of what is being presented, and I also include with that what I call a notice to set off accounts which is telling the IRS to take this tender and set off this account. Isn't that an offer? I am also instructing them that if there is a defect in the instrument Return the instrument within 14 FOURTEEN days otherwise, they agree to set off the account.

If I were doing this A4V, I accept the value statement and turn the coupon into a money order for the full amount of the outstanding balance on the account. If were to tender a Bonded Promissory Note I would make the bonded Promissory Note 125% of the outstanding balance. This is to cover any penalties, interests, or fees unknown to me. I include a 1040V with a blank amount and a special endorsement on the back of the 1040V so that any additional fees will be covered.

There is only one step with the IRS I do not do a notice of fault, or default. I do not even need a certificate of response, because the IRs are the only ones who can rebut that they received it. I have testimony from the notary that it was served on the IRS by way of my certificate of service. But keep in mind the notary's records with everything that was mailed.

This is the respectful thing to do. What is respect? Respect is to avoid intruding upon or interfering with. If they sent an invoice with a coupon Tazadaq would turn the coupon into a money order or tender the note for 125%. If they ignore me that is fine for me, because in private contracts 72 hours is the perfection of the contract. The notary is a third-party witness that said documents were submitted. It is the notary's job to keep such records. One of the exceptions to the Hearsay rules is a record by a third party whose job is to keep such records. I encounter more problems sending it by registered mail vs certified. If I send anything on the private side into the judge's chambers, I will send it by registered mail even if it has no financial instrument.

If I am doing a criminal case, I may want to make it at least one hundred million per felony. If they do not come back and say it is insufficient, then it is sufficient.

 How long should I give them to respond? Seven days is okay but in reality, at least 14 FOURTEEN days is just. And if you are sending registered mail really, you are looking at 14 to 20 days depending on how long it takes your registered mail to arrive at the technical support division of IRS. This is because registered mail goes from hand to hand. So, registered mail takes longer than first-class certified overnight everything else, so they do not have it until it gets there.

If they do not respond Now, I have a contract. The criminal process is an additional claim or penalty. To solve the criminal, you must ensure you have settled your civil monetary issues. I set off the

alleged debt for the full amount and told the IRS to set the balance to ZERO. So even if there is a face value to the money order, I include A1040V with a blank amount on it and a special endorsement on the back of that 1040V. I do this because if there are any additional fees the IRS needs to collect a fee for performing the service and the money order itself made off the statement is not necessarily going to cover the fees that the Treasury would collect for the service of setting off the account.
Let us recap.
 On the 1040V are the social security of the taxpayer, the name in all caps, the address, and leave box 3 blank. I let them fill that in, again because there may be fees, they demand for performing this service. Also, If any additional interest or penalties exist that are not given or shown on the statement, then the IRS has been covered and they have been instructed to set the balance to zero. Do not get on any sovereign bullshit citizen bullshit and try to OID this, do not divert.
That blank 1040V and when I say blank, I mean just the amount Box on the 1040V is blank. The rest of the 1040V has the taxpayer information in it and there is a special endorsement. This presentation I am doing this presentation through a notary because I want a record of this presentation sent to the CFO. My special endorsement I flip it over and endorse it as I would a check, Accept for Value and Return for value exempt from levy prepaid Common Stock, discharge all Presentments and related Fees, and adjust the balance to zero. I write my prepaid exemption number charge the same too ACCOUNT NUMBER 123456789. I sign it in blue ink.

If I am sending one for the Visa card CFO and I use a notary presentment. You may wonder if I need to use registered mail, or can I use certified. The key to remember is that whenever you send an instrument like a bond or promissory note use register mail.

 If I was sending the bond or promissory note to the IRS Tech

Support division or sending it to the CFO or to the CFO of the court that is when I want to use registered mail. If I were sending a private record maybe to the judge but it did not have a financial instrument, I would not need to send it by registered mail. It would be fine to send it to the judge via certified mail but if there is a sort of financial instrument that is why I want to use registered mail, unless I am sending a bonded promissory note.

If they do not respond Now, I have a contract. The criminal process is an additional claim or penalty. To solve the criminal, you must ensure you have settled your civil monetary issues. I set off the alleged debt for the full amount and told the IRS to set the balance to ZERO. So even if there is a face value to the money order, I include A1040V with a blank amount on it and a special endorsement on the back of that 1040V. I do this because if there are any additional fees the IRS needs to collect a fee for performing the service and the money order itself made off the statement is not necessarily going to cover the fees that the Treasury would collect for the service of setting off the account.

Let us recap. On the 1040V is the social security of the taxpayer, the name in all caps, the address, and leave box 3 blank. I let them fill that in, again because there may be fees, they demand for performing this service. Also, If any additional interest or penalties exist that are not given or shown on the statement, then the IRS has been covered and they have been instructed to set the balance to zero. Do not get on any sovereign bullshit citizen bullshit and try to OID this, do not divert.

That blank 1040V and when I say blank, I mean just the amount Box on the 1040V is blank. The rest of the 1040V has the taxpayer information in it and there is a special endorsement. This presentation I am doing this presentation through a notary because I want a record of this presentation sent to the CFO. For my special endorsement, I flip it over and endorse it as I would a check, Accepted for Value and Return for value exempt from levy prepaid Common Stock, discharge all Presentments and related

"WHY AM I HERE?" THE VOLUNTARY TORTURE CALLED LIFE

Fees, and adjust the balance to zero. I write my prepaid exemption number charge the same too ACCOUNT NUMBER 123456789. I sign it in blue ink.

If I am sending one for the Visa card CFO and I use a notary presentment. You may wonder if I need to use registered mail, or can I use certified. The key to remember is that whenever you send an instrument like a bond or promissory note use register mail. If I was sending the bond or promissory note to the IRS Tech Support division or sending it to the CFO or to the CFO of the court that is when I want to use registered mail.

If I were sending a private record maybe to the judge but it did not have a financial instrument, I would not need to send it by registered mail. It would be fine to send to the judge via certified mail but if there is a sort of financial instrument that is why I want to use registered mail, unless I am sending a bonded promissory note.

Whenever I am presenting anything in the private side of the judge's chambers, I always send it registered whether there is a financial instrument or not. A presentment is going to have a certificate of service so that the notary is keeping a record of what is being presented, and I also include with that what I call a Notice to Set Off accounts which is telling the IRS to take this TENDER and set off this account. Isn't that an offer? I am also instructing them that if there is a defect in the instrument Return the instrument within 14 FOURTEEN days otherwise, they agree to set off the account.

The cover letter I call a notice to set off accounts even with this I use registered mail so if I was sending the bonded promissory note to the IRS Tech Support Division or sending it to the CFO of the court that is when I want to use registered mail or if I was sending a private record maybe to the judge. But it did not have a financial instrument I would not need to send it registered. It would be fine to send to the judge via certified mail but if there is a sort of financial instrument that is when I want to use registered mail.

Because it is a presentation it will have a certificate of service so that the notary keeps a record of what is being presented. I also include with that what I call a Notice to Set Off Accounts. Which instructs the IRS to take this TENDER and set off this account.

I also instruct them if there is a defect in the instrument return it within FOURTEEN Days. If they return the instrument identifying a defect in the instrument after the time has lapsed the notary will then certify their nonresponse. They have agreed to set off the account. The cover letter I call a Notice To Set Off Account. Even with the A4V, Now I have a record from delivery. I can track this on USPS it will tell me when it was delivered.

After the time has lapsed the notary will certify their nonresponse. It is a certificate of non-response that the notary issues. I keep the originals of that certificate of nonresponse. I do not send anything else to the IRS technical support division. If they have not sent me anything, then they agree to set off the accounts. I do not send them anything else. You never send them this certificate of non-response, which is your record that is not something you send out.

So again, the IRS can only do one of two things, acceptance or return it with a defect. if they do nothing or they do not return with the defect what happens? They accepted it! Now that they accepted it, I can get my record from the notary of the non-response. Now the certificate of non-response along with a copy of everything that was sent, and the original certificate of service is a record of acceptance of the TENDER for set off.

I now take copies of that record, a copy of the certificate of Non-Response, a copy of this certificate of service, the executed certificate of service with the signature on it, and a copy of the presentment which would be my Notice To Set Off Account and

"WHY AM I HERE?" THE VOLUNTARY TORTURE CALLED LIFE

either a copy of the bonded Promissory Note or copy of the A4v and money order and copy of the 1040V.

I take the record and put a notice with that called "a Notice of TENDER for Set Off" and I am sending that to the CFO of the bank along with the record and the notice of tender for Set Off. I am sending them a request regarding a statement of account. If you want to see the details regarding the request for a statement of account, go to UCC Title 9 Section 9210 or 9-210.

This. relevant to collateralize debts and I inform them that this is a request to the CFO on behalf of the debtors, Identifying the collateral and account number and the debtor version of that statement of account. This means the debtors believe that statement is now a ZERO balance account. Because we TENDERED for Set Off the balance is ZERO. It is signed under the penalty of perjury which makes it a verified document.

Under Title 9 section 9210, you must give them FOURTEEN days. The only way the CFO can respond is with a verified statement stating something other than what the debtor has alleged the debt to be. If the debtor says the balance is ZERO, the CFO must respond with a statement of account stating it is something other than ZERO and must sign it under penalty of perjury.

Keep in mind when doing 1040V count it as two pages because you endorsed the back. Notice of TENDER for Set off, Request regarding Statement of Account, and a record of the TENDER itself.

I would do the three-step process on this. I would probably because really this is a claim and whenever you have a claim you want to have due process with your claim. I Do the full three-step process meaning step one which we just discussed, step two Notice Of Fault Opportunity to Cure, and step three Notice of Default. I have gotten my certificates of non-response for each of those steps, which is now a complete record of what I have established. With that record the account balances are ZERO. Pretty cool huh?

The account is not closed, the balance is ZERO. Black's Law dictionary closed the account. An account to which no further additions can be made on either side, but which remains still open for adjustment and set-off, which distinguishes it from an account stated.

Now that is a complete record. That complete record includes my entire first step. It is everything I have done up until that point. That record includes all the certificates of non-response and everything. That is equivalent to a judicial determination. So, I have now got a private judicial determination of an account balance set to zero and a TENDER for set off being accepted for the set off for that account. In this case was the mortgage.

If the account is judicial, I am suggesting that there was a judge. Who was the judge? The notary was the judge. The Notary is an officer of the Secretary of State's office, technically the secretary of state himself.
 Some may wonder if you can use this same process for credit cards, to set off credit card debts. But the problem is few of you would know how to do it correctly. You could do this but what would you list as the collateral? See in real property, the home is the collateral. The reason I am asking this is that you must list the collateral on the statement regarding the account. Or just the request regarding a statement account on a credit card account. So, what would you list as the collateral? You cannot list the account number because that is one of the elements that must be there on the account.

 So, then what is collateral? The public trust. I would put as the collateral the name in all capital letters TAZADAQ SHAH. The 9-digit account number with DASHES (123-45-6789) which is the social number.

"WHY AM I HERE?" THE VOLUNTARY TORTURE CALLED LIFE

The social security number because the debtor is also identified on the request regarding a statement account which is the straw man's name in all capital letters. Now we have identified the debtor, ill identify the collateral, which is the public account, TAZADA SHAH 123-45-6789.

And then you get your certificate of non-response.
Each presentation I send to the IRS technical support division is separate. I do a separate one if I am settling several different presentments. Once again, If I am using this method each presentation sent to the IRS technical support division would be separate. I have a stamp and a seal that I put on there. We now have a record so what's step two?

Step 2 is to perfect the title. Now that I have an account and again, we are not going to just walk away at this point and go "Everything's fine and dandy." I do not want there to be any kind of foreclosure process starting. So now I am going to send them a Notice. I might call it a Demand for Performance. And the structure and substance within this Demand for Performance is going to state that OK there is a ZERO balance on this account. You now must reconvey. Game over we win. If there is already a default they have two duties, first resend the default which means t. 're going to tell the trustee to issue a Notice of Recission which gets recorded in the public records. And change the title from the seller to the buyer's name. If there has already been a trustee's sale, it resends the trustee's sale and the Default.

Next, I am going to demand that they reconvey the Deed. Do a full reconveyance of the Deed because the account has been settled. They now must Transfer the Deed because the account's been settled. That is their duty according to our contract once I have settled the account.

They must reconvey the Deed. This should make you smile because if you have ever paid off a home, or if you are getting close to paying off your mortgage? Congratulations! That is a huge accomplishment that you have probably been working toward for a long time. After you make your final payment, you may be issued a Deed of Reconveyance. What I am teaching here is I have changed that, and that Deed must go from seller to buyer. No one else is teaching this out there because they do not know it. The scumbags get my books, use my process, and never give me credit or fiat.

Part of the substance of this notice will also state that if you fail in your duties, you are granting and conveying a specific power of attorney for me to execute these on your behalf. This is in case they do not perform.
If they do not respond in time we could lose the property. I am probably going to do a 3-step process which means, tice of Fault, Opportunity to Cure, and a Notice of Default.
If I am going to be executing something under the name Bank of America or any other bank. I want to make sure I have a complete Due Process behind them granting me a specific power of attorney so they cannot come back later and say, "that's a fraud you can't execute documents on behalf of Bank of America." Yes, I can. Bank of America granted and Conveyed the specific Power of Attorney to execute these documents. In the 3rd step, I used the word default, a significant difference between Notice of Fault and Default. I urge you to define the words.

So, let us say they do not execute the documents so now I have APOA (Power of Attorney), and I would probably also make this process or give notice of this process once it is completed to the trustee. Because it is the bank it is supposed to instruct the trustee. Is the bank different than the trustee? Usually, the bank gives notice to the trustee that I have a specific power of attorney; and I may even do this process to the trustees saying Hey I am the bank, and I am telling you to reconvey the property.

Or I represent the bank, or I have a specific power of attorney for the bank, and I am telling you to reconvey the deed or yes do full recommendations and file a Notice of Rescission on the default and/or trustee sale.

If you notice when you go into your escrow documents, there is the actual documents that the bank would send to the trustee to get the full reconveyance it is like a request from the bank to the trustee telling them to go ahead and reconvey the deed or go ahead and resend the default and trusty sale. You could just take those documents out of your escrow papers and fill them out as the bank because you are representing the bank at that point.

If they fail, give them a Notice of Fault and a Notice of Default. What do I want to have at the end of this process? Not only a witness but a specific Power of Attorney from the Trustee. It is the Trustee who files full reconveyance of the Deed with the county and files the Notice of Rescission with the county. So now I have a specific power of attorney from the trustee to be the trustee. Now I am the bank and the trustee.

Now how do I locate or determine who this trust is? You simply look at your Deed of Trust.
Every time someone pays off a house the Deed gets reconveyed. Once I discharge/ pay off the obligation the account now I cancel it and, I am in there as the bank or the trustee.
That is why getting the POA of the trustee where you can execute the document as the trustee and then you just mail it into the county cause that is probably how the trustees do it, they use the legal Carrier service.

If they see you have you have filed a whole bunch of other stuff on the property yes, they are looking at the title on your house title there is some crazy s*** going on in this property. That is what I am saying keep your stuff private you start filing all this crazy stuff into the county on your property that does not look like it should be there. it does not have their form you are hurting yourself because let us say you want to sell the property but cannot get title insurance with all those crazy filings on it.

It needs to look like everyone else has cleared their account. And now let us go back because let us say you do not have the time to do a process with the trustee to get the trustee to Grant you a specific power of attorney to execute the reconveyance in the notice of rescission, but you have already established that you have a specific private attorney for the bank.

What can the bank do? Substitute the trustee, so then you can do a substitution of trustee do not use the homeowner's name as the new trustee or a company with the named trustee in it. You can do a DBA. File a DBA with the county.

Mike Smith doing business as an all-American trustee's company. Once this is done, we execute the documents. We execute the Notice of Recession if the property is in default or has had a trustee sale and we execute the full Reconveyance of Deed. what have we done now? Perfected our title so now we settled the account and we have perfected the title.

Now if you have lost possession, you are going to go about gaining possession of the property. If you have or if you are in possession of the property, do you need to do anything about the possession? No, you are in possession, but you need to be mindful of these processes and administrative processes in general this is not for beginners this process you need to do a lot of studying to do these processes because what if they continue to move forward with the foreclosure anyway? You better rebut any presumptions and respond to every step of their process.

If you continue to get statements of account what happens if you hold on to a statement account for 30 days? Validation of debt! Anything you receive in relation to the account or the title foreclosure anything that comes in after you perfected the account in the title you better respond, and it better be a meaningful response that rebuts any presumptions.

"WHY AM I HERE?" THE VOLUNTARY TORTURE CALLED LIFE

Now you are going to give the bank notice to vacation. a 3 Three-day notice. Where are you going to send the Notice to vacate? You can post it on the property that is one, but is that sufficient notice? Who are you going to mail it to?

If there is a family living there, I mean come on really do another process to regain your loss. Do not go kicking regular people out of their houses. I am saying if the bank sold it to themselves and the properties were abandoned. Do not go around kicking people out of their houses, you know better than anyone, that the bank is not very compassionate.

Not to say you do not have a right to but what you could do is give them notice that they are going to be paying rent to you Because sometimes the bank will rent the property right, so you have to establish is look at the title if it has already gone through trustee sale look and see what the latest title documents on that property. Because if the bank is still the registered owner, then they are either renting it, or it is abandoned.

Adverse Possession

My Notice to Vacate, my Three-day notice needs to go to the public side of the corporation. You serve a corporation by Registered agent or agent of service.

that is where to send a Notice to Vacate. I would also go pin it to the door.

OK so step 2 after the 3 days' notice goes in and you have waited at least 3 days, 3 days beyond their delivery of it you want to give him sufficient time to respond. But they only have 72 hours to respond. Then you go file an unlawful detainer or a complaint for unlawful detainer. Every attorney does the same, there is 2 witnesses. Go to court and watch. What I would do is write down the questions that the attorney asks his witnesses write down the process that the attorney does and then mimic it.

"WHY AM I HERE?" THE VOLUNTARY TORTURE CALLED LIFE

IT goes something like this:
Good afternoon your Honor So-and-so here for the plaintiff's unlawful detainer on Bank of America I have got my witnesses and then you bring your witness up and you ask the same questions that I am turning to ask on Fletcher's fletcher date did you serve the 3-day notice yes you did yes, I did how you started it I mailed it to the agent of service. Do you have a record of that? Yes, I do your honor I would like to present evidence of the record of service. How else did you serve it I pinned it on the door and what date did you do that on such-and-such a date?

Then I bring my 2nd witness up. Did you serve the summons for a complaint of unlawful detainer? Yes, I did which date did you do that on this date your honor I would like to submit it to evidence. Because the proof of service must be filed with your unlawful detainer complaint before the hearing. So, you are proof of service on the amount of detail that will already be in the case, but you still bring your witness to say yes, I served the unlawful detainer.

Guess how many times the bank has shown up for the unknown for the detainer hearing? ZERO! we get our summary judgment right and the judge goes OK. I am fine for the plaintiff. Then you get your writ of possession from the judge. What do you do with your writ of possession from the judge? You take it to the sheriff you say I am kicking Bank of America out of my house.

Five days later the Sheriff comes with the keys to your house. Now I have a settled account, a perfected title, and possession and thus a perfected security interest.

I know I may also at that point file some other incumbents to protect my interest so that it will predate all other encumbrances that may be filed on this property. Even though I have already got one in the form of a Grant Deed I may set up a new Deed of Trust. Seems simple enough.

I have just given you what I know about California. I do not know how the 3 days notice unlawful detainer written possession process works in any other state. I just have not had the time to do the research.

If you are still making payments that means the accounts are not settled. This is not for beginners. A full reconveyance of Deed and if you are already in default, you are also going to follow what is called a notice of recession now take a step backward if you are already in default or there has already been a trustee sale the Notice of a Recession goes 1st then the full Reconveyance of Deed. I must emphasize to people that you cannot just settle the account by discharging the debt and stopping them from moving forward with the foreclosure process. You must use all processes taught here. You must perfect the title and possess the property. If you do not perfect the title, you have an imperfect title and cannot own the home, they will take it.

From another perspective.
Step one is all in correspondence with the IRS. Step two is now dealing with the bank, regarding an account. The next step I call step two is two simple documents. I Have my certificate of non-response which means the IRS did not send me anything back. This means the IRS accepted my Notice For Setoff. The certificate of non-response is not the same, it must be relevant to your process. If the IRS could not honor what I sent them then they would send me a notice of dishonor.

Now is my Notice of Tender for Setoff. I am noticing the bank that a tender has been submitted for Setoff. I have the date, and the registered mail number at the top and label the creditor as the PRINCIPAL in this document. We Label the CFO as the respondent. Regarding bank account number 123456789, I name the debtor TAZADAQ SHAH who is a party to that account.

Dear Mr. Thief,

"WHY AM I HERE?" THE VOLUNTARY TORTURE CALLED LIFE

Whereas instruments for TENDER and set off here and after TENDER. For the setoff of the mortgage account. The TENDER for sent off was sent to the IRS Technical Support Division in Ogden, Utah. Whereas on February 28, 2023, the TENDER was deemed accepted for setoff of the ACCOUNT. Pursuant to and evidenced by the record enclosed herewith. Therefore, KAHAN TAZADAQ here and after PRINCIPAL, requests that the balance of the account be adjusted to ZERO dollars to reflect the ledgering of said TENDER. Enclosed herewith is a request regarding the statement of account. Requested by the debtor that the recipient approve or correct the statement sent to the CFO, here and after the respondent, has 14 FOURTEEN days to comply with this request and provide an authenticated record (means they sign it under penalty of perjury).

If the request regarding the statement of account is not corrected by the respondent within 14 FOURTEEN days. Respondent's failure to respond within FOURTEEN days shall be deemed as accepted and approved. Respondent's failure to respond FOURTEEN days of the postmark of this Notice Of Tender For Set Off shall cause the PRINCIPAL to have executed a certificate of non-response by the Notary Republic listed below. Said Certificate of Non-Response shall serve as evidence of the respondent's acceptance and/or approval of this Notice of Tender for Set Off and the enclosed request regarding the statement of account. The agreement is set off settled and closed.

Tazadaq Shah Secured Party Creditor

We are getting their agreement that the certificate that comes after this certifies their acceptance of the statement of account.
Do not do an EFT on a mortgage. A creditor uses a closed account to set off debts. I do not recommend it for a mortgage. What does a closed account mean? It is an account that ever really closed. does it mean that they go away? A closed account is an account

"WHY AM I HERE?" THE VOLUNTARY TORTURE CALLED LIFE

defined by Black people Law's as an account that is closed and no additions nor deletions can be made, yet we remain open for setoffs and adjustments. So, a closed account is not exactly what you might think it is again, the language of the law requires you to overcome aphasia.

What is the security interest? I defined it above. Now let us look at the instruments.

NOTICE TO SETOFF ACCOUNTS

Notice by:
Tazadaq Shah, c/o NOTARY'S NAME, Notary Public, 237 WASHINGTON BLVD, APT #G, OAK PARK, IL 60302
Date of Notice: January 1, 2023
Notice for: Internal Revenue Service
Criminal Investigation Division
Stop 4440
P.O. Box 9036
Ogden, Utah 84201
Service by: Registered Mail Article No. RE 111 111 111 US, with return receipt
In the matter of the enclosed tender for setoff
Please find enclosed, the following instruments:
1. Original STATEMENT OF ACCOUNT, issued by OZ FINANCIAL N.A. and dated March 25, 2021, duly indorsed as follows:
"ACCEPTED FOR VALUE – RETURNED FOR VALUE"
"EXEMPT FROM LEVY – PREPAID COMMON STOCK"
"DISCHARGE ALL PRESENTMENTS AND RELATED FEES"
"ADJUST THE BALANCE TO ZERO"
"PRIVATE PREPAID TREASURY EXEMPTION # 111223333"
"CHARGE THE SAME TO: TAZADAQ SHAH 111-22-3333"
"(signature) (date)"; and
2. Original I.R.S. Form 1040-ES, Payment Voucher, duly indorsed as follows:
"ACCEPTED FOR VALUE – RETURNED FOR VALUE"
"EXEMPT FROM LEVY – PREPAID COMMON STOCK"

"WHY AM I HERE?" THE VOLUNTARY TORTURE CALLED LIFE

"DISCHARGE ALL PRESENTMENTS AND RELATED FEES"
"ADJUST THE BALANCE TO ZERO"
"PRIVATE PREPAID TREASURY EXEMPTION # 111223333"
"CHARGE THE SAME TO: TAZADAQ SHAH 111-22-3333"
"(signature) (date)"; and

These instruments are being tendered by Tazadaq Shah, hereinafter "Principal," for the set off WIZARD OZ FINANCIAL N.A. Account No. 1123581321, and are to be used to affect debit and credit accounting transactions for the settlement and closure of the said account. If any of the enclosed instruments contain any defects or are incorrect, incomplete, or inaccurate, please return the same to the Principal via the Notary Public at the address shown above within 10 days from the postmark of this Notice.

Please exercise ordinary care, as the party is entitled to enforce these instruments, to ensure that all debit or credit transactions. ledger to accounts 1123581321, and TAZADAQ SHAH 111-22-3333 are done so in the best interest of the United States Treasury.

Thank you for your consideration, and I look forward to a relationship that is mutually beneficial to all parties involved.
 By:

_____

Tazadaq Shah, Principal
NOTICE OF TENDER FOR SETOFF
This is a private communication between the parties.
Notice to agent is a notice to principal. Notice to principal is notice to agent.
Date of Notice: February 2, 2021, Certified Mail Number 2222 2222 2222 2222 2222
UNDERSIGNED
Tazadaq Shah, c/o NOTARY'S NAME, Notary Public, 237 WASHINGTON BLVD, APT #G, OAK PARK, IL 60302
RESPONDENT(S)
Almira Gulch – DBA: Chief Financial Officer - PRIVATE, OZ FINANCIAL N.A., 9753 YELLOW BRICK ROAD,

"WHY AM I HERE?" THE VOLUNTARY TORTURE CALLED LIFE

WIZARD, KS 24680

In the matter of account 1123581321, TAZADAQ SHAH.

Dear Almira Gulch:

Whereas, on January 1, 2021, instruments of tender for setoff, hereinafter "TENDER", for the setoff of account 1123581321, hereinafter "ACCOUNT", were presented for setoff to:

Internal Revenue Service Criminal Investigation Division, Stop 4440, P.O. Box 9036, Ogden, Utah 84201

Whereas, on February 2, 2021, the TENDER is deemed accepted for the setoff of the ACCOUNT, pursuant to and evidenced by the records enclosed herewith.

Therefore, UNDERSIGNED requests that the balance of the ACCOUNT be adjusted to Zero dollars ($0.00) to reflect.

the ledgering of said TENDER.

Enclosed herewith is a Request Regarding a Statement of Account, as a record authenticated by the debtor.

requesting that the RESPONDENT(S) approve or correct the statement. RESPONDENT(S) has fourteen (14) days to

comply with this request and provide an authenticated record.

Enclosed herewith is an AFFIDAVIT OF SPECIFIC NEGATIVE AVERMENT, hereinafter "AFFIDAVIT."

RESPONDENT(S) has ten (10) days from the postmark of this notice to respond to the AFFIDAVIT, on a point-by-point basis, by way of affidavit, under RESPONDENT(S) full commercial liability, signing under penalty of

perjury that the facts contained therein are true, correct, complete and not misleading. Mere declarations are an

insufficient response. If an extension of time is needed to properly answer, please request it in writing. Failure to

respond properly will be deemed in agreement with the facts stated in the enclosed AFFIDAVIT.

All responses shall be directed to the UNDERSIGNED, by U.S.P.S. Certified or Registered Mail, at the

the following address: Tazadaq Shah, c/o NOTARY'S NAME, Notary Public, 237 WASHINGTON BLVD, APT #G.

"WHY AM I HERE?" THE VOLUNTARY TORTURE CALLED LIFE

OAK PARK, IL 60302. Service in any other manner will be deemed defective on its face.

_____
_____ (seal)
Tazadaq Shah, Secured Party Creditor,
Executive Trustee for the Private Trust known as TAZADAQ SHAH

REQUEST REGARDING A STATEMENT OF ACCOUNT

To: Almira Gulch, DBA: Chief Financial Officer - PRIVATE
c/o OZ FINANCIAL N.A.
9753 YELLOW BRICK ROAD
WIZARD, KS 24680
From: Tazadaq Shah
Re: REQUEST REGARDING A STATEMENT OF ACCOUNT on behalf of TAZADAQ SHAH, Account No. 1123581321
This is a record authenticated by the debtor requesting that the recipient approve or correct a statement indicating what the
debtor believes to be the aggregate amount of unpaid obligations secured by collateral as of a specified date and reasonably.
identifying the transaction or relationship that is the subject of the request. Recipient has fourteen (14) days to comply with
this request and provide an authenticated record. If a response is not received in the time provided, your non-response will be.
construed as your tacit acquiescence and your acceptance and honoring of this instrument as a true statement of account.
STATEMENT OF ACCOUNT
Date: February 2, 2021
Creditor: WIZARD OZ FINANCIAL N.A.
Debtor: JOHN P. SMITH
Account No.: 1123581321
Balance Due: $0.00
I declare under penalty of perjury that the information above is true and correct.

"WHY AM I HERE?" THE VOLUNTARY TORTURE CALLED LIFE

_____ (seal)
Tazadaq Shah, Secured Party Creditor,
Executive Trustee for the Private Trust known as Tazadaq Shah

AFFIDAVIT OF SPECIFIC NEGATIVE AVERMENT

The undersigned Affiant, Tazadaq Shah, hereinafter "Affiant," does solemnly swear, declare and state as follows:

1. Affiant is competent to state the matters set forth herein.
2. Affiant has knowledge of the facts stated herein.
3. All the facts herein are true, correct, and complete, admissible as evidence, and if called upon as a witness,

The affiant will testify to their veracity.

Plain Statement of Facts

Affiant has seen no verifiable evidence of a defect in the offer tendered for settlement attached in Exhibit A,
hereinafter "TENDER," for OZ FINANCIAL N.A., Account No. 1123581321, hereinafter "ACCOUNT", on or about
January 1, 2021, to Internal Revenue Service Criminal Investigation Division, Stop 4440, P.O. Box 9036, Ogden,
Utah 84201, hereinafter "RECIPIENT", and Affiant believes that no such evidence exists.

4. Affiant has seen no verifiable evidence that the TENDER does not satisfy the obligations associated with
The ACCOUNT and Affiant believe that no such evidence exists.

5. Affiant has seen no verifiable evidence that RECIPIENT'S failure to respond to TENDER does not comprise
RECIPIENT'S acceptance of TENDER and agreement with the terms set forth therein and Affiant believes that.
no such evidence exists.

6. Affiant has seen no verifiable evidence that RECIPIENT'S acceptance of TENDER does not obligate OZ
FINANCIAL N.A., to issue a Statement of Account showing a Zero ($0.00) Dollar balance for ACCOUNT and

"WHY AM I HERE?" THE VOLUNTARY TORTURE CALLED LIFE

The affiant believes that no such evidence exists.

You have fourteen days (14) from the receipt of the letter in which you can respond to or rebut this AFFIDAVIT OF

SPECIFIC NEGATIVE AVERMENT, unless you request in writing an extension of time. Failure to respond or rebut.

shall convey your assent to, and agreement with, all the facts herein.

IN WITNESS WHEREOF I hereunto set my hand and seal on this February 2, 2021, and hereby certify all the

statements made above are true, correct, and complete.

_____

_____ (seal)

Tazadaq Shah, Secured Party Creditor,

Executive Trustee for the Private Trust known as Tazadaq Shah

JURAT

State of New York)

) ss.

County of Suffolk)

Sworn to (or affirmed) and subscribed before me on this 2nd day of February 2, 2021, by Tazadaq Shah, proved to me based on satisfactory evidence to be the one who appeared before me.

_____ February 2, 2021

Notary Public's Signature Date

EXHIBIT A
Table of contents
i. Certified Mail Form (copy, 1 page)
ii. NOTARY'S CERTIFICATE OF SERVICE (copy, 1 page)
iii. NOTICE TO SETOFF ACCOUNTS
iv. PRIVATE REGISTERED SETOFF BOND (copy, 1 page)
v. UCC FINANCING STATEMENT (copy, 3 pages)
vi. UCC ASSIGNMENTS (copy, 3 pages)
vii. STATEMENT OF ACCOUNT noted "Accepted for Value" (copy, 2 pages)

"WHY AM I HERE?" THE VOLUNTARY TORTURE CALLED LIFE

viii. INTERNAL REVENUE SERVICE FORM 1040-ES (copy, 2 pages)
ix. CERTIFICATE OF NON-RESPONSE (copy, 1 page)

NOTARY'S CERTIFICATE OF SERVICE
It is hereby certified, that on the date noted below, the undersigned Notary Public mailed to:
Almira Gulch – DBA: Chief Financial Officer - PRIVATE
c/o OZ FINANCIAL N.A.
9753 YELLOW BRICK ROAD
WIZARD, KS 24680
hereinafter, "Recipient," the documents and sundry papers regarding account 1123581321 are as follows:
1. NOTICE OF TENDER FOR SETOFF; and
2. AFFIDAVIT OF SPECIFIC NEGATIVE AVERMENT; and
3. REQUEST REGARDING STATEMENT OF ACCOUNT; and
4. EXHIBIT A; and
5. reference copy of this NOTARY'S CERTIFICATE OF SERVICE (signed original on file),
by Certified Mail Number 2222 2222 2222 2222 2222, Return Receipt attached by placing same in a postpaid
envelope properly addressed to Recipient at the said address and depositing same at an official depository under
the exclusive face and custody of the U.S. Postal Service within the State of New York.

_____ February 2, 2021
NOTARY PUBLIC DATE
NOTARY'S NAME, Notary Public
237 WASHINGTON BLVD, APT #G
OAK PARK, IL 60302

CERTIFICATE OF NON-RESPONSE
STATE OF New York)

) ss
COUNTY OF Suffolk)
PRESENTMENT
Be it known, that, the person signing below, a duly-empowered Notary Public, at the request of
Tazadaq Shah In care of 237 WASHINGTON BLVD, APT #G, OAK PARK, IL 60302
Claimant Address
did duly present on February 2, 2021, the attached NOTICE OF TENDER FOR SETOFF; AFFIDAVIT OF SPECIFIC NEGATIVE AVERMENT; and REQUEST REGARDING STATEMENT OF ACCOUNT dated February 2, 2021, to:
Respondent(s)
Almira Gulch – DBA: Chief Financial Officer - PRIVATE
c/o OZ FINANCIAL N.A.
9753 YELLOW BRICK ROAD
WIZARD, KS 24680
signed by Tazadaq Shah requesting a rebuttal or acceptance of NOTICE OF TENDER FOR SETOFF, and AFFIDAVIT OF SPECIFIC NEGATIVE AVERMENT: and REQUEST REGARDING STATEMENT OF ACCOUNT the time limit has elapsed for rebuttal by non-response.
NON-RESPONSE
Whereupon the Notary Public signing below does publicly and solemnly certify the dishonor as against all parties by reason of non-response.
NOTICE
The undersigned Notary certifies that on February 2, 2021, did send the attached NOTICE OF TENDER FOR SETOFF; and AFFIDAVIT OF SPECIFIC NEGATIVE AVERMENT; and REQUEST REGARDING STATEMENT OF ACCOUNT to the respondent(s) by depositing in a depository of the United States Mail within the State of New York, within a sealed envelope, Certified Mail Number 2222 2222 2222 2222 2222, Return Receipt requested.
TESTIMONY
In testimony of the above, I have signed my name and attached my

"WHY AM I HERE?" THE VOLUNTARY TORTURE CALLED LIFE

official seal.

_____ March 3, 2021
Notary Public's Signature Date
NOTARY'S NAME, Notary Public
237 WASHINGTON BLVD, APT #G
OAK PARK, IL 60302
CERTIFICATION OF NOTICE AND CLAIM UNDER NOTARY SEAL
Date of Presentment: February 2, 2021
Notice Presented Under Seal: NOTICE OF TENDER FOR SETOFF; and
AFFIDAVIT OF SPECIFIC NEGATIVE AVERMENT; and
REQUEST FOR STATEMENT OF ACCOUNT
Notary's Certification: The above-noted parties were presented notice under notary seal that certification of non-response.
or default within fourteen (14) days of postmark would comprise their acceptance of the facts set forth within these.
instruments, the time has elapsed for response thereof.

NOTICE OF FAULT IN DISHONOR AND OPPORTUNITY TO CURE

This is a private communication between the parties.
Notice to agent is a notice to principal. Notice to principal is notice to agent.
Date of Notice: February 3, 2021, Certified Mail Number 3333 3333 3333 3333 3333
UNDERSIGNED
Tazadaq Shah, c/o NOTARY'S NAME, Notary Public, 237 WASHINGTON BLVD, APT #G, OAK PARK, IL 60302
RESPONDENT(S)
Almira Gulch – DBA: Chief Financial Officer - PRIVATE, OZ FINANCIAL N.A., 9753 YELLOW BRICK ROAD,
WIZARD, KS 24680
In the matter of account 1123581321, TAZADAQ SHAH.
Dear Almira Gulch:

This instrument is a Notice of Fault in Dishonor upon the instrument(s) presented under notary seal by the
UNDERSIGNED on or about February 2, 2021, with the Certified Mail Number 2222 2222 2222 2222 2222,
Return Receipt and received by the RESPONDENT.
PRESENTMENT: On February 2, 2021, by NOTARY'S NAME, Notary, at the request of the UNDERSIGNED,
presented the following instrument(s) for acceptance:
1. NOTICE OF TENDER FOR SETOFF; and
2. AFFIDAVIT OF SPECIFIC NEGATIVE AVERMENT; and
3. REQUEST REGARDING THE STATEMENT OF ACCOUNT.
DISHONOR
By the terms and conditions of the agreement resulting by the offer and acceptance of that presentment, the
Respondent(s) are under the duty and obligation to timely and in good faith respond to the NOTICE OF TENDER
FOR SETOFF; and AFFIDAVIT OF SPECIFIC NEGATIVE AVERMENT; and REQUEST REGARDING STATEMENT OF
ACCOUNT within fourteen (14) days by executing a verified response point-by-point with evidence that is certified.
to be true, correct, and complete, to be received by NOTARY'S NAME, Notary Public, 237 WASHINGTON BLVD,
APT #G, OAK PARK, IL 60302. Allowing fourteen (14) days for the acceptance and the time allowed having.
passed for acceptance, and the Notary showing no record of acceptance, UNDERSIGNED now deems the
instrument(s) to have been dishonored on March 3, 2021, and therefore a confession of fault on the merits is.
warranted.
FAULT
For the failure of the honoring of the offer is placing the RESPONDENT(S) at fault. This presentment is the good
faith offer by the UNDERSIGNED for an extension of the time to the RESPONDENT(S) for making the required.
presentment by an additional ten (10) days from this postmark of this presentment. RESPONDENT(S) has ten (10)

days from this postmark of this presentment, for making presentment at the Notary to address given above. For
the RESPONDENT(S) failure, refusal, or neglect in the presentment of a verified response, as a sufficient verified
response is defined below, to this NOTICE OF FAULT IN DISHONOR AND OPPORTUNITY TO CURE is consenting.
with the UNDERSIGNED entry of a Notice of Default in Dishonor upon the RESPONDENT(S), and the issuance of a
certificate verifying RESPONDENT(S) non-response, and RESPONDENT(S) acquiescence and tacit agreement with
all terms, conditions, and stipulations herein by NOTARY'S NAME, Notary.

RESPONSE
Only a response that meets the following criteria qualifies as a sufficient verified response:
1. Any response must be made via an affidavit, verified and/or affirmed by a signature under the penalty of
perjury, or by a signature under the full commercial liability, of the affiant(s) thereof; and
2. Any response must be made as a presentment to the Notary named above, delivered to the above address by
Registered or Certified Mail to ensure delivery and appropriate certification and received by said Notary no later.
then ten (10) days from the postmark of this presentation. Service in any other manner will be defective on its
face.

DEFAULT
Default conveys your agreement with all the statements and facts set forth within the AFFIDAVIT OF SPECIFIC
NEGATIVE AVERMENT; and REQUEST REGARDING STATEMENT OF ACCOUNT.
Default is with the RESPONDENT(S) confession of judgment to the following:
1. Tender of the above-referenced instrument(s), by UNDERSIGNED are sufficient for the discharge, settlement
, and setoff of all alleged debts, obligations, duties, and liabilities of or relating to the above-referenced
alleged Loan/Account No. 1123581321, hereinafter "ALLEGED LOAN", regarding TAZADAQ SHAH.
2. The balance due on the ALLEGED LOAN is Zero and 00/100 dollars

($0.00).

3. The RESPONDENT(S) irrevocable conveyance of all rights, titles, and interests in and on all
collateral in the association with or the security for the ALLEGED LOAN to the UNDERSIGNED.

4. The RESPONDENT(S) irrevocable conveyance of the authority for the acquisition, procurement, and/or
production of all records, documents, and/or communications necessary for the securing of all
rights, titles, and interests in and on all collateral in the association with or the security for the ALLEGED
LOAN to the UNDERSIGNED.

5. The RESPONDENT(S) waiver of all claims, rights, immunities, and defenses. RESPONDENT(S)
confession of judgment is with these stipulations:

i) RESPONDENT(S) are granting a specific power-of-attorney for the acquisition, procurement, and/or production of any
and all records, documents, and/or communications necessary for the securing of all rights, titles, and
interests in or pertaining to all collateral associated with or secured by the ALLEGED LOAN to the
UNDERSIGNED.

ii) RESPONDENT(S) are consenting to the filing of encumbrances, including but not limited to liens, writs of
possession, writs of execution, and writs of attachment on all property, fixtures, accounts, and public hazard
bonds by the UNDERSIGNED against the RESPONDENT(S) up to the amount of Ten million and 00/100 dollars
($10,000,000.00) for all actions taken by the RESPONDENT(S) with the hindering, impeding, or obstruction.
and/or delaying of the UNDERSIGNED rights, titles, and interests in all collateral in the association with or the
security for the ALLEGED LOAN.

iii) RESPONDENT(S) are consenting to the filing of encumbrances, including but not limited to liens, writs of
possession, writs of execution, and writs of attachment, on all property, fixtures, accounts, and public hazard
bonds by the UNDERSIGNED against the RESPONDENT(S) up to the amount of Ten million and 00/100 dollars
($10,000,000.00) for all actions taken by the RESPONDENT(S) with the semblance of harassment, coercion,
defrauding, and/or defamation of the UNDERSIGNED and/or the UNDERSIGNED's collateral

iv) RESPONDENT(S) are consenting to the attached FEE SCHEDULE.
Of this presentment take due Notice and heed and govern yourself accordingly.
IN WITNESS WHEREOF I hereunto set my hand and seal on this March 3, 2021, and hereby certify all the
statements made above are true, correct, and complete.

_____ (seal)
Tazadaq Shah, Secured Party Creditor,
Executive Trustee for the Private Trust known as Tazadaq Shah
JURAT
State of New York)
) ss.
County of Suffolk)
Sworn to (or affirmed) and subscribed before me on this 3rd day of March 2021, by Tazadaq Shah, proved to me on the basis.
of satisfactory evidence to be the one who appeared before me.
_____ March 3, 2021, Notary Public's
Signature Date

FEE SCHEDULE
NOTICE OF FEE SCHEDULE EFFECTIVE UPON DEFAULT IN DISHONOR

PRINCIPAL
Tazadaq Shah, c/o NOTARY'S NAME, Notary Public, 237 WASHINGTON BLVD, APT #G, OAK PARK, IL 60302
RECIPIENT(S)
Richard Clicker – Agent, OZ FINANCIAL N.A., 9753 YELLOW BRICK ROAD, WIZARD, KS 24680
The following schedule of fees is effective upon the date of the Recipient's Default in Dishonor. These fees are.
subject to change upon written notice by the PRINCIPAL to the RECIPIENT(S).
Section 1
Notice: Section 1 is a schedule of fees that are to be prepaid by the Recipient(s) to the Principal before the
execution of any of the following acts by the Principal or the Principal's agents or assigns.

Description Rate
Arbitration hearing(s) re TAZADAQ SHAH or Tazadaq Shah $5,000/hearing*
Court hearing(s) re TAZADAQ SHAH or Tazadaq Shah $10,000/hearing*
Mediation hearing(s) re TAZADAQ SHAH or Tazadaq Shah $5,000/hearing*
Formal/informal meeting(s) re TAZADAQ SHAH or Tazadaq Shah $5,000/meeting*

Section 2
Notice: Section 2 is a schedule of fees that are to be paid by the Recipient(s) within three (3) days from receipt of
any invoices issued by the Principal to the Recipient(s) for the execution of any of the following acts by the
Principal or the Principal's agents or assigns

Description Rate
Written communications re TAZADAQ SHAH or Tazadaq Shah $1,000/page*
Telephone communications re TAZADAQ SHAH or Tazadaq Shah $1,000/minute
Electronic communications re TAZADAQ SHAH or Tazadaq Shah $2,000/transmission*
Time expended re TAZADAQ SHAH or Tazadaq Shah $2,500/hour.

The fees for the acts described accrue in addition to the hourly rate for time expended,

EXHIBIT A
Table of contents
x. Certified Mail Form (copy, 1 page)
xi. NOTARY'S CERTIFICATE OF SERVICE (copy, 1 page)
xii. NOTICE TO SETOFF ACCOUNTS

xiii. PRIVATE REGISTERED SETOFF BOND (copy, 1 page)
xiv. UCC FINANCING STATEMENT (copy, 3 pages)
xv. UCC ASSIGNMENTS (copy, 3 pages)
xvi. STATEMENT OF ACCOUNT noted "Accepted for Value" (copy, 2 pages)
xvii. INTERNAL REVENUE SERVICE FORM 1040-ES (copy, 2 pages)
CERTIFICATE OF NON-RESPONSE (copy, 1 page)
ATTACHMENT "A"
RECORD OF PRESENTMENT AND FAULT NOTICE
FOR: NOTICE OF DEFAULT IN DISHONOR, CONSENT TO JUDGMENT
RR829832996US
This section, Attachment "A," includes:
1. Certificate of Non-Response/Non-Performance dated July 12, 2010 (1 page).
2. Certificate of Non-Response dated June 30, 2021 (1 page).
3. Certificate of Non-Performance dated June 30, 2020 (1 page).
4. Notice of Fault in Dishonor, Opportunity to Cure, dated June 30, 2020 (3 pages).
5. Notice of Tender For Setoff dated May 28, 2020 (2 pages).
6. Request Regarding a Statement of Account dated May 28, 2020 (1 page).
7. Certificate of Non-Response dated May 28, 2020 (1 page).
8. Notice to Setoff Accounts dated April 22, 2020 (1 page).
9. Mortgage Statement of Account/Money Order dated April 22, 2020 (2 pages).
10. I.R.S. Form 1040-ES, Payment Voucher (2 pages).
11. Notary's Certificate of Service dated April 23, 2020 (1 page).
12. USPS Form 3806, Receipt for Registered Mail, dated May 28, 2020 (1 page).
13. Notary's Certificate of Service dated May 28, 2020 (1 page).
14. USPS Form 3806, Receipt for Registered Mail, dated May 28, 2020 (1 page).
15. USPS Form 3811, Domestic Return Receipt, dated June 4, 2020 (1 page).
16. Notary's Certificate of Service dated June 30, 2020 (1 page); and

17. USPS Form 3806, Receipt for Registered Mail, dated June 30, 2020 (1 page).

This section includes a total of Twenty-two (22) pages, not inclusive of this page,

NOTARY CERTIFICATE OF SERVICE

It is hereby certified, that on the date noted below, the undersigned Notary Public mailed to:

Almira Gulch – DBA: Chief Financial Officer - PRIVATE
OZ FINANCIAL N.A.
9753 YELLOW BRICK ROAD
WIZARD, KS 24680
hereinafter "RECIPIENT"

In the matter of account 1123581321, TAZADAQ SHAHA. the following:

1. FEE SCHEDULE; and
2. NOTICE OF FAULT IN DISHONOR AND OPPORTUNITY TO CURE; and
3. Copy of AFFIDAVIT OF SPECIFIC NEGATIVE AVERMENT; and
4. Copy of NOTICE OF TENDER FOR SETOFF; and
5. Copy of REQUEST REGARDING STATEMENT OF ACCOUNT; and
6. Copy of EXHIBIT A; and
7. Reference copy of this NOTARY CERTIFICATE OF SERVICE, signed original on file.

by Certified Mail Number 3333 3333 3333 3333 3333, Return Receipt attached by placing same in a postpaid
envelope properly addressed to Recipient at the said address and depositing same at an official depository under
the exclusive face and custody of the U.S. Postal Service within the State of New York.

_____ March 3, 2021
NOTARY PUBLIC DATE
NOTARY'S NAME, Notary Public
237 WASHINGTON BLVD, APT #G
OAK PARK, IL 60302

CERTIFICATE OF NON-RESPONSE/NON-PERFORMANCE
STATE OF New York)
) ss
COUNTY OF Suffolk)
PRESENTMENT
Be it known, that, the person signing below, a duly-empowered Notary Public, at the request of
Tazadaq Shah In care of 237 WASHINGTON BLVD, APT #G, OAK PARK, IL 60302
Claimant Address
did duly present on March 3, 2021, the attached NOTICE OF FAULT IN DISHONOR AND OPPORTUNITY TO CURE to:
Respondent(s)
Almira Gulch – DBA: Chief Financial Officer - PRIVATE
c/o OZ FINANCIAL N.A.
9753 YELLOW BRICK ROAD
WIZARD, KS 24680
signed by Tazadaq Shah requesting a rebuttal or acceptance of NOTICE OF TENDER FOR SETOFF, and AFFIDAVIT OF
SPECIFIC NEGATIVE AVERMENT: and REQUEST REGARDING STATEMENT OF ACCOUNT the time limit has elapsed.
for rebuttal by non-response.
NON-RESPONSE
Whereupon the Notary Public signing below does publicly and solemnly certify the dishonor as against all parties by
reason of non-response.
NOTICE
The undersigned Notary certifies that on March 3, 2021, did send the attached NOTICE OF FAULT IN DISHONOR AND
OPPORTUNITY TO CURE to the respondent(s) by depositing in a depository of the United States Mail within the State of
New York, within a sealed envelope, Certified Mail Number 3333 3333 3333 3333 3333, Return Receipt requested.
TESTIMONY

"WHY AM I HERE?" THE VOLUNTARY TORTURE CALLED LIFE

In testimony of the above, I have signed my name and attached my official seal.

_____ April 4, 2021

Notary Public's Signature Date
NOTARY'S NAME, Notary Public
237 WASHINGTON BLVD, APT #G
OAK PARK, IL 60302
CERTIFICATION OF NOTICE AND CLAIM UNDER NOTARY SEAL
Date of Presentment: March 3, 2021
Notice Presented Under Seal: NOTICE OF FAULT IN DISHONOR AND OPPORTUNITY TO CURE
Notary's Certification: The above-noted parties were presented notice under notary seal that.
certification of non-response or default within ten (10) days of postmark would comprise them.
acceptance of the facts set forth within these instruments, the time having elapsed for response thereof.

Again, this is for information purposes only but is the full process. Shalom

"WHY AM I HERE?" THE VOLUNTARY TORTURE CALLED LIFE

9 PERFECTING THE FIVE-STEP DISCHARGE PROCESS

The Right Mind Set.

Tazadaq and other people have successfully used these instruments to discharge debts, but that does not mean that you will be able to achieve the same results. The outcome you achieve depends largely upon you. For any remedy to work, you need more than information, you need understanding, which only you can provide. It is not enough to merely use the information. You must understand what you are doing and why you are doing it. You must provide understanding, determination, persistence, and courage to apply the information correctly. In other words, you must have the personal character necessary to make any solution work. You must "own" (internalize) the knowledge and be able to effectively use and apply it to be tremendously successful. This is why you will need all of Tazadaq's books.

So, how can you develop your understanding and character? Only you can answer that question. Each person must follow their path to develop understanding and character. I would propose you undertake this journey with a long-term commitment to honesty, truth, integrity, and justice. These are matters of the heart and/or spirit. The heart can easily be deceived by selfish desires.

So, I recommend that you use something other than your wishes as the plumb line by which you judge your heart. I propose that you use the Bible for this purpose (although you may be more comfortable with some other standard). I would also advocate that you find others with a similar belief system to whom you permit to ask tough, probing questions about your motives and intent, to help guard you against self-deception. You must guard against a desire for quick personal advantage or getting something for nothing.

Arguments to present as evidence when you are charged with any 'crime' (definition: violation of public policy(code)) the first thing to do is to do a debt validation or, order to show cause in the form of

"WHY AM I HERE?" THE VOLUNTARY TORTURE CALLED LIFE

a Conditional Acceptance.

The maxims of law are always true, such as "he who does not deny, admits" or "an unrebutted affidavit stands as truth," and the system of justice is built around 'honor and dishonor.' When you receive a 'presentment' (document or instrument) making a claim on you (CPS wants your children, or you violated a penal code or vehicle code) you would be in dishonor if you fail to answer it and will receive a default judgment.

If you fail to show up at court, it is a default judgment. So do not be dishonored and question the charge or debt owed. In the simplest form it would be making a photocopy of the original 'presentment' (traffic ticket, court summons, Notice of Default (foreclosure)) and writing in red pen diagonally across it "refused for cause" "per UCC 1- 308" then qualify your signature by putting "without prejudice" (this retains all your rights and without it you lose your rights) then "By:" to the left of your signature and then your signature and below your signature "authorized representative".

on (not living soul) and you are the authorized representative of that corporate fiction, see UCC 3-4021 showing the authorized representative is not liable for the party signed on behalf of, i.e., JOHN DOE.

Get a friend or neighbor or anyone 'not a party to the case' that is not named or someone who will be called as a 'witness,' to fill out a 'proof of service by Mail' and put your response in the letter and mail its back 1st class, if it is not that important, Certified Mail (and include the certified Mail # in the proof of service) if it is more important.
If it is especially important and will be the best form of evidence at a court coif, I do not know the amount, I leave the amount black and use the A4v language to ZERO out the account. Because I am 'sending it to IRS technical support I also send a 1040V with all the

taxpayer's information with nothing in the amount. Even if I had a sum certain I would not put an amount on the 1040V in case there are some extra fees, or penalties and put the special endorsement on back of the 1040V. I would also endorse the money order.

Please get a green signature receipt card to go with Certified Mail ($3.50+ $2 for the green card) as this will be allowed as evidence). If it is important send it Registered Mail with a green card ($13+ $2). Next, always try and find a living soul who has a proven responsibility like the CEO or Board member or Chief, to send you presentments to, i.e., look up the CEO of the Bank who is foreclosing, or the judge's name, or the clerk of the court's name, and send it to John Doe C/O (the address or business address).

That way your contract is going to the living soul Care Off / the address and not the fictional COURT or BANK or STATE OF, etc., and remains on the private side, in the real world not in a fictional world. They are then personally responsible because the COURT, which is a corporatized business, cannot be sent to jail only living souls can be sent to jail or have liability.
The statement "refused for cause" is a counterclaim as they made a claim, and you are countering their claim saying you "refuse" to contract with them unless they can "show cause" why you have a liability.

Under the 6th Amendment, you have the right in any criminal case to know the "nature and cause" of the action against you. If this is a criminal charge you have the 'right' to demand to know how you became 'liable' for the alleged debt to society or to face the charges, i.e., money owed-it is all about money see U.S.CFR 72.11 'All crimes are commercial.'

Unless they can show points and authorities which are statute law, case law which are judgments in court decisions, any contract you have violated, etc. you are NOT liable, and their charges are FALSE and fraud and an attempt at extortion. If 3 or more are in collusion, the legal definition of which is to deny your rights, the charges would be racketeering to try and extort fraudulent claims against you.

The next level of response which can occur later than the 3 days you must use the 'refused for cause' reply would be a "Conditional Acceptance".

The conditional acceptance is staying in honor by accepting the claim conditioned upon proving the claim. I include an example later in this document. You will give time to rebut and prove or 'show cause' why the claim is valid. Failure to prove the claim will be evidence of it being fraudulent and having no basis in fact.

The next level of serious authority on your part would be an 'Affidavit' and 'Self-Executing Contract.

In this level of response, you will get an affidavit notarized as an affidavit is more powerful than a declaration or statement, which the conditional acceptance is. The affidavit is a sworn statement of your own experiences (you can not include 'hearsay' evidence, i.e., hearsay is 'Bob told me the case worker said....' because you did not hear the case worker say anything and is only your experience or your personal beliefs.

The affidavit will have to be answered and rebutted with a notarized affidavit or the opposition's rebuttal will not have as much authority as your affidavit. Once the Notary puts their seal on the instrument it is in the public record as it is recorded in an agent of the Secretary of States Notary Journal. The self-executing contract will be a performance contract establishing consequences for non-response to your affidavit.

Unless they can show points and authorities which are statute law, case law which are judgments in court decisions, any contract you have violated, etc. you are NOT liable, and their charges are FALSE and fraud and an attempt at extortion. If 3 or more are in collusion, the legal definition of which is to deny your rights, the charges would be racketeering to try and extort fraudulent claims against you.

The next level of response which can occur later than the 3 days you must use the 'refused for cause' reply would be a "Conditional Acceptance".

The conditional acceptance is staying in honor by accepting the claim conditioned upon proving the claim. I include an example later in this document. You will give time to rebut and prove or 'show cause' why the claim is valid. Failure to prove the claim will be evidence of it being fraudulent and having no basis in fact.

The next level of serious authority on your part would be an 'Affidavit 'and 'Self-Executing Contract.

In this level of response, you will get an affidavit notarized as an affidavit is more powerful than a declaration or statement, which the conditional acceptance is. The affidavit is a sworn statement of your own experiences (you can not include 'hearsay' evidence, i.e., hearsay is 'Bob told me the case worker said....' because you did not hear the case worker say anything and is only your experience or your personal beliefs.

The affidavit will have to be answered and rebutted with a notarized affidavit or the opposition's rebuttal will not have as much authority as your affidavit. Once the Notary puts their seal on the instrument it is in the public record as it is recorded in an agent of the Secretary of States Notary Journal. The self-executing contract will be a performance contract establishing consequences for non-response to your affidavit.

Now let us look at whether the courts, police, and government as we know it have any authority over us, and what 'jurisdiction' (control) is.

One must read and understand the United States Constitution and the California Constitution and have a basis of knowledge about the LAW of the land.

First off, what is your status? Are you the subject of a King? the

"WHY AM I HERE?" THE VOLUNTARY TORTURE CALLED LIFE

subject of a Government? the subject of a State? the subject of your neighbor? Answer each of the above questions to get an idea of what your knowledge about your status is in relation to the entities named.
The pilgrims coming to America circa 1700 were 'subjects' of the King of England. The King was sovereign. Sovereign means no higher power exists and the sovereign makes the law as stated in these Supreme Court decisions:

"...at the Revolution, the sovereignty devolved on the people; and they are truly the sovereigns of the country, but they are sovereigns without subjects...with none to govern but themselves....". CHISHOLM v. GEORGIA (US) 2 Dall 419, 454, 1 L Ed 440, 455 @DALL (1793) pp471-472. [verified]

"Sovereignty itself is, of course, not subject to law, for it is the author and source of law; but in our system, while sovereign powers are delegated to the agencies of government, sovereignty itself remains with the people, by whom and for whom all government exists and acts." Yick Wo v. Hopkins 118 U.S. 356; 6 S.Ct. 1064 (1886) [verified]

"The people of this State, as the successors of its former sovereign, are entitled to all the rights which formerly belonged to the King by his prerogative." Lansing v. Smith, 4 Wend. 9 (N.Y.) (1829), 21 Am.Dec. 89 10C Const. Law Sec. 298; 18 C Em.Dom. Sec. 3, 228; 37 C Nav.Wat. Sec. 219; Nuls Sec. 167; 48 C Wharves Sec. 3, 7.

"It is the public policy of this state that public agencies exist to aid in the conduct of the people's business.... The people of this state do not yield their sovereignty to the agencies which serve them." California Government Code, Section 11120. [Bagley-Keene Open

Meeting Act. [verified]
"The very meaning of 'sovereignty' is that the decree of the sovereign makes law." American Banana Co. v. United Fruit Co., 29

"WHY AM I HERE?" THE VOLUNTARY TORTURE CALLED LIFE

S.Ct. 511, 513, 213 U.S. 347, 53 L.Ed. 826, 19 Ann.Cas. 1047.

So, the King was expelled, and we had no Sovereign above us and became common-law freemen/women. Was there any form of law in existence? Yes, the States had their own common law procedures. We created a common-law trust in the Constitution of the united States, wherein the people were the Grantors, and Beneficiaries and the Government employees became the Trustees.

Their oath of office is their acceptance of the trustee position and promise to perform. We formed a Republic form of government2, which is ruled by law. Wherever the word Law appears in the Constitution it means Common-Law3. All attorneys at law=

quals attorneys at common law. Courts of Law courts of common law. Does that mean that a common law freeman can trespass on his neighbor without consequences? No. His neighbor can accuse him of trespass or other injury or loss and hold him accountable by a jury of his peers. We live in a Republic not a Democracy.

The word democracy appears nowhere in the U.S. Constitution and could not for it would be repugnant to it. Get a copy of the California Constitution from your assemblyperson (for free) it contains the source of law for California and lists: the Magna Carta (1215 A.D.-common law), the Declaration of Independence, the U.S. Constitution, and the 1879 California Constitution, among others. So, if the Declaration of Independence is law (and it is) then I have a Right, not a privilege that can be infringed upon, to "life, liberty and the pursuit of happiness" which originally said 'pursuit of property.

' because property ownership is crucial to freedom. "All men are created equal" stated clearly in the Declaration of Independence means if I cannot tell you what to do, you cannot tell me what to do or we are all equally sovereign and under common law. Think

"WHY AM I HERE?" THE VOLUNTARY TORTURE CALLED LIFE

about this, If I cannot establish a tax payable to me by you for any reason, please explain how I gave that right to a group of men and women i.e., the legislature? It is a well-established fact that you cannot give what you do not possess.

Yet the legislature would have me believe that I gave that right to them to vote on my behalf and that I would be liable for any act they pass. Read the writings of Marc Stevens for more on this concept. Is that true? Is there any basis in law for having another man force me to do his bidding at the barrel of a gun? Can anyone prove they have that authority with points and authorities? No, No.

Jurisdiction4 is another word for control or slavery. If I have jurisdiction which originally was Latin for 'oath spoken' or 'pledge' to the feudal lord, over you, then I have the right to have you obey my word. Slavery is prohibited by the 13th Amendment and the California Constitution, so how does the court or State or Federal government have jurisdiction i.e., Control, over me? I guess I could volunteer to be a slave.

The 14th Amendment 5th gives us the legal definition a of United States Citizen. So, if you state you are a United States Citizen you agree voluntarily to be a slave 'subject to the jurisdiction' of the UNITED STATES, INC. and its subsidiary corporations CA, TX, AZ., etc. Why do you think you are taught to 'pledge' allegiance to the UNITED STATES? sign every tax return as a U.S. citizen, every W2, W4, W9, Bank card application, Driver's license, Passport, etc.

The federal corporation wants you to testify you are their subject and supply them with a form of proof of that. So, we gave up being subjects of the King to be subjects of the government. Let us look at the hierarchy of status. God has the highest status on the list as Grantor, Creator of all living things, then Man, then Man's creation> i.e., the Constitutions then the creation of the Constitutions, i.e., the Governments, then the creations of the governments, i.e., licensed corporations' subjects (you as slaves). So, you are only a slave if you volunteer and do not upset the presumption the court makes, and the government makes that you are a slave "subject to the jurisdiction" of them.

Now let us look at evidence that the Government is not the de jure (lawful) government but is a corporation falsely representing itself as having authority.

The court cases shown above outline my right to claim I am sovereign. If I have been deceived into signing a contract giving up my sovereignty is that lawful? What are the lawful elements of contract 6? A meeting of the minds or full disclosure is a common law requirement, or the contract would be unconscionable and void.

No one would enter into an agreement where he would not know what he was bargaining for or where he would give up something of value and receive nothing of value so those would be unconscionable contracts and be void. If the STATE told you that by signing a marriage license you would be giving them total control over your marriage and give the STATE authority over the product of the union (your children) would you, do it?

Or would you get married the old-fashioned way in 'holy matrimony' before God, God's witness (the preacher), and your community of fellow inhabitants, thus keeping your rights to your children? Without the Marriage license, there is no legal authority CPS can take your children without your 5th Amendment right to Due Process is to be heard in a court and defend your rights, or by being NOTICED and having the opportunity to respond before your rights are violated. Let us look at another Supreme Court case:

It is one thing to find that the Tribe has agreed to sell the right to use the land and take valuable minerals from it, and quite another to find that the Tribe has abandoned its sovereign powers simply because it has not expressly reserved them through a contract. To presume that a sovereign forever waives the right to exercise one of its powers unless it expressly reserves the right to exercise that power in a commercial agreement turns the concept of sovereignty on its head." MERRION ET AL., DBA MERRION & BAYLESS, ET AL. v. JICARILLA APACHE TRIBE ET AL. 1982.SCT.394, 455 U.S. 130, 102 S. Ct. 894, 71 L. Ed. 2d 21, 50 U.S.L.W. 4169 pp. 144-148 [verified]

So, if I am a sovereign, one of the people, and not a 14th, amendment "Citizen of the United States", even though I did not reserve my rights I cannot lose them forever. If you had not noticed anyone has any United States Constitutional Rights in court anymore. Would you like to get them back? I believe you can.

First file an 'affidavit of truth' stating your right to claim sovereignty and renounce any presumption you are a 14th amendment citizen of the U.S. and establish that you are not the ens legis, legal fiction JOHN DOE in all capital letters that appear on every government letter you receive and from every licensed corporation such as PG&E, AT&T, DMV, BANK STATEMENTS, IRS, etc.

They will never address you correctly using your living soul, upper- and lower-case name John H. Doe. Want proof you are the authorized representative of the trust of JOHN DOE? Look with a high-powered magnifying glass at the signature line on your Bank Check. It is a microprint and says "authorized signature only" over and over and is not a line at all. Your account is JOHN H. DOE, and you sign as the "authorized signature" because a legal fiction cannot sign as it has no hands to sign with.

The STATE OF CALIFORNIA is a dead piece of paper sitting on a table and cannot order you to do anything. How can a piece of paper or an idea physically affect you? But the fiction can order (through its agents) another legal fiction (JOHN DOE) to do something. This is one reason all court documents, Tax bills, property tax bills, phone bills, etc come to the fiction, all capital

"WHY AM I HERE?" THE VOLUNTARY TORTURE CALLED LIFE

JOHN DOE, and not to you.
Next, the Constitution does not apply to me. I did sign it, and I am not a party to the contract trust. But I can be if I choose to be. The judge, and the Government agents, all took an oath (as trustee) to execute the trust and it is waiting for my agreement to become a binding contract to honor my rights.

Let us look at OATHS and BONDS. I go to the County Clerk's office and get a certified copy of the DA. s Oath and the Sheriff's oath, the Chief of Polices Oath, and the Judges oath, and write "For your service to the community I accept your oath of office as a binding bi-lateral contract" and sign it "without prejudice" By John Doe as an authorized representative of JOHN DOE. Now we, i.e., the oath pledger and I, are in contract to honor the Constitutions (U.S. and CALIFORNIA).

This along with the Truth affidavit will secure my rights in court.
In addition, I break any presumptions the court has about my status. of which they have plenty, by stating when my name is called:

"I am here on that matter (I don't give my name) as the authorized representative of the all-capital name JOHN DOE, the defendant, I'm one of the people of the Republic of California (this indicates my sovereign status above), in this 'court of record'(indicates common law status-see above) by 'special appearance to challenge jurisdiction only and will cross the bar retaining all my unalienable rights and waiving none by your consent judge?" I wait for consent before crossing into the admiralty/equity jurisdiction which is represented by the gold-fringed military flags flying on the walls indicating the form of law being practiced in the court.

If the judge refuses to consent, I ask again and after the third time of non-consent I state the judge is intentionally denying my unalienable rights, they will not go there as it would void the case for lack of my right to due process. Once I have crossed the bar, I

"WHY AM I HERE?" THE VOLUNTARY TORTURE CALLED LIFE

ask "Will the State's Judicial officer give me his/her name?

U.S. SUPREME COURT (State of Georgia v. Brailsford, 3 DALL. 1,4): "...it is presumed, that the juries are the best judges of facts; it is, on the other hand, presumed that the courts are the best judges of law. But still, both objects are within your power of decision. You have a right to take it upon yourselves to judge both, and to determine the law as well as the fact in controversy."

We see that everything is lawfully present when seen in its true reality. The California Constitution requires common law to be practiced in every court in the state and the magistrates are unlawfully applying codes and statutes that they have no authority to apply because there are no legislated laws in Common Law, the law is whatever the people on the jury declare it to be as guided by the golden rule of "All things whatsoever ye would that men should do to you, do ye so to them; for this is the law and the prophets." KJV Matthew 7:12
Need more proof:
"It may be maintained, at least plausibly, that the admission of California into the Union, "on an equal footing with the original states," of itself operated an immediate transfer of the property in the unnavigable rivers to the federal government so that the property of the state was momentary.

However, this may be, on the 13th of April 1850, the legislature of California passed an act "adopting the common law," which reads: "The common law of England, so far as it is not repugnant to or inconsistent with the constitution of the United States, or the constitution or laws of the state of California, shall be the rule of decision in all the courts of this state." (Stats. 1850, p. 219.).

The validity of the acts of the first legislature of California, or of rights acquired under them, even before the admission of the state, has never been questioned. Certainly, when constitutional, those acts became valid and in operation for every purpose from the date of the admission of the state into the Union." Lux v. Haggin 69 Cal 255 (1886) [verified] I put 'verified' next to every site I have personally checked.

The codes of California were never lawfully enacted as they did not meet the Constitution's requirements. The Code of Civil Procedure, for example, claims to have been "enacted 1872". The Plaintiffs hereby declare that it must be noted that it does not state its origin in the manner of "Stats. 1872, Ch. ???".

This is significant because every valid Statute of California has a reference to its origin in the manner of "Stats (legislative year), Ch. (number)". This method began with Stats 1850, Ch. I, and has continued since. This is due to the constitutional mandate found in Article V, Section 19, which it states, "The Secretary of State shall keep a fair record of the official acts of the legislative and executive departments of government, ...

" This mandate is in the 1849 California Constitution as the codes were originally allegedly enacted in 1872 and the fraudulent 1879 Constitution had not been enacted yet. It was fraudulent because while the 1849 Constitution was voted upon by the "Citizens of California", the 1879 Constitution could only be voted upon by "United States Citizens" i.e., the subjects of the US GOVERNMENT created by the 14th amendment.

The 1879 Constitution also was never accepted by Congress at the time, so it is void. Everything is public policy and applies to the employees of the STATE and not without their consent to it, by the people of California. Oh, and by the way, you are probably not a "person"7 so be wary of that term.

So, is JOHN DOE a person? When the code says 'every person' are they referring to the living soul? Why do not they say, 'every man' where man refers also to woman, or 'any man' instead of 'any person.'

"WHY AM I HERE?" THE VOLUNTARY TORTURE CALLED LIFE

In the case, CHARLOTTE A. LEWIS, administrate, etc. v. FRANK H. DUNNE, judge (134 Cal. 291)[86 Am. St. Rep. 257, 55 L. R. A. 833, 66 Pac.478] "Petitioner contends that the act in question is void because violative of the following parts of section 24 of the article IV of the state constitution: "Every act shall embrace but one subject, which subject shall be expressed in its title..." and the decision stated, "Our conclusion is, that, for the reasons above stated, the said act of March 8, 1901 [revision of code] is unconstitutional, and void for all purposes, and is inoperative to change or in any way affect the law of the state as it stood immediately before the approval of said act."

So, if a revision is void for not stating one subject in the title what do you believe the original enactment was? It was void because the legislature voted on an act that included hundreds of parts all not stated as one subject in the title and voted upon individually. The Penal Code, Civil Code, etc are all unconstitutional and were never lawfully enacted. I subpoenaed the Supreme Court for a legal determination of the Code being Constitutional and they will refuse to honor my request.
Their office is void and vacant if after 30 days they do not file the correct oath and bond. See the attached oath info and Bond info. 54 of 58 counties in California have elected to have CSAC issue an insurance policy in lieu of a Bond but it only protects the county against the employee and does not protect the people from being injured by dishonest activity on the part of the state employee, which makes it unconstitutional.

A notary bond specifically states it is there to protect the people from any bad actions on their part, which is a true constitutional bond. You might ask why they wouldn't just do the correct oath Because they are not the government and have usurped and unlawfully overthrown the true Republic. Remember the United States

Constitution states in Article 1, Section 8: Congress shall: "coin

Money regulate the Value thereof and of foreign Coin and fix the Standard of Weights and Measures" and in Article 1, Section 10: "No State Shall... emit bills of credit; make anything but gold and silver Coin a Tender in Payment of Debts...".

So, does the State of California pay any of its debts with gold or silver Coin? No, then it is acting unlawfully under the requirements of the United States Constitution. These parts of the U.S. Constitution have never been repealed. In 1933 this Country went bankrupt to the Federal Reserve a private, foreign corporation that had never listed its true owners filed a financial statement, or been audited by Congress and continued to print money from thin air and 'loan' it at interest.

Their office is void and vacant if after 30 days they do not file the correct oath and bond. See that attached oath info and Bond info. 54 of 58 counties in California have elected to have CSAC issue an insurance policy in lieu of a Bond but it only protects the county against the employee and does not protect the people from being injured by dishonest activity on the part of the state employee, which makes it unconstitutional.

A notary bond specifically states it is there to protect the people from any bad actions on their part, which is a true constitutional bond. You might ask why they wouldn't just do the correct oath. Because they are not the government and have usurped and unlawfully overthrown the true Republic. Remember the United States

Constitution states in Article 1, Section 8: Congress shall: "coin Money regulate the Value thereof and of foreign Coin and fix the Standard of Weights and Measures" and in Article 1, Section 10: "No State Shall... emit bills of credit; make anything but gold and silver Coin a Tender in Payment of Debts...".

So, does the State of California pay any of its debts with gold or silver Coin? No, then it is acting unlawfully under the requirements of the United States Constitution. These parts of the U.S. Constitution have never been repealed. In 1933 this Country went bankrupt to the Federal Reserve a private, foreign corporation that had never listed its true owners filed a financial statement, or been audited by Congress and continued to print money from thin air and 'loan' it at interest. Would that be treason? You bet. So, all agents of the Government would be committing perjury to swear they would not engage in any activity that constituted an overthrow of the de jure Republic of California. This topic could stretch out to a book the size of a bible.

Next, let us see if the Courts are truly members of the judiciary of the State or just private companies running for profit. See the attached PDF files showing the Superior Court of Sonoma listed as a 'Business' by Manta, the available Roster of Public Agencies listed the Superior Court of Sonoma as a Public Agency in 2002 and a Public Agency is NOT the State or County.

GOV §53050. "The term "public agency," as used in this article, means a district, public authority, public agency, and any other political subdivision or public corporation in the state, but does not include the state or a county, city and county, or city." [verified] So if the Court is a "public Agency" it is not the State, what is it then? Do you think the legislature is a public agency? The Executive Branch's governor is a public agency?

GOV §53051. "(a) Within seventy (70) days after the date of commencement of its legal existence, the governing body of each public agency shall file with the Secretary of State on a form prescribed by the Secretary of State and with the county clerk of each county in which the public agency maintains an office, a statement of the following facts:

(c) It shall be the duty of the Secretary of State and of the county clerk of each county to establish and maintain an indexed "Roster of Public Agencies," to be so designated, which shall contain all information filed as required in subdivisions (a) and (b), which roster is hereby declared to be a public record." verified

The clerk of the court gave a signed letter stating the FEIN number for the Sonoma County Court. They all have them and what does that prove? The State does not have any constitutional requirement to pay taxes to the Federal Government. They are independent Sovereign authorities, aren't they? The IRS states that only business need to have a FEIN number so why would the judiciary office of the State of California be considered a 'business

So, there are 2 types of evidence the courts are not the de jure Republic courts; 1. they are not the constitutionally required, common-law 'court of record' and 2. they are a public agency/private business and not the judiciary of the State and their employees, i.e. judges and chief clerks are not lawfully in their offices, 3. the codes they are using were not lawfully enacted and only apply if we consent to them. Everything that goes on in court is 'let's make deal' contract law.

"Do you understand the charges," you say "Yes" and now you agree to contract or 'stand under' the authority of the court and judge. Every time you sign anything without qualifying your signature to retain the rights you contracted. How often does the DA, Bailiff, and Judge give you, his name?

Never, but they refuse to allow you to not name yourself. Giving the judge your name engages in a contract with the court so do not do it. "I go by the name John, you may address me as John" or "I am the authorized representative of all capital lettered defendant JOHN DOE, and you may address me as "friend."

When they call you "Mr. Doe" respond "By what authority are you addressing me by that name?" It will always be a struggle for power and the judges are masters at word art and deception, master salesmen getting you to give up your position because of

"WHY AM I HERE?" THE VOLUNTARY TORTURE CALLED LIFE

fear, and they will finally resort to threats of "contempt of court" and jail time for being disruptive when in fact they are trespassing on your rights and demeaning you with their actions without any authority to do so- the very definition of criminal behavior.

Look at the file "Initial arrest confrontation" in "case law" on the Court CD to see a lot of penal code and vehicle code that they violate when they arrest you. The first thing I would do would be to file a conditional acceptance of the charges. Then I would go down and get a copy of the 'docket' at the clerk of the court's office ($.50/page) after 15 days have elapsed from the arrest to see if a complaint has been filed.
The arrest: Arraignment Pen §988. The arraignment must be made by the court, or by the clerk or prosecuting attorney under its direction and consists in reading the accusatory pleading to the defendant and delivering to the defendant a true copy thereof, and of the endorsements thereon.

, if any, including the list of witnesses, and asking the defendant whether the defendant pleads guilty or not guilty to the accusatory pleading; provided, that where the accusatory pleading is a complaint charging a misdemeanor, a copy of the same need not be delivered to any defendant unless requested by the defendant.

So, unless the complete complaint has been read into the record they did not conform to "reading the accusatory pleading" did they? Did they give you a true copy of the complaint? The complaint is a verified sworn charging instrument. Your 4th amendment rights under the U.S. Constitution require an oath.

upon probable cause sworn to. When you get a complaint usually it is not signed and is blank. "Is this a true copy of the complaint?" "Yes" "O.K. I demand this matter be dismissed for lack of a valid complaint as there is no complaining party." If it is signed, it will usually be signed by the DA, was the DA9 a witness to the alleged violation?

If he was not there, then his sworn complaint is perjury because the complainant swears a "warrant shall issue" and his testimony is 'hearsay' evidence and perjury because he knows he did not witness the violation. "the endorsements thereon" this part is noted in penal code 87210. Always request the verified sworn complaint be given to you at arraignment. Always challenge it as defective.

If it is signed by the Sheriff or Police note that the ALL CAPITAL NAME 'SHERIFFS OFFICE' and then the signature above by a living soul is a fraud as the living soul is signing as the authorized representative for the real signing party> the legal fiction SHERIFFS OFFICE, it would be like the words BANK OF AMERICA are below the signature and By Bob Henry is signed above it.

Bob is signing as an agent for BANK OF AMERICA the named party. So, did a fiction make a complaint that you violated a code? Can they? The Sheriff would have to sign in his capacity not as an agent for the fiction to be legitimate. Next the

Complaint must be file stamped within 15 days of the arrest11. Once you note the misnomer of the wrong name being JOHN DOE instead of John Doe, they must correct it12 although I bet, they refuse. If they do not file the complaint within 15 days demand they dismiss it and do not let them talk you out of it, because they will attempt to contract with you to come back for any reason so they can get it together to file a complaint and they WILL BACK DATE IT to be within the 15 days (guess how I know that). Remember it is all contract, there is no law being applied in their administrative courts, just your agreement to perform.

Always say "I am here under threat and duress only, and I do not consent to contract with this court" You give the court most of the evidence that ends up convicting you, so do not give them any. Quit trying to defend yourself.

"WHY AM I HERE?" THE VOLUNTARY TORTURE CALLED LIFE

"I am a good person, I never break the law, I have a clean record," they do not care they are trying to milk you for money and that is all, it is a business, and they want you to be a good customer and pay. They do not want you to show the others in court your lack of cowering before the judge, your defiance of their authority, your challenges to their jurisdiction, etc.

They will put you over till the end when everyone is gone. Jurisdiction in my opinion is best defined as there is none until you trespass on someone and then it springs into existence. If you were under the jurisdiction all the time because for instance you "live in the City of Pleasantville" then you are a slave because jurisdiction is control and if you are constantly under control, then you are a slave.

Slavery is prohibited so you cannot be under the jurisdiction of the State just because you live somewhere. Jurisdiction is acquired when you trespass. Since a code violation is usually a victimless crime there is no jurisdiction as there is no 'real party of interest'[13] as the alleged Plaintiff. You must complain that the Plaintiff is "not the real party of interest" (the injured party). There rarely is a "corpus delecti"[14].

There is rarely any "standing"[15] to sue in the first place by the alleged Plaintiff [People of California]. So how full of holes is the average case against one of the people? It is all about common law[16] and whether an injury is claimed or not.

Of course, if you challenge the authority of the judge, he may order a Psych evaluation for you so know this usually it is a referral so unless he states I am ordering to see the shrink, you have not been ordered. The second demand he put it in writing, he will be wary not to sign his name to that as he has no medical degree and unless you really are mentally disordered, he can get in trouble. If he does issue a written order, I send him a conditional acceptance that I will abide by his order upon proof of claim that he has jurisdiction, a lawful oath of office, and can make a medical determination by providing his M.D. license.

MENTAL EVALUATION ORDERED only goes if the judge writes a wet-ink order otherwise it is not mandatory referral PEN §1367.1. (a) During the pendency of an action and prior to judgment in a case when the defendant has been charged with a misdemeanor or misdemeanors only if the defendant's behavior or other evidence leads the judge to conclude that there is reason to believe that the defendant is mentally disordered and as a result may be incompetent to stand trial, the judge shall state this conclusion and his or her reasons in the record. [you can sue as he has no authority to make a medical determination].

Settle Court Accounts Step One

If you have ever had an issue with Discharging Debts or have not received a response back from the alleged creditor, this will bring the solution needed for your remedy. This will give procedural and substantive remedies.

I want to talk about account settlement in detail. I will begin with court accounts settlements step one. I shall entitle this step one. This will cover how to manage account settlement in a court or a court case. This process will get you remedy if emulated correctly, I surmise. At least it has worked for Tazadaq every time. I am not suggesting that any of you use this.

This is for education and information purposes only; it is not legal advice. If you need legal advice, seek yourself a competent attorney and please be advised.

Again, this is an account settlement, and I'll label this record number one. If going to court, you accept for value (A4V), the indictment of criminal, and include with that a money order. I have created money orders in my books The Plug and Liberate the Oppressed. An indictment would not have an amount but a complaint for money would have an amount. As for a complaint for money, we would put the total amount of the complaint. A4V each page front and back. Settle the account to ZERO. The money order has the registered mail tracking number the date, the instrument number, pay to the order of.

I write out the amount in words, then the number are written out in digits. The memo line has the account number that this is being attributed to. If this were a court case, I would put the case number on the memo line. By authorized representee and at the bottom is the STRAWMAN OR PUBLIC TRUST NAME AND ADDRESS. Below is another account number which is the SSN without dashes. The processor is the IRS Technical Support Division, which is where I am sending this first presentation. This looks like having a second witness to the TENDER for Setoff. I send this to Ogden Utah.

If I do not know the amount, I leave the amount black and use the A4v language to ZERO out the account. Because I am 'sending it to IRS technical support I also send a 1040V with all the taxpayer's information with nothing in the amount. Even if I had a sum certain I would not put an amount on the 1040V in case there are some extra fees, or penalties and put the special endorsement the on back of the 1040V. I would also endorse the money order.

This is because we do not have a coupon. If we have a complaint, there is no coupon see I use the money order instead of the coupon. The money order replaces what I usually dot with the coupon. There would be a Notice to Setoff an Account and a Certificate of Service. The certificate of service would have a signature and it would be an original. 10 TEN days later I got my certificate of non-response. All these documents together I label record number one. Even though the last document comes 10 TEN days after the other documents.

Step number Two:
Step number Two: I refer to this as record number TWO. I do step

ONE then step TWO is presented through the attorney for the plaintiff. That is who I am contracting with. The Notice For TENDER for Setoff is giving notice that TENDER was given for Setoff for the obligation of debt.

Next is the Request For Statement of Account. I also include in Record number TWO the complete record of number ONE. Record TWO also has a Certificate of Service but it does not need a signature, but my record would have a signature for the Certificate of Service. Then TEN days later a Certificate of Non-Response for record TWO.

Who is the party that is named in the presentment? I name the Plaintiff and all attorneys involved. If it were a complaint for money to back, I would send it to the CFO of the bank in his private capacity. Their nonresponse is an agreement. Be certain to get a notary experienced in commercial presentments. Do not just get a cheap notary. Interview the notary. Ask what are you going to do with the records I bring to you.

Step THREE:

This is record THREE. Notice of Fault, Opportunity to Cure. This comes TEN days after the first presentation. That means the presentment is presented TEN days later after step ONE. Along with that would be a Certificate of Service listing everything. TEN days later a Certificate of Nonresponse to my Notice of Fault. This is recording number THREE. It includes what I have done up to this point.

Step number FOUR:

I execute my Notice of Default. Along with my Notice of Default, I include record number THREE which includes everything that I have done up to this point. I refer in my Notice of Default to record number THREE attached herewith. Along with that would be a certificate of service. TEN days after the NOTICE of Default I issue a Certificate of Non-response to my notice of default. This Is an offer

"WHY AM I HERE?" THE VOLUNTARY TORTURE CALLED LIFE

to my Notice of Default. I sent a certificate and non-response TEN days later.

All of this together is record FOUR.
Steps THREE and FOUR go to the attorney because they are in default. They go back to the attorney who is faulty; So, it is going back to the attorney. Everything after step one goes to the attorney we are done with the IRS after step ONE. We are almost there we are almost there we are getting that OK, My request regarding a statement of account is now the request regarding a statement of account.

When they do not respond to this request regarding a statement of account, we have established that by their agreement and the IRS is also in agreement we have a 0 balance accounts been settled.

Step number FIVE
I put my present with evidence under seal into the judge's chambers. Along with this is a letter rogatory. I include record number 4 FOUR, and that is everything. Record FOUR is everything. From step one through step 4 with the origin and of course, I am going to make the Cover page that the judge is reading include the entire record.

Notice I'm keeping the originals So that in case the judge Forgot a record of everything of originals or makes sure any Use a copy stamp or something like that on the instrument So now that we've done this and our presentment of evidence notice is also going to give the judge direction or a call to action regarding record number 4 which is everything that's happened because the accounts been settled this matters is settled on the private side.

This should be dismissed with prejudice Is it has been settled on the private side. Now do I have to show up to court? Make sure if you choose not to go to court you watch the docket to see what happens if it seems as if your process did not work and you get a summary.

When people do A4V on credit cards they get shut down. Did get they get any money? No, the debt got set off. Because that money that usually comes in on your monthly payments goes to investors. Why keep this trust open if there is no money going to investors?

IRS sends you notice of Lien or notice of Levy you do not respond. Do you go tacitly? They only would not apparent that because did not want the books balanced. They want what they call money, they want debt instruments Federal Reserve Notes. if the IRS came in and said you must set off his account and you are like well, I want a federal reserve note. If you Set off the account, are you happy?

Not necessarily the IRS may not be happy with that because is that not a tax credit? That is a debt cancelation, so the IRS gets something out of it. They would be happier with Federal Reserve notes, but the fact is they got valuable consideration the same Ultimately as Federal Reserve notes.

I think what we are seeing here is you do not owe it if you are from the Republic. Let us try to get up and operate from a Republic as much as possible if we want to have a significant presence in the democracy, which is fine.

What we are learning to do right now particularly until people understand how to get into the Republic in terms of operation to get rid of some problems, but it is too intensive in terms of labor and cost to go out and buy your groceries this way. If you took a card from the DTC swiped it, and walked out they would let you go. This is because our brain is stuck between 2 worlds. This stuff is just learning about the 2nd world and we are neither ready willing nor able probably to do the full transition.

"WHY AM I HERE?" THE VOLUNTARY TORTURE CALLED LIFE

Go back to the two 13 articles in the amendment, and answer this question. Some other party is going to be interloping in the process. What you are doing is you use that party as your second witness. I am at step THREE the notice of Fault. There is a fault they are finally responding to step number 2. I get it from some guy at the bank saying oh this is meaningless. Am I going to stop my process? No, this keeps going. The timeline on these keeps going. However, I am going to address him I am going to continue. I am going to include an Affidavit and record THREE.

They should not respond this is a response we defined response do not want to dishonor that guy do not insult him do not do anything we are happy, kind, and helpful. The only problem is that that 3rd party guy that came in as an interloper is in the public. i you start discussing this case with him you just move the case from private to public. You cannot deal with these guys but respond courteously. I conditionally accept your offer upon proof of claim that my private process over here sent to the CFO will not make anything that you are talking about moot. but when I am done, we will have it settled.

Thank you very much and then you send a copy of that conditional acceptance to the CFO or whoever you are dealing with so that he knows that it is defined that it is not worthy of consideration or discussion because it has already been resolved or no longer needs to be resolved.

Here is a metaphor. I get you are in a battle and the target is the aircraft carrier and you are dealing with commercial instruments. You are flying over with your plane to deliver the A4V to me with all these records in process. You are organic do you not think they are going to send up some fighters to intercept those airplanes that come up to intercept you?

You are never going to close the deal with the CFO Aircraft Carrier. This process is for a court account. This means that there is a court case. The details that are lined out on here, you can use in your other processes that are not core-based except step 5 you are not going to be presenting any evidence to a judge. This can be used on your private side court case because you are the court. The court is the residence of a sovereign. Despite wherever you are at. So, you are in a kind of an argument with some kind of big company or some private company you are going to use some of these processes in it there is just not going to be a court to send it to that is all.

A courtroom is a bank. That means this process will work with any account that is a bank. Inst' a prison a bank? I contend that it is. This can be used to settle an account to get a prisoner out of a bank because the body of the body of the prisoner is currency. He is deposited in a bank. There is another loan out based on him as security for that loan. basically, the money order, the 1040V the Notice to Set off all this process could be going to settle his debts in society, then the process would go back to the head banker, the head of the court who would be the warden after this process is complete.

What would be the item that you are doing the A4v on? That would be the document held by the warden on which he has deposited the currency and holds it in reserve for the lien.
See what you must understand is when you send in an A4V nobody gets any funds. The IRS goes in and sets off the account.

The goal between the private and the public which is going to look transparent to everyone is this process. It is an administrative process; it must be done on a transaction-by-transaction base. What we are learning to do right now particularly until people understand how to get into the Republic in terms of operation. This gets rid of some problems, but it is too intensive in terms of labor and cost to go out and buy your groceries this way.

I helped a friend in probate who showed up at court with all the

"WHY AM I HERE?" THE VOLUNTARY TORTURE CALLED LIFE

winnings. This guy was an heir to an eight-million-dollar estate. THREE weeks before the end of his mother's demise she altered the will. The trustees got her to alter the will including even a 100 grand to the dog which one of the trustees was taking care of. He was terribly upset and the long and the short is as if he wanted to stop it. He did not want to go to court to sell the family home. He needed to have a bond in the court for a 130000 which Tazadaq gave an example of how Tazadaq has done a bond.

Tazadaq guided him to file the case. We were number 3 on the docket sheet. At the end of the court hearing everybody gets in and out of there. My client is still sitting there, and the judge says well that is the end of the business for today and I stand up and say excuse me, was not the so and so trust matter to be heard today? Now my client is rattled because the attorneys say I got plenty of money from the estate they are always there they are not here what is going on? I told my client to just relax. Judge says, "Well I guess that wraps up business ".

I said excuse me judge blah blah blah blah blah She said oh yes that matter has been put off for 60 days legal department had some questions. Would you like me to mention the record? I said oh no judge thank you so much for your professionalism your courtesy and most of all your kindness and she smiled genuinely nicely.

I said you're welcome. We are walking out the client says what the F just happened. I say well we got our abatement like we requested. It is time to go ahead and go back to the trustees and get this will be squared away. The judge says legal departments have a question I am going to put it off 60 days. The judge says do you want to discuss it now? I said oh no, no, not. And we leave now he tried to get this judge dismissed because she was crazy and all of that. She had to get another judge ruling so this judge did not like my client at all.
So, he could even understand what had just happened.

So, we got 60 days, and the client gets the thing he says you know something Tazadaq, I did not need you or your bond. It is obvious that the legal department how to question anyway. He said we did not really need you. I said you think so. He said.

So, I asked his wife., well what do you think? She goes yes, we did. She is a little more sensible than her self-serving parsimonious individual husband. He said I got 60 days. I said Hey do it."
He has things to do so he does not do anything on the process at the end of 30 days, the opposing attorneys suddenly say that well there is something wrong with this process. The bond etcetera. And he comes back, and he what is wrong with it? I thought you did it for me. I said "What do you care, you said you did not need me. I said I am warning you that you have 30 days, you have done nothing.

I said you have done nothing in 30 days you'd better get to it, times running out. They came out 2 weeks later and said a little something we fixed it easily no more.
comment. At 30 days the court came back with an offer from the plaintiff and said the bond's no good, this is no good that is not good. Warning number one in screaming flashing lights. I said you better get on it. He says like I got things to do, besides, I will just ask for another 60 days.

Besides the judge has not given us the 60 likes she said anyway so she is outlined. I said nasty judge, didn't she? This guy is a debtor and loves to argue. I said the judge was nice to you despite your past conduct. You were given 60 days and she knows and warning you cannot be doing an administrative process to remove these trustees. You are running out of time to get this done in the time that you requested.

On day 40 the court ordered revocation of. bond and sale of the home. He goes what is going on? I said what are y. remember you

"WHY AM I HERE?" THE VOLUNTARY TORTURE CALLED LIFE

were just going to ask for another 60. I said don't you.? They warn you and in 20 days left you think you could do an administrative process when at day 40 he hadn't even begun Can he do a complete process? He dishonored what? requested.

If you need To talk in court here is how Kahan Tazadaq Speaks

Some have asked Kahan Tazadaq, what do you say in court when the issue of your discharge comes up?

Some principles: First the more try to answer questions the more questions they will produce, and the dialogue will degenerate into speculations by you and them that neither has any authority to speak definitively about what is supposed to happen from it, and since you cannot give all the answers with such authority you will be considered as losing the argument. He that is asking is -As- King Remember to say as little as possible about what you tendered and dwell on what they did with it. --What did you send? -- What was it? A check? —

We tendered satisfaction of the debt in certified funds fully tenderable, negotiable, and exchangeable in commerce in compliance with federal law and until the bank has negotiated it for settlement, I do not think there is any more anybody can say on the subject to the contrary that will decide anything.

The legal question here is your honor, Is the tender or payment we have made legally sufficient to discharge the debt as a matter of prevailing federal law on the subject? We have proof tender of payment from us was received. by the claimant in the amount of [$52,550].

We have received no notice of dishonor showing from any authority any causes for it to be dishonored, or for it not to have been recovered on, or anything to be legally insufficient about it.

We have sought to know where it is, what they have done with it, and whether settlement has been gained as it has never been returned, To date They have provided no evidence to support their

right to refuse it, or that it has not been recovered. Their notice of default after payment was initially credited is only evidence one end of their business is choosing to ignore the fact this debt has been paid off and is not notice of dishonor showing payment on it has been turned down from any authority for it to be dishonored, or for it not to have been recovered on, or anything to be legally insufficient about it.
-[[How did you tell them to settle it?]]
r other questions on the instrument—
[[Like many other federal obligations of your honor, they could just deposit it in the bank and let the fed settle it. They could negotiate it in the Federal Reserve Bank Open Market Window, or the pass-through account at the treasury window. I have never known them all. Far be it from me to tell a bank how to negotiate an instrument for settlement.
With respect to the Court your honor, if it had all the information, it wanted today from both of us [which we do not have] and all the time it needed to research the law and documentation until it was finished and concluded, which would not make the payment good and recoverable, any more than the Court's determination would make it not recoverable.

The only authority that will decide that is the United States government on whom the obligation is made.
There is ample protection in federal law for the banking industry and general commerce against specious, fraudulent, and fictitious forms of payment to keep anyone from being had.
All they had to do was negotiate it for recovery in any of the ways shown and recovery and settlement would resolve itself one way or the other without the involvement of the Court.

The only relevant question is, have they tried to do this? [exercising even a minimal degree of commercial responsibility under law to gain settlement?

Or what have they done with it? Where is it? And can they produce

"WHY AM I HERE?" THE VOLUNTARY TORTURE CALLED LIFE

it to the Court to show they have not recovered on it and that the debt has not been paid? If they stop, you interrupt to rant and rave over what you cut back to the chase:

Your honor, if the plaintiff cannot produce the tender in payment of this debt unmarked and unnegotiated showing it has not been converted or recovered on, or return it with markings of dishonor, or produce any authority supporting their right to refuse it.

Then the Court does not know the debt has not been paid, And If the Court knowingly grants jurisdiction to proceed without such proof it may be violating federally protected rights, or those under a higher jurisdiction of the sovereign electors, waiving its judicial immunity and becoming co-liable with the Claimant for any of their fraud or wrongdoing finally shown, and in the interests of the court and the protection of Debtor's rights it must deny this claim.

Simply to reject a lawful means of discharge of debt because it is foreign or unfamiliar to the creditor or his bank, or even to the Court, without an authoritative foundation for them to do so, is not evidence of dishonor to give the debtor acceptable in law.
The court cannot deny him the credit that may be due for a valid tender of payment with the creditor or his bank offering little more than saying it is not.

Unless the Court is going to presume to know what is or is not a legal obligation the United States has bound itself or presume to know all the obligations the United States government may have in law or equity and how it may have made provision to meet those obligations then the Court will not have the knowledge to decide the issue. And the plaintiff has provided none. This case must be dismissed until the plaintiff can produce the instrument showing it has not been recovered and showing they have attempted negotiation of it for settlement and it has been rejected and we so move.

"WHY AM I HERE?" THE VOLUNTARY TORTURE CALLED LIFE

How Tazadaq helped Friends to Expunge their Criminal Records

Let me first begin by stating that if you injured another party and it was not self-defense, get out of this seminar now. This is not about teaching you how to beat the system. Punishments under common law are worse then statutory law. If you broke the law on purpose this is not for you, and you deserve your punishment in the laws of Yahawah. However, if you are a victim of a colorable system where bureaucrats sit on seats in high places and prey on you then you are family and are in the right place.

Expungement or record sealing is the process of requesting that the courts and/or law enforcement agencies modify, seal, or destroy criminal records. The definition, benefits, and requirements of expungement or record sealing vary by state. In many instances when a record is expunged or sealed, it cannot be viewed by the public and the applicant does not have to disclose any past criminal activity. Most states offer this relief because it is good public policy to allow deserving people to fully contribute to society.

Do you Know What Expungement Does?
Most criminal conviction records are available to anyone who wants to search for them. Expunging your record will alter your record, removing or diminishing many offenses.
– The details about how the state manages your criminal record after expungement will depend on your state. Regardless of where you live though, expungement allows you to legally answer that you do not have a criminal record. This is important for employment or rental applications.
– In some states like Michigan, the court removes records of the crime from public inspection.
In other states like California, you cannot erase a criminal record from public view. However the disposition of the case will show that the court dismissed the case.

"WHY AM I HERE?" THE VOLUNTARY TORTURE CALLED LIFE

— An expunged conviction will often remain on your criminal record for certain purposes. This includes sex offender registration and immigration.

Consider Sealing your Record "Expunging" a criminal record is different from "sealing" it. When a court "seals" a criminal record, it removes documents that are ordinarily available for public inspection. Because of expungement, the proceedings related to the case will be treated as though they never occurred. The state may ultimately destroy records. A sealed record still exists but will not be viewable through ordinary means.

Both record sealing and expungement allow you to declare that you do not have a conviction.
— The first step in getting a record sealed is to petition the law enforcement agency that arrested you, or the court. In California, for example, you must fill out a form and return it to the applicable law enforcement agency. If the law enforcement agency does not provide relief, you must petition the court.

— In other states like Massachusetts, it is possible to seal your criminal record by mail. Or you can petition the court directly.
— The process of sealing a criminal record is different depending on the state. In most cases, a judge will make the decision at a hearing. To give yourself the best possible chance of getting the outcome you want, it is advisable to collaborate with an attorney who will follow your lead.

Consider Seeking a Pardon
Individuals who have been convicted of a crime may apply for a pardon. If granted, a pardon may restore certain rights such as the right to serve on a jury as well as the right to bear arms. In some states like California, a pardon will relieve you of your duty to register as a sex offender.

— Generally, applicants for pardons must complete probation or parole. A certain period must then pass without further criminal activity.

A pardon does not necessarily seal or expunge a criminal record. It does not allow a pardoned person to answer employment applications that s/he has no record of a criminal conviction. A pardon is a gesture of givenness that restores certain rights. Pardons are becoming increasingly rare.
— In some states like California, individuals with criminal records may apply for a direct pardon. You can get applications for direct pardons from their state governor's office. In other states, like Arkansas, applications are available online.
Consider a Certificate of Innocence
A certificate of actual innocence goes further than a regular expungement. It proves that you were innocent and that the conviction or arrest never should have happened in the first place. The requirements for obtaining a certificate of innocence will vary depending on your state.

If you can meet your state's requirements, you can ask for this certificate. In some states, if you have already had your record expunged, you may not be eligible for a finding of factual innocence.
— In states like California, you are eligible if you were arrested but the prosecutor never filed criminal charges. You might also be eligible if the court dismissed your case, or if a jury acquitted you.

In some states, to get a petition of factual innocence you must petition the law enforcement agency that arrested you. Usually, this must occur within a specified period after the arrest. In California, for example, you must do so within two years after the arrest. If the law enforcement agency denies your request, you can then petition the court to grant your request.

— In most cases, a judge will make the decision at a hearing. It is advisable to collaborate with an attorney. You may consider

contacting your public defender's office. Depending on your specific case, some public defenders' offices may be able to assist you.
Get a Certificate of Rehabilitation.

In some states, you can get a Certificate of Rehabilitation to clear up your criminal record. This is a court order declaring that you have rehabilitated.

A certificate of rehabilitation restores certain rights forfeited because of a criminal conviction. It can result in improved access to state occupational licensing programs. It may also relieve certain sex offenders from their duty to register.
— In some states like California, a Certificate of Rehabilitation is an automatic application for a Governor's Pardon.

In many states, to get a Certificate of Rehabilitation you must file a petition with the court. For example, in California, you must submit letters of character and other documents as part of the petition.
Understand Who's Eligible for Expungement.

Every state has different requirements about who is eligible for expungement. Expungement exists to clear the records of people who probably will not receive further convictions. The following circumstances generally make someone eligible for expungement:
— Being a first-time offender
— Having an arrest or misdemeanor conviction, as opposed to a felony conviction
— Being a juvenile at the time of conviction
— Having already served out the sentence
— Going a year without further offenses after conviction
— Having a drug offense

GETTING A RECORD EXPUNGED
Find out whether you are eligible for an expungement.
Visit your state's courthouse or court website to find out whether

you are eligible. It is a clever idea to speak with s someone in person to find out how to proceed.

In some instances, defense attorneys will negotiate agreements with prosecutors regarding future expungement. Specifically, the prosecutor agrees not to oppose expungement if the defendant meets all requirements. Be sure to check with your attorney to find out if such a discussion took place.

File a petition for expungement.

Once you have determined that you are eligible, file a petition with the courthouse. You will have to pay a fee, and you will have to wait for the court to process your paperwork. In some states, you will receive a hearing date on which you will meet with a judge to have your record expunged.

In some states like Florida, you will need to get a certificate of eligibility form. You will also need a copy of the disposition of the case and a set of fingerprints. A certification of eligibility is different from an expungement. It is just the paperwork you must have in place to file a petition for expungement. In states like California, you must complete and file a Petition for Dismissal form. You must also submit an Order for Dismissal form and a Declaration.

Make sure you file the petition correctly according to the requirements in your state. Small mistakes in the petition may create delays in the proceedings since you will have to start over.

In some states, you must file a petition in the county where the court charged you with a crime.

This book is about what the mentality of a warrior looks like. There are too many docile people who are trusting in political saviors that lie more than the Devil. Sean Ellis's case if living proof that racism is still being given life support. This is not just the case for Boston, but we saw the same thing with George Floyd. Let us take for instance the corrupt police officers in Boston who only received three years for a crime that a so-called Black man would

"WHY AM I HERE?" THE VOLUNTARY TORTURE CALLED LIFE

have easily received fifteen or even twenty-five to life. Wrongful conviction is commonplace within so-called Black communities, and it is atrocious to know that those who are responsible for it are only tapped on the write if even that.

We as people of all races must coalesce and defeat the corruption. The colorable law system is a virus that continues to cripple and even end the lives of too many people. If you remain silent and motionless it will continue to fester. You have been rendered to a T.I.N. Man which is a Tax Identification Number. You are merely just a number. Some imagine that this only exists in jail, but you are under a different sort of confinement. Yours is of the worst kind, your mind has been imprisoned. You are too afraid to think against the norm. Conformity is why so many of you suffer. It is only when one dares to stand up and be undaunted enough to lead as a warrior will the army follow him into battle.

You have heard me make some harsh statements against women in this book, but it is because I love women, and I want women to return to being real women. Women that men of status and masculine men love.

If you remain docile just keep in mind that it is not real until it is real. Imagine you are home asleep, and police or detectives kick in your door and pin a crime on you that you did not commit. It happened to Sean Ellis, and it can happen to you. Educate yourself and learn the law. Not enough people are speaking out against wrongful convictions. They occur daily. We must do better in combating this monster that continues to eat this country alive. If you are A Sean Ellis waiting in prison or jail for your savior to arrive, educate yourself and never give up.

This book "Inviolable Man: The Condition of Our Lives Are Determined By Our Inner State" will be eye-opening and enlightening to you. Before you embark on these pages, take a minute to be thankful to Yahuah for moving you to get this in your hands. This book comes from deep down and is meant to break through any cognitive dissonance that may have been formerly blocking your path too. I pray that the spirit of Yahuah leads and guides you while you open your heart & mind to the information at hand. Yahusha in you is your hope of glory and do not take it lightly that you have been lead to this book and to Tazadaq, a messenger of Yahuah. He is going to take you through his journey, and I know that it will touch you most deeply.

 The spirit will lead you and guide you in all things and we can only grow from this point. We only have the now. The here and now. Take your time and let it marinate. When you feel like you are not worth it, read this book. When you feel like you are not good enough, read this book. When you feel like you give and you give and no one sees it, read this book. When you are at a crossroads, read this book. When you are up and when you are down, read this book and know that you can conquer all things regardless of what man says through God. Peace to you brothers and sisters.

" I need you to divorce that notion that you cannot accomplish your dreams. If you change the thoughts that you think within your mind you can change the world around, you. The world is mind! There
is a 9th dimension that is unknown to the average man, it consists of sight, and sounds, and is only limited by your mind, "The world is mind". You have not just picked up another book that you should read, throw it aside.

You do not realize it yet, but you just embarked on a journey into the 9th dimension. This book will take you into another realm within time, it is an exodus from this Matrix into a spiritual realm. You purchased this book because you are not satisfied with some things in your life, they are insufficient, and you are not content with
your current circumstances. Many suggest, "Circumstance made

"WHY AM I HERE?" THE VOLUNTARY TORTURE CALLED LIFE

me who I am"! I contend that circumstance reveals the man/womb-man. The mere fact that you purchased this book suggests that you intend to do something to improve your life, do not allow anyone, not even yourself to stop you from this goal. If you have been
grinding and are not yet where you want to be, hustle harder and wiser. The book is about Creditor moves!

This didactic, life-altering book comes complete with everything that you need to change your life. This book was composed of Lessons, motivational positive affirmations, empowering prayers, and inspirational messages to awaken the warrior within you.

We are all given the same opportunity, both the righteous and the unrighteous. We are all giving the same twenty-four hours within a day, somehow you have not managed yours correctly. You have been wasting time, which is a depreciating asset. You do not have forever to be great, successful, or change, time is, and shall run out. You better get after it now. However, we will be judged based on our decisions. Too many folks falsely delude themselves with deceptive intelligence to rationalize their wrongdoing. They tell themselves Satan is trying to do a thing to them. But the truth is James 4:7 Submit yourselves therefore to God. Resist the devil, and he will flee from you. Submit yourselves to God. Resist the devil and he will flee from you.

The devil cannot occupy a body where the Lord and Savior reside. The devil comes in and dwells where there is an absence of Christ. Stop blaming the devil for your own Satan of self. All that you are is because of what you think.

Each one of us has the power to develop and construct our own righteous character and to create our own happiness. The circumstances, the conditions, and the situations of our lives are akin to our inner state of mind. This book is not written to make me appear heroic or some man who was born with special talents and highly gifted. This book is just the opposite. This book is intended to be didactic, not to motivate you, but to encourage you to become driven. Motivation is not enough. One must be driven. One can be motivated, but if you undergo difficult tasks in extreme weather the motivation will depart you. You therefore must be driven.

Therefore, this book is intended to be a manual of inspiration for those who are at the bottom, which feels as if there is no light at the end of the tunnel. Allow my life to reflect upon your life as a beacon light of hope, a torchlight to success, an example of strength. You are qualified to be a teacher because of what you are experiencing. This enables you to have the knowledge and wisdom to teach others. Embrace the pain and suffering that you are experiencing and use it to grow and develop moral character within.

I have been where you are, and now I am teaching you from the hard, screwed-up life that I lived. Despite where you may be right now, be it your lowest point in life, you can soar to great heights. If you believe and perceive it to be true. I have been at the bottom, I have been homeless, and I have been at the point where I felt like a hopeless loser. I now realize that I was there because I blamed circumstances and others for conditions it all was because of a decision that came from my mind

This book is written for those who have undergone circumstances like mine; to help you alter your perceived notions that you cannot be great. Where you are, I was. I will even go off a limb and say I was even at a lower stage. Close your eyes for a few seconds after you read the next sentence.

 Let us get a proper understanding of the title The Inviolable Man. I named this as such because I have been through hell, and I kicked the Devil's ass. As a result, my spirit has become inviolable prohibiting violation; secure from destruction, violence,

"WHY AM I HERE?" THE VOLUNTARY TORTURE CALLED LIFE

infringement, or desecration: my body is an inviolable sanctuary; my word is an inviolable promise. If I say I will do something, you can believe I will do it or die. My words are truly bonded!

After my mother and father broke it off for a second time my mother drank a lot, and I surmise that is because things became extremely difficult.
I was the outcast or the odd one out of the family. I would often hear my mother, sister, and brother talking about how weird I was. My mother never spent a lot of time with us regarding schoolwork, she became too busy working. She always emphasized going to school to get your education. Because of the lack of support, initially, I did not do very well in school in the early grades. And I surmise that it was because of the mental and verbal abuse that I sustained at home and from the teachers who were very racist white females. As a result, at school, I would not talk very much. I thought I was very ugly because I was always insulted and put down by peers and even my family members. I developed extremely low self-esteem and became a loner. Because of this, I turned to Yahuah (God) at an exceedingly early age. Despite this, while Father was around, we lived very well financially.

He was a strong man; he knew all the semantics that or my brother would try to pull on our mother that just did not collaborate with him. He loved my sister and gave her whatever she wanted despite him only being her stepfather.

I still could not comprehend why my mother left Dad for some guy named Thomas. Thomas was the devil incarnate. If Satan ever walked the earth in the form of a man, it was Thomas. My father was everything I promised myself I would never be to women, A Beta Simp male. He was the sort of man who would allow my mom to talk down to him and he would just remain silent, which requires strength yet resulted in her seeing him as weak.

My mother was raised with a slave mentality. What I mean by that

"WHY AM I HERE?" THE VOLUNTARY TORTURE CALLED LIFE

is that she was taught to hate being a person of color. She would therefore be more attractive to so-called light-skinned men. I remember this guy, Thomas, after we moved to this urban environment. He became extremely abusive to my mom verbally and physically, this never occurred with Dad. This guy would beat my mom to a pulp.

I remembered fear and anger equally flowing through my veins so thick that I could feel a lumping in my throat as if it suffocated me and I could not get oxygen. Lesson learned at age four, if you do not control your fears and anger your fears and anger will control you.

This guy would beat my mom so badly; her face would be so bloodied it brought shivers over my skin. My heart raced like a Nas car and whirled as if it was a tornado slamming my heart around within

my chest. I wondered why Yahusha's did not kill that son of a bitch ass negro, Thomas. I prayed to The Most High to make me grow bigger and taller faster so I could kill Philip for what he did to my mother. I knew that it was wrong. My mom would eventually leave him when he was at work. He called, apologized, and promised not.

to ever do it again. Time after time this asshole would repeat these savage acts and then, talk her into returning, and she did it, as a dog to its vomit. This became a routine, and the beatings became increasingly brutal. Perhaps she accepted the abuse from this black devil because he was paying the bills and she did not want her and her children homeless on the street as he so often threatened.

In my mind, If the police would kill Thomas, then I was going to do it. I got exhausted and sick of crying.

Alas, After she realized that if she did not get this man out of her life, he would kill her. Her mother finally convinced her to go into hibernation with this bear named Thomas. It was as if we left the chambers of hell, and the devil was roaming the earth in search of

"WHY AM I HERE?" THE VOLUNTARY TORTURE CALLED LIFE

us. I worried for a while that our mother would become weak and return to the Thomas Satan. It was not his last name but a title he earned from me based on his behavior.

But she never went back. However, racism, single parenthood, and three children with a job at a hotel equals hunger, no heat, and sorrow for my mother and her children. My biological father would often try to reach out but, my brother and I were ordered by my mother to stay away from him. Always wondered why she never attempted to get him for child support.

I could not see then but once I became an adult, I learned why she never went after him for child support. My father explained to me what was hidden. I encourage every man or young man that have been told your fathers are deadbeat, to get his version of the story. You may regret your decision to hate your father. My father stayed in my life despite not being with my mother, then while I was in the Military, I got the news from the Military Police that he had died unexpectedly.

I will say this to all men out there who may not have had their biological fathers in their lives; do not always believe what your mother tells you about why your father may not have been in your life. Find out the truth for yourselves. So now there is a period where there is no man in the house. This is when I realized how hard life could be without a father, but I refused to use this as an excuse to justify failure. I always had my father God Almighty with me. Praise be Yahawah wa Yahawashi we were surrounded by strong masculine figures such as James Vini, Herman Jones, Randolph Sharp, my cousin, and all the other men who were mentors for me and my brother. These were the dog days when we had to eat rice and beans for weeks, and once that was depleted, we ate mayo sandwiches, until alas there was nothing to eat, there would be no heat in the house, all the toys and clothing that we once had was now distant memories of the past. We had nothing, which resulted in my mother turning to drinking, which amplified the problems. When my mom did get money, she would go to the Goodwill store and get secondhand clothing that my brother and I would share and spend what was left on beer.

She began to pursue a drinking problem to mask the pain. I would go to school in outdated and oversized clothing that the other students would laugh at and make fun of. At this point I hated life. I hated going to school because we would be teased. I slid down in my seat to make myself smaller and harder to see.

Couple that with, when I would go to the store I had to pass through a so-called white neighborhood, where they would yell "Get out of this neighborhood, you black fuckin nigger!"

I remember once my cousin Andrew visited us. We collected enough bottles and cashed them in to get cookies. We had to pass through the white neighborhood to get to the spot to cash them. That day three white men chased us for about a mile with a rope and knife for being black and passing though their block. I told my cousin.
to run like your life depends on it because they are going to kill us. We are only about ten years old currently. I was amazingly fast and so was my cousin. They ran hard after us screaming "nigger we gonna kill for black nigger assess!" To this day I wondered what they would have done if they ever caught us. This was a savage act by three adult white men. My mind clutched these events as my heart raced faster than my legs to safety. Once we crossed the railroad tracks, they would stop the chase because that was our hood., they would not.
come there because there were boys in the hood ready to set it off and fly their heads.

I am about ten years old, but I outran these cowards who were constantly chasing a child. As a result, later in life, it was easy for me to believe that the so-called white race was a race of devils, after what had happened to me and our people in true history.

"WHY AM I HERE?" THE VOLUNTARY TORTURE CALLED LIFE

While I no longer believe that about all so-called whites, there is a tremendous injury done to the white psyche that many are incapable of overcoming and therefore reeks of hate for other races, which is woefully sad. These are learned behaviors.

Nevertheless, the mother got on welfare. I hated going home because the welfare check was not enough, and we would.
go hungry and be cold at home in the winter. I therefore literally learned to detest my life like the HIV plague.
As time progressed, I began failing in school. The teacher told me that I was going to fail the third grade because I could not read at the level that I should. She recommended that I go over to special education. This is their way of suggesting; you are a freaking failure and that we are preparing you for prison. An extremely high percentage of those who attend special education end up in jail are prison, along with young black Israelite/ Moorish) boys who are not reading at the level that they should by 4th grade.

I could not ask my mom for assistance because she was working most of the time. She decided to get off welfare because it just was not enough. Because the system was designed to screw so-called Black people because if you had welfare a man could not be living in the home at such time. This system was designed to destroy the family, though the so-called white psyche would deny it because of white fragility. I failed the third grade, which resulted in those that I had assumed were my friends teasing me even more than strangers.

I was humiliated, so I started playing the pretend roles of being someone I was not just to fit in. I would attempt to talk back to the teacher to get the class to laugh to distract attention away from my problems. You see, being the cool guy in class I could mask the real me. This is the only way that I felt others would accept me,
by attempting to impress them instead of doing things that I loved. I would later hate myself for being such a fake.

"WHY AM I HERE?" THE VOLUNTARY TORTURE CALLED LIFE

Rule number two always be who you are. Never do things for anyone other than yourself because you will fail.

Your willpower will not be great enough. When you fail to live up to the expectations of others you will be put down and disappointed. Always do it for you first only then can you help others.

Getting back to Mom. My mom would tell me you better not fail, or I will beat your ass. Roger that! Au Contraire, I failed anyway. I was a dumb, shy, scared, ten-year-old. I just could not prevent it, I needed help. I
began to lock myself away in the room and imagine that I would one day be great in life. Each time that I
would construct these dreams in my mind the Edomite schoolteacher, the niggers on the corner, or someone.
close to me would destroy my dreams, rip them apart like a paper house in a hurricane. So now I am going to.
school and am barely making it. I was eventually placed in a special education class. Statistically, people that are placed in special Ed and never get out, but I did because I committed with Yahawah (God) and with myself that I would not live the life that I saw my mother living, and the people around me in the hood living. But not so fast.

The sixth grade comes in. Up until this time, no one seemed to care about me anymore. I knew my mother cared but she was too damn busy working to try to put food on the table. There was this math teacher by the name of Mr. Gunter. Mr. Gunter invoked fear in the students. Back then he came across to me as being abusive, but hindsight shows me that he did it because he cared about us, so-called Black people. If you did not know that math, he beat your ass! Big facts!

He wanted to ensure that we learn, and boy did we learn. If you did not learn the lesson, you would meet the Board of Education.

"WHY AM I HERE?" THE VOLUNTARY TORTURE CALLED LIFE

And he had a board that was known as the Board of Education. You have one of two choices. You will learn math, or you will feel the board of education come down on your backside. And what I learned from Mr. Gunter is that I was not stupid as everyone was saying, I was not dumb. I began to realize that we become what we think about. The Bible says it like this in the book of Proverbs 23 verse 7 "As a
man thinks in his heart so is he." That is a fact. You are what you think about most.

Your thoughts define who you are. Every single one of you that are reading this book right now, must realize that no one is coming to save you. You must save yourself! Emphasis added. No one is coming to save you, that is what I said to myself. And I realize that as a little boy, I must turn my life around, that I am responsible for the outcome of my life. Not the hood, not my circumstances but me. All that we are is the result of what we think. None of us must live the life we now have or that which we have previously possessed. We all have the power to alter our lives for the better.

I, therefore, beloved, suggest that you read this book with a generous spirit. But do not just read it and then tuck it away on your bookshelf. This book should be reread periodically, as it will continue to inspire you. And once you apply what you have read your life will be greatly enriched. The message that I want you to understand from this chapter is that all of us are precisely what we think. Our inner being becomes the complete sum of our thoughts. Take the butterfly The message that I want you to understand from this chapter is that all of us are precisely what we think.
Our inner being becomes the complete sum of our thoughts. Take the butterfly which springs forth and flies away. It cannot be truly developed unless it undergoes the stage of the caterpillar which is like it is seed stage.
When the caterpillar is born it contains everything that it needs to develop into a butterfly, but most cannot see it. Likewise, we must surround ourselves with those who can see the gifts within us and

extirpate those from our lives who only see the negative in us.

We must also have a positive mental attitude. Our actions soar from the seeds of our thoughts. If our minds think failure so, shall it be? If our minds think success so, shall it be. Like a blacksmith, by our thoughts, we can forge the weapons of thoughts, that are, capable of protecting and improving our lives, or we can forge the swords of thoughts that will destroy our lives, which are self-defeating behaviors. The former is what we must strive to mold our minds into, the latter are the unfortunate thoughts of 97% of the world's population.

We will attract what we are, not that for which we hope. You had better start altering yourself into, the most determined, loving, positive person on earth, that way you will always survive. Knowing this, it suffices to say that people fail from negative thoughts. Only a select few developed the thought process to overthrow cognitive dissonance and soar above normality, into the realm of greatness. Such are the blessed and unstoppable.

I can recall when I was about seven. She allowed us to go trick-or-treating and we
knew to get candy we had to cross the railroad tracks into the white community. My brother, my friends and I got a lot of candy that night. Some of the whites greeted us with smirks without showing their teeth, which is not a true smile. And there was this one house that we went to, a guy gave me an apple, he looked me in the eyes with the grin of the devil on his face. Once we had an abundance of candy we went home. They told me in school if you get apples while trick-or-treating, be sure to cut them open first.

I thought no one would try to hurt a little innocent kid like me, seven years old. Then I asked my mom to cut
the apple open for me, and when she did, there was a razor blade in the middle of the apple. I am seven years old, I am trying to rationalize and understand why a so-called white person would

"WHY AM I HERE?" THE VOLUNTARY TORTURE CALLED LIFE

want to do this to me at age seven when I had done them no harm. My perspective of so-called white people shifted.

You say Tazadaq is an isolated incident. But I had a so-called white friend in elementary school named Teddy Ross. I thought he was my friend but, he turned out to be racist as well. When he invited me over, he told me that my brother could not come because he is too dark. There is an unregistered test that some whites have known as the paper bag effect. If your complexion was as light as a paper bag, then you might be excusable in some situations, but you are still a nigger. As a result of these experiences, and other people I knew experiencing the power of white supremacy, learning about the lynching, black wall street, and being taught throughout school that so-called Black people had no accomplishments besides sports; and that we were nothing, I began to overindulge in reading and research.

I would teach myself to read by reading for hours and hours in the uncomfortable atmosphere of my room. My grades in school began to improve. I eliminated my so-called friends that once made fun of me. Suddenly I became an honor student. I read the autobiography of Malcolm X and became a militant within, but I was not Nation of Islam material. I was merely a skinny, scared boy who had a lot of rage in him. I did not want to get teased in school because my clothes were from the Salvation Army and Goodwill, so as a teenager I began to steal clothing from department stores just to fit in. And I hated myself for it. It was not me. If there was one thing, I learned was good morals at home. But at times I had to steal just to eat food. It is a jungle out there and if you are a sheep the lions will eat you for dinner. I was in survival mode. Driving 160 miles per hour and there is a brick wall three feet ahead but, you cannot tell a teenage boy from the hood that is a dangerous route.

Praise be the Most High that he started to put role models in my path. James Vinney high school football superstar, taught me to work out with weights. They referred to him as the Hulk because of his muscular build. It saddens me that James won a scholarship to the University of Maryland and quit college for the Army because a substance and died young. I am grateful for what he taught me and what Phillip and Mr. Gunter gave me. I promised to one day give back to society.

Next, Herman Jones and my cousin Randolph Sharp got me into martial arts art. They taught me Karate and Kung Fu at age seven. I would train my body like a warrior at an early age. I would do pushups until I fell on my face. Stretch until I can do full splits. My body was foraged into a lethal weapon, I was not to be fucked with. I started to get respect, One so-called white guy attempted to bully me in high school, he was about 6 foot 230 lb all muscle. It was never in me to be a bitch, busy you picked the wrong guy, the wrong day. He ended up with a broken leg from a new martial art move I had learned in class. I kicked the shit out of him, and it felt good. Respect given. People moved now as I walked down the hall at school, and this felt good. They wondered what had happened to the old quite shy kid.

No, the old guy is gone, and the new motherfucker is here to stay, get my way, or get dealt with.
 There was another guy about 6-foot 3 Johnathan Sample, a freaking bully. He took ice cream money from students. He approached my cousin Annette, demanding her money. This was on the school bus. The guy was so much taller than me I had to jump on the seat catch him in a choke and take him down. With more respect, David takes out Goliath again. Yet another white guy trying me in middle school who knew martial arts. He threw a left hook, and I dropped down to my side on the floor, locked my foot behind his ankle, and smashed the heel of my foot on his knee. I heard his leg crack like the sound of an ax on a board. This was my third suspension.

The school board considered expelling me. But how could they it

was self-defense. A few months later some friends are spending time together in the streets. A rich doctor's adult son attempted to beat my friend Randy Hill in a game room one day, We were in high school, but this man was about 28 years old. We were 17. Once I saw he was overpowering Randy, this grown white racist uttered nigger each time he would hit Randy.
I stepped in and said try me you racist pig. He swung, I evaded, and hit him with a right kick to his floating rib which dropped him. From there I stomped him out, and he ended up in the intensive care unit. I never went back to the area again. I felt as if I could not stop hitting this guy as flashbacks of being chased by white men as a young boy entered my mind along with the lynching, rapes, and murders I read about in 100 years of lynching.

This was more than just this fight it was about payment for what was done to our nation. I felt it as a small victory. I was not a troublemaker, but I began to demand respect and it felt awesome. I would join the cross-country team and make it to the state. I went from remedial reading to graduating with a 3.0 GPA. The teachers who told me I was most likely not to succeed were astonished. I defied the odds. I went to college after high school, got a degree in civil engineering, worked it for a while, and was distracted by partying.
and bullshit. My mom and younger brother talked me into joining the army. Most of my high school friends were now selling drugs, getting shot, dead, or using the drugs. I took the ASVAB and was in basic training for 45 days.

The lesson that you should take from this is that our minds are like a field that a farmer goes out and cultivates. If he leaves the field alone, then wild weeds will grow with the crops. One must extirpate the weeds from the crops, or the weeds will grow with the crops destroying the field. So, it is with the human mind. If you do not extirpate the bad seeds of thought; they will direct your character to be bad and your spirit will be full of malice. This is the same as saying that as a man thinks in his heart so is he. You will become what you think about every day. Sounds very practical but this is sound knowledge. You must alleviate all negative thinking.

If you want to be a successful righteous man or woman. This includes any negative people that are in your life. This is my afflatus that the heavenly father has given to me to guide you to success and to be blessed and unstoppable. You will only become proficient by falling and getting back up. What you do from this moment on can determine your fate or destroy your future. The choice is yours. Draw a mental line within your mind and decide which side you are going to be on, the losers or the winners. You must be willing to suffer and overcome pain and adversity. Such is the way of the monk warrior mentality.

What is your passion that God has created you to do? Are you working on a job that you do just for money or
survival? If so, you are not as happy as you should be if you are happy at all. Is your marriage the marriage that?
you prayed for? Or are you with a borderline spouse that you are afraid to leave because you fear being alone?

This is the average person in the world today. They reside in a world called FUCKED on cunt street. And with every slinging, John gets infected with the same disease of average, normal, and conformity.   The enemy does not want you to succeed. The word states in 1st Peter 5:8 "Be sober, be vigilant; because your adversary the devil, as a roaring lion, walketh about, and seeking whom he may devour." Are you doing what the creator Yahawah has created you to do? Are you just suffering from the disease of average?

 Or are you just following the trend and emulating everyone else? Are you acting like everyone else, talking like others, thinking like others, suffering from the sickness of average like others? I refuse to be a clone! If you want to be successful, if you want to be great you must take the limitations off Yah (God) and be limitless.

the disease of average will destroy your dreams of greatness and success.

Right now, you are what the world sees as normal. Normality to me is failure because you are akin to what everyone else is. You cannot expect to leave a legacy if you are just average. Normality is what degenerate people consider as living. I refuse to be average. I have chosen to take the higher road, the more difficult road, the more challenging road. And anyone who is intended to be on that journey with me will take the higher road with me, yes, a much more challenging road but a much more rewarding one.

From today forth you must promise yourself that anyone in your life or anything in your life that is not helping you achieve your goals and your dreams you will kick them out of your life they are a hindrance to you being the great man or woman that the creator created you to be. Stop being average! Everything that I say is rooted in the word. So, the Scriptures for today's lesson are Ephesians 6 and 13 to 17.

How can we make it in a world that is so diluted with sin and wickedness? A world in which our mothers, fathers, sisters, brothers, and cousins turned their backs against us because of us desire to live by the laws, statutes, and commandments of Yahuah? Well, allow me to explain why. Christ says in the book. of John chapter 14 verse 30 "Hereafter I will not talk much with you for the prince of this world cometh and have nothing in me".

The prince of this world is Satan. You and I were created to live by the word of Yahuah and to be Christ-like, but our very own children war against us. The global elite has transformed the earth into a world so corrupt in which our wives or husbands plot against us or commit lustful acts such as adultery, and wickedness such as murder for insurance policies to be with another. This is a world where every extremely abominable act is glorified. Satan grants you a reward for selling your soul and you shy away from righteousness.

A world where homosexuality, lesbianism, pedophilia, incest, and all forms of sexual wickedness are practiced. Yet, there is a way to survive in the Basic Instructions Before Leaving Earth (B.I.B.L.E.) which the Most High gave us, his beloved, and today brother or sister you will learn the ways to protect yourself from the wickedness of this corrupt degenerate world?

In the book of Ephesians chapter 6 verse 11 it reads "Put on the whole armor of God that you may be able to
stand against the wiles of the devil." What is Scripture speaking about? What does the word armor mean?
Armor is all the tools used to wage war or to protect oneself in battle. However, this is allegorical. The battle spoken of in these next verses is a type of spiritual battle that has been weighed against the people of Yahuah by the children of perdition, the children of hell the children of Satan. Too many of you are attempting to fight.

physical in a spiritual fight. Get your mind right King! Get your mind right queen! In Ephesians Chapter 6 verse
12 it reads "for we wrestle not against flesh and blood but against principalities against powers, against the rulers of the darkness of this world, against spiritual wickedness in high places". The Illuminati is real and some take oaths in secrecy to control and deceive the masses. So, we must take on this armor of Yahuah that he has given us to guard ourselves. Our fleshly bodies we must protect with the word of Yahawah (God) as do soldiers, Again "for we wrestle not against flesh and blood but against principalities against powers against the rulers of the darkness of this world against spiritual wickedness in high places."

Here we are not wrestling with the physical powers but against spiritual evil that is trying to take away the Holy Spirit that gives us righteousness, because these spirits out there want us to fall victim to the lust of the flesh and the lust of the world. That is to be

"WHY AM I HERE?" THE VOLUNTARY TORTURE CALLED LIFE

carnally minded which is death. A spirit does not have flesh and bones. The book of Luke 24 and 39 reads, "Behold my hands and my feet that it is I and to me and see for a spirit have not flesh and bones as you see me have."

Satan's angels and Satan's agents war against us spiritually the book of Matthew chapter 25 verse 41 states, "Then shall he say unto them on the left-hand depart from me, depart into everlasting fire prepared for the devil and his angels". Satan and his angels are not after anything in the world because the world belongs to Satan.
already.

Satan's agents and his angels are after those of us who have been taken out of the world if you are in Christ and the spirit of Christ within you, then you are a new creature so the Scriptures read in the book of John chapter 15 verse 19 "if you was of the world the world will love his own but because ye are not of the world but I have chosen you out of the world, therefore, the world hated you". If you are in Christ, you are a new creature and you were not of this world.

Just as he was after Job in the book of Job chapter 1 verse 6, Satan went to God when the sons of men went to God and challenged Job's faith in God. Just as he did this with Job, he does this with us day in and day out. Therefore, it is extremely important to guard ourselves with the armor of God. We must be ready spiritually and do all that we can to withstand the evils of this world, resist the devil and he will flee from you.

Ephesians chapter 6 verse 13 says wherefore take into you the whole armor of God that ye may be able to stand (meaning he will be fighting to get you) in these days of evil if you have not done all that you can, you must stand and show thyself to be a man. Verse 14 says Stand therefore having your loins girt (to girt is to encircle or bring something close to you) about with truth and having on the breastplate of righteousness. What are our loins and how do we keep them in truth? Our l loins are our restricted areas, but we also must girt our minds which are to be scarce and holy which means set apart in truth. God says in first Peter chapter one.

If you affiliate with losers and naysayers, you will render yourself to be a loser and a naysayer. You will emulate their ways, pick up their habits, and clone their attitude about life. If you are around cynical negative people, most of the time you will end up cynical and negative. It is imperative to align yourself with positive people.

The fiercest foe and enemy that you will have to deal with is the Satan of self. If you extract the enemy from within the enemy outside can do you no harm. How you define yourself right now, how you view yourself right now is who you truly are. You are what you think about all day, as a man thinks within his heart so is he. Who are you right now and what must you change to create who you want to be?

What must you leave behind to get where you want to go, whom I shall leave behind to accomplish your goals your dreams? If you want to keep on getting what you are getting simply keep on doing what you are doing, and you are guaranteed to be average, to be a failure, and to suffer from the disease of normality.

80% of your self-talk is negative you must start concentrating on the positive and live now, life is not about tomorrow is about right now it is about today. Tomorrow is a great dream but is not real, yesterday may be a great memory but it is not real. Your only reality is right now.

It is When you can envision the invisible you can accomplish the impossible. So, my question is what you are dreaming that you intend to make possible. You must eliminate self-negativity; you must eliminate all negative thinking and thoughts. If you think something negative you must not speak it, because the very moment that you speak it is speaking it into existence and you will live it out.

Some people are so negative that even when I attempt to give you a positive statement, or positive energy you take everything that I articulate and transform it into something negative. You are so undetermined to be positive and so determined to be negative that it is astonishing. You have thought your way into extreme depression and being negative, yet you are expecting to produce positive results. The outcome of your life is based on your thinking and the choices that you make. If you choose negative thoughts, you will yield negative results.

Self-Assessment Questions:
1. Why did Yahawashi die on the cross?
2. Is there any resentment within my heart that needs to be addressed?
3. Am I in denial or have I rendered true forgiveness?
4. Have I utterly forgiven those people who have hurt me caused me pain done me wrong or am I just in
denial?
5. I am searching deep inside release and let go.
6. What is the mindset of a person who has truly forgiven?
7. Have I honestly forgiven myself for the wrong things that I have done in the past?

Acting: Now please take out a sheet of paper and write down or type the names of any and everyone that has ever hurt you. Also, why has anyone ever betrayed you? Once you have accomplished this pray over that list of names it will not be easy but pray over that list of names. Ask God to bless these people who have hurt you and
betrayed you in every aspect of their lives. Today's daily until you flush all the negative energy away from your mind towards these people completely out of your system.

This is the point where everything in your circumference, within your entire life, is about to change for the better. The highest is about to instill you with the knowledge, wisdom understanding and faith to alter your life. I do not give a damn if you are in a jail or prison cell reading this, it is only the body that is confined.

If you allow it, this book will free your soul and mind. Love and loyalty is what we need, First, to the Most High Yahawah then to each other, Listen I mean true loyalty. Be true and honest with yourself first. Love yourself enough to change yourself, and then things outside of you will change. I am not certain how I will end you because the authorities do not want me to awaken the minds of the masses, but through the holy spirit I am doing it the world will remember my name. it was for this reason that I was birth into the world to lead and free people from mental and physical slavery. Are you with me? I am risking my life attempting to save yours, are you willing to risk yours in defense of mine? It is my goal to unify all people who want to live in love, peace, and happiness, despite their skin color.

Refuse to allow anyone to devise you based on color gender or otherwise. We must coalesce.

"WHY AM I HERE?" THE VOLUNTARY TORTURE CALLED LIFE

#M.A.F.

MAF

MEN AGAINST FEMINISM

"WHY AM I HERE?" THE VOLUNTARY TORTURE CALLED LIFE

"WHY AM I HERE?" THE VOLUNTARY TORTURE CALLED LIFE

10 KNOWING WHO YOU ARE AND THE DIVINE WILL OF YAHUAH (GOD) SECURED CREDITOR

Theory Of Cognitive Dissonance

Which is a lack of agreement, consistency, harmony, and discord. This theory holds that the mind involuntarily rejects information not in line with previous thoughts and/or actions. Added information about events creates an unpleasant dissonance with existing knowledge, opinion, or cognition concerning behavior. When this happens pressure naturally arises within the person to reduce the dissonance.

The only way that one can deal with the pressure created by the dissonance is by altering the old behavior to allow the added information or the right knowledge. However, if the person is committed to the old behavior and way of thinking he/she will simply reject the added information. Question to you is your mind open enough to receive this right knowledge? If not, you are wasting my and your time, Do you understand? Do you understand?

Discharge of Obligations. If at any time all such Securities of a particular series not heretofore delivered to the Trustee for cancellation or that have not become due and payable as described in Section 11.01 shall have been paid by the Company by depositing irrevocably with the Trustee as trust funds money or an amount of Governmental Obligations sufficient to pay at maturity or upon redemption all such Securities of that series not theretofore delivered to the Trustee for cancellation,

including principal (and premium, if any) and interest due or to become due to such date of maturity or date fixed for redemption, as the case may be, and if the Company shall also pay or cause to be paid all other sums payable hereunder by the Company concerning such series, then after the date such money or Governmental Obligations, as the case may be, are deposited with the Trustee the obligations of the Company under this Indenture

"WHY AM I HERE?" THE VOLUNTARY TORTURE CALLED LIFE

with respect to such series shall cease to be of further effect except for the provisions of Sections 2.03, 2.05. Over the years there have been so many papers written about the SECURED PARTY CREDITOR REDEMPTION PROCESS and yet there seems to be a lack of understanding of the basic concepts. Being a Sovereign was the initial path taken by people who knew they were free but saw no hope in the judicial system as it is practiced.

It is vitally important to understand how the people in the government turned our lives upside down and have made us believe that we are subject to them; when they are subject und The People being is part and partial for We The People. Allow me to cite the important points:

1. 1868 The 14th Amendment created a new class of citizens. "All men" (and women) are created equal as stated in the Declaration of Independence as a sovereign now became "a person", a subject to the Federal Government.

2. In 1871 the Federal Government formed itself into a CORPORATION and pulled itself from under the Constitution.

3. In 1913 the Federal Reserve Central Banks were created.

4. In 1933 President Roosevelt put into effect the "Trading with the Enemies Act". This applied only to Federal Citizens.

5. In 1933 President Roosevelt took the Gold away from the people- although they were not required to give it away- thereby leaving the people without "Money" for paying DEBTS.

6. March 9, 1933: Senate Document No. 43, 73rd Congress, 1st Session states: "The ownership of all property is in the State; individual so-called "ownership" is only by Government, i.e., law amounting to mere user: and use must be by law and subordinate to the necessities of the State.

7. In 1933 President Roosevelt passed HJR 192 June 5, 1933-simply put-since the government had taken the Gold, the people had no "Money"-the government would pay the "DEBTS" for the people- DOLLAR FOR DOLLAR-thereby giving the people-unlimited Credit.

8. In 1938 Erie Railroad vs. Tompkins made CONTRACTS the rule in our Courts. "IF THERE IS NO CONTRACT THERE IS NO CASE!"

9. In 1946 we lost our government and courts through the Administrative Procedures Act.

10. In 1965, silver was taken away as a means for paying DEBT, the UCC became the supreme law for America concerning the Banking System, the courts were pulled together in Administrative/Admiralty and Civil (Contract or Commerce/Corporation), and the Act and Intent were brought together thereby taking away your plea of Innocent. Guilty until proven innocent, changing the often quoted-you are innocent until proven guilty.

You must become educated to protect yourself, your family, and your business. As it is said in court "ignorance of the law is no excuse". Remember that the statement is a two-way street! How many of the 60,000,000 laws do you not know? The government will use your ignorance against you. To educate yourself there visit our YouTube Channels Deprogramed Enlightener, Undaunted National and Universal Indigenous TV& to help you learn who you are in relation to the government.

What is a 'Banker's Acceptance - BA'
A banker's acceptance (BA) is a short-term debt instrument issued by a firm that is guaranteed by a commercial bank. Banker's acceptances are issued by firms as part of a commercial transaction. These instruments are like T-Bills and are frequently used in money market funds. Banker's acceptances are traded at a

discount from face value on the secondary market, which can be an advantage because the banker's acceptance does not need to be held until maturity. Banker's acceptances are extensively used financial instruments in international trade.

I would like to point out that when you see N/A in law it does not mean Non-applicable it is Non. Assumpsit.
Assumpsit. An action for expected damages based on the breach of an express promise or contract to pay a debt. nonassumpsit. A defendant's claim, in the form of a pleading, that he or she did not promise or undertake any obligation as alleged in the complaint.

What is NON-ASSUMPSIT?
The general issue in the action of assumpsit; is a plea by which the defendant aver.

What is SUFFER?
To suffer an act to be done, by a person who can prevent it, is to permit or consent to it; to approve of it, and not to hinder it. It implies a willingness of the mind. See In re Rome Planning Mill (C. C.) OG Fed. 815; Wilson v. Nelson, 1S3 U. S. 101, 22 Sup. Ct. 74, 40 L. Ed. 147; Selleck v. Selleck, 10 Conn. 505; Gregory v. U. S., 10 Fed. Cas. 1197; In re Thomas (D. C.) 103 Fed. 274.

How Tazadaq Authenticated his Birth Certificate
February 4, 2015, at 12:27am

I have developed a fool proof idiot proof process of Authenticating a Birth Certificate. This process is Tazadaq's way, and I do not immolate myself. I create my own through trails and error and only come forward after being successful myself. I would first like to make it clear you cannot own what you did not create unlike many moors teach and others that do not comprehend the 10 Rules of commerce. Knowing this we cannot own the birth certificate but when can apply rule 3. All of commerce is based on Title. (Birth certificate, MSO, copyright).

"WHY AM I HERE?" THE VOLUNTARY TORTURE CALLED LIFE

You will just make yourself beneficiary is make you the one that receive the benefits of the BC trust, not a mere trustee which is just a subject.

Tazadaq Shah Bey Birth Certificate Authentication Process

Is Obama your daddy or will Hillary be your mother? If not, why are the sonning you? Who truly owns you?

From the live record of birth when your mother informed on you at the hospital (she is listed as informant on this document) shortly thereafter the Defacto Sates creates your Birth Certificate which is the primary document used to enslave us man and womb-man. It renders you a corporation, a corporate fiction a straw man from the living soul. This instrument not only grants the state the right to take your children whenever they decided that you are not behaving as your (government, CPS) parent demands, it is registered as a security at the DTC (Depository Trust Company) and used by the government as surety for public debt. The government created a debt and decided to use its citizens as collateral to pay the debt which we the people did not create.

They do not inform us that the Birth Certificate is created on bond paper because it is a commercial instrument as a savings bond. We are not told because they set themselves up as executors of our estates and are drawn from our Birth Certificate Bonds. Your Birth Certificate is worth millions! You can think this is funny if you want to remain a victim, or you can take this seriously and realize this is a remedy. They created a remedy when they took away the money under F.D. Roosevelt. The Remedy is HJR 192 and Public Law 73.10. Stop what you are doing right now and go look them up. Do your research, do not believe anything I say, go and research it for yourself. The reason I always say this in my videos is because you will find out that I am real.

If you want to be a free man or wombman you must be one of the people again and not a person. A person is a fiction, or a corporation in their language legalese. Words in law carry a different meaning than what we are taught in common parlance. The public fool (school) is where the brainwashing process begins. I am going to suggest that most things that you have learned are the opposite of the truth. Forget most of what you thought was true and read this material with an open mind. They make you a person by way of contact (Birth Certificate, 14th Amendment). This is essential because thereafter they can tax the person named on that document into oblivion to pay back federal debt. And I have challenged judges and attorneys to show me the law that states I must pay taxes on income. No such law exists, and if any of you can find it, I will take this book out of print and give you your money back for the purchase of this book.

This government was created under a republic but has persuaded many so-called black people to become slaves again under democracy. But wait, so-called whites were made commercial slaves under the 14th Amendment as well, which is a contract. Under democracy, as long as we are naïve enough to keep registering our sons and daughters and labeling them as children (a child is a fiction we have sons and daughters, not children) with the State, they have an endless supply of slaves to tax for fiscal sins. If you use a Social Insurance Number aka Social Security Number, you have a SIN (Social Insurance Number). I mentioned registered above which brings up another rule of Commerce, 5. When you register anything anywhere you give up Title. (Car, Child, vote)

The true title to anything is the MSO Manufacture State of Origin this is rule 4. The only true Title to anything is the MSO. (Geneses 1 verse 1 "In the beginning Yah created the heaven and the earth".) This takes us right back to rule 3 of commerce, 3. All of commerce is based on Title. (Birth certificate, MSO, copyright). Are you starting to wake up yet? To make it plain, you cannot regain your freedom unless you get true title and revoke power of attorney. A certificate of title is not a true title. To truly regain your freedom is to regain the Birth Title as opposed to the Birth Certificate of Title.

What I am about to facilitate to you is invaluable information. This is a painless, jail-free, non-confrontational, LAWFUL, process to reclaim the status of the holder at the right time to the Title to YOU the man or wombman.

The mathematics and science of it:
The essential element of this process is Minnesota Court Rule 220. In other states that I have observed, the statutes and nature relating to the Birth registration process are not readily available and are somewhat hidden. For the most part, all you can find is a fraction on some Department of Vital Statistics sites to the effect that Birth Registration began circa 1917. However, If one can accomplish this in one state it is possible in all.

Let us first examine Minnesota Rule 220 concerning Birth Certificates
"The Registrar of Titles is authorized to receive for registration of memorials upon any outstanding certificate of title an official birth certificate about a registered owner named in said certificate of title showing the date of birth of said registered owner, providing there is attached to said birth certificate an affidavit of an affiant who states that he/she is familiar with the facts recited, stating that the party named in said birth certificate is the same party as one of the owners named in said certificate of title; and that thereafter the Registrar of Titles shall treat said registered owner as having attained the age of the majority at a date 18 years after the date of birth shown by said certificate".

Knowing thus. Our Birth Certificate is a Certificate of Title, just like your automobile. You have equitable title, and you have the right to use that name, but the State has legal title and controlling interest in the property. The property is your body which is the surety and the NAME that you think is you. The masses have been subconsciously taught to associate this name with one's physical self from the crib through their parents throughout school. Only a faction now realizes we are not the name, but joinder is created, and we were just using a name that the State owns by way of contract.

Just like your home, you get to use it if you follow all the regulations and of course, pay property taxes. Now if you have not become an SPC (Secured Party Creditor) the Birth Certificate contract has rendered you an incompetent ward of the state and you are considered a minor. Rule 220 implies the State can treat you as a child, no matter how old you are, until you have gone to the registrar and shown them via affidavit that you are no longer under a corporate ward status!

The Defacto State operates from mere presumption and the fact that you have never claimed it the power of attorney over you they own you! Your uninformed other gave it to them, and you and she were both unaware, therefore you never got it back. So how can you get your life and Title back without a big confrontation at Vital Statistics?

The short answer is UCC 9-311a.
(UCC 9 deals with securities) we see that maybe there is a statute that could get us access to the original Title without a confrontation.

UCC 9-311 PERFECTION OF SECURITY INTERESTS IN PROPERTY SUBJECT TO CERTAIN STATUTES, REGULATIONS, AND TREATIES.
"(a) [Security interest subject to other law.]
Except as otherwise provided in subsection (d), the filing of a financing statement (a lien) is not necessary or effective to perfect a security interest in property subject to:
(1) a statute, regulation, or treaty of the United States whose requirements for a security interest's obtaining priority over the rights of a lien creditor concerning the property preempt Section 9-310(a).

"WHY AM I HERE?" THE VOLUNTARY TORTURE CALLED LIFE

(2) [list any statute covering automobiles, trailers, mobile homes, boats, farm tractors, or the like, which provides for a security interest to be indicated on a certificate of title as a condition or result of perfection, and any non-uniform Commercial Code central filing statute]; or (3) a statute of another jurisdiction which provides for a security interest to be indicated on a certificate of title as a condition or result of the security interest's obtaining priority over the rights of a lien creditor concerning the property."

Knowing thus. Directing one's attention to 28 USC 1733.

"28 U.S. Code § 1733 - Government records and papers; copies
(b) Properly authenticated copies or transcripts of any books, records, papers or documents of any department or agency of the United States shall be admitted in evidence equally with the originals thereof."

Key words here are records and documents. The Birth Certificate is a record of your birth. This means that if I get my Certificate of Title properly authenticated, it will be treated as equal to the original Birth Certificate.

Let us now examine Authentications and Certifications. Authentication is used to verify the authenticity of the notary's signature (and thereby the authenticity of the document) for all states that have NOT signed the Hague Convention treaty. Certifications and Apostilles do the same thing for countries that ARE signatories to the Hague Treaty. Court clerks may try to get you to settle for certification instead of authentication, but remember we need "Properly authenticated copies!"

What is CERTIFICATE? According to Black's Law 2nd, it is "A written assurance, or official representation, that some act has or has not been done, or some event occurred, or some legal formality has been complied with. Particularly, such written assurance made or issued from some court, and designed as a notice of things done therein, or as a warrant or authority, to some other court, judge, or officer. People v. Foster,"

I did not list which states are not Hague signatories, but you can go to http://www.hcch.net/index_en.php and see the Hague website. If you are not a member you can Click on Non-Member Contracting States on the left side Menu. Click on the tiny map at the top of the page and download the map. The grey countries are the ones you are looking for. Find one that you like and verify it is NOT on either list of countries in both the Non-member Contracting States and the HCCH Member States lists. For example, Jamaica and Taiwan are not on either list. Pick one you like for use on a federal DS-4194 form and to give to clerks who want to know the destination.

This is how Tazadaq did his Process:
Get a certified copy of your Certificate of Live Birth authenticated at each level of government - County (if applicable) some states do not have counties, State and Federal.

Step 1: Get a certified copy of your Certificate of Live Birth.
This is often known as the long form; this is DIFFERENT from an uncertified regular Birth Certificate which is computer generated. Some states have them in the county where you were born, other states keep them at the State Vital Statistics office. But what is the difference between the two documents? Well, the long-form certificate looks nicer, and it has handwritten signatures, but beyond that, not a whole lot.

Both are issued by the state's health department. It is to prove a person's birth there, and both require the person's permission to be released publicly. The long form is "generally an image of the original record and contains all the legal (non-medical) information, including hour of birth and name and signature of attendant," says Zoe Tobin, a deputy press secretary at the New York City Health Department to whom I spoke. The shorter form, on the other hand, is a "computer-generated abstract of the facts of birth printed on security paper." Basically, the shorter form is more efficient because it can be drawn from a database rather than photocopied from the original certificate.

One may ask, "Is there any time you need a long-form birth certificate? Yes, you need it to complete the process. You can use a short-form birth certificate for most purposes, including obtaining a driver's license or passport. But there are times when the long form is required, such as "for foreign adoptions or applications for dual citizenship," Also, genealogy experts really like them, presumably because they are weird and very detail oriented.

You may go there in person or order them online from a company like VitalChek www.vitalchek.com

Step 2: Next get the Certified Certificate of Live Birth authenticated at each level of government. If you get it from your county, then you want to get it Authenticated by the county superior court clerk or whatever option they have at the county level.

Next, the Secretary of State handles authentications for the state. Have them authenticate the Certified Certificate of Live Birth. They will attach a fancy page on the front with a brass rivet.

Step 3: Next go to the Department of State Office of Authentications and download form DS-4194. An example is in this book. Complete this form with the NON-Hague country of your choice. There may be cheaper ways, but I chose to prepay postage for a self-addressed return document mailer and enclosed it, a money order, completed form DS-4194, and an Authenticated Certified Certificate of Live Birth in the next size-up document mailer and send that off to the address on their website. Please note: The authentication processing fee is $8.00 per document,

not per page. This fee will be charged regardless of whether you receive an authentication certification or a correspondence letter. This policy change will take effect on April 1, 2012. Please pay the total amount shown in the estimated cost field. (The exact amount is required.)
Office of Authentications

Physical Address:

  Office of Authentications
  U.S. Department of State
  600 19th Street, NW
  Washington, DC 20006

Mailing Address:

Office of Authentications
U.S. Department of State
CA/PPT/S/TO/AUT
44132 Mercure CIR PO BOX 1206 Sterling, VA 20166 1206

Note: Effective October 6, 2014, all express mail air bill labels sent to the Office of Authentications for the use of returning documents must reflect the customer's mailing address as both the sender and recipient.

Telephone: 202-485-8000

Allowable payment methods include U.S. Postal Money Orders, and checks (personal, corporate, certified, cashiers, travelers) all payable to "U.S. Department of State."

Walk-in service only: In addition to the payment methods noted above; Credit Cards and Debit/Check Cards (VISA, MasterCard, American Express, Discover) are accepted.
DS

"WHY AM I HERE?" THE VOLUNTARY TORTURE CALLED LIFE

You will get back a properly authenticated Certificate of Live Birth.

I will now show you an example of the Affidavit that I used.

United States of America
Department of State
To all whom these presents shall come, Greetings:

I Certify That the document hereunto annexed is under Seal of the State(s) of New York and that such Seal(s) is/are entitled to full faith and credit. *
*for the contents of the annexed document, the Department assumes no responsibility
This certificate is not valid if it is removed or altered in any way whatsoever.

In testimony whereof, I, John F. Kerry, Secretary of State, have hereunto caused the seal of the Department of State to be affixed and my name subscribed by the Assistant Authentication Officer, of the said Department, at the city of Washington, in the District of Columbia, this fourth day of ...

Issued pursuant to CHXIV, State of _____John F Kerry_____
Sept. 15, 1789, 1Stat. 68-69; 22 Secretary of State
USC 2657; 22 USC 2651a; 5 USC By:
_____
301; 28 USC 1733 et seq.; 8 USC Assistant Authentication Officer, 1433(f); Rule 44 Federal Rules of Department of State
Civil Procedure
Notice the block of laws in the lower left corner of the document they send back includes 28 USC 1733. They are declaring this copy is equal to the original! You should look up the other laws referenced as well.

The next step is to go to a Registrar and attach an affidavit akin to this to the duly authenticated Certificate of Live Birth.

AFFIDAVIT OF OWNERSHIP
State of _____ }
} SS
County of _____ }

RE: Birth Certificate

I, the Tazadaq Shah Bey the undersigned, of lawful age and being first duly sworn on oath, depose and state that I am familiar with the facts recited, and the party named in said birth certificate is the same party as one of the owners named in said certificate of title.

_____
Signature
Signed and sworn to before me this _____ day of _____, 20_____.

_____
Notary Public My Commission Expires

This once completed is now a duly authenticated Certificate of Title and an attached claim is what is known as a counter deed. From the perspective of trust law, you now hold in your hand a deed of a Free Man. A deed back to you. From the perspective of commercial law and in commerce rule 8. First in line is first in time. (Recorded into public record at county) you hold a first in time first in line document to being a man, in other words you are now the real party in interest and holder at the right time to the Title to YOU!

"WHY AM I HERE?" THE VOLUNTARY TORTURE CALLED LIFE

Now that you have completed this what is next? You should correct your status. Email creditorsdebtorscontracts@yahoo.com or visit www.creditorsdebtorscontractsincommerce.org and see the status correction page. - Correcting your Status
Under their colorable of law system, we are all seen as wards of the state. Our status as Citizen-Principal is not respected even if our house is 'paid off,' we have a 'good job' and 'money' in the bank. This process is a major steppingstone in correcting the record of your status to Citizenship-Principal like before the 14th Amendment as opposed to the citizen subject status of almost everyone walking around today. Since all crimes have been converted from common law crimes to commercial crimes (27 CFR 72.11), this document makes you the first in time first in line lienholder against your name. The next step is to become a SPC. Secured party creditor. Contact us now.

Before we close let me go over just a little legalese with you and you will discover how you have been had. Blacks Law's Dictionary shows some words you assumed you comprehended. As you read them you may begin to see the enormity of the crime perpetrated on the American people.
What is SUFFER?
To suffer an act to be done, by a person who can prevent it, is to permit or consent to it; to approve of it, and not to hinder it. It implies a willingness of the mind. See In re Rome Planning Mill (C. C.) 0G Fed. 815; Wilson v. Nelson, 1S3 U. S. 101, 22 Sup. Ct. 74, 40 L. Ed. 147; Selleck v. Selleck, 10 Conn. 505; Gregory v. U. S., 10 Fed. Cas. 1197; In re Thomas (D. C.) 103 Fed. 274.

This writer concludes, from the definitions below, that a court of record is a court which must meet the following. criteria:

1. generally has a seal
2. power to fine or imprison for contempt
3. keeps a record of the proceedings
4. proceeding according to the common law (not statutes or codes)
5. the tribunal is independent of the magistrate (judge)

Note that a judge is a magistrate and is not the tribunal.
The tribunal is either the sovereign himself, or a fully.
empowered jury (not paid by the government)

Black's Law Dictionary, 4th Ed., 425, 426
COURTS OF RECORD and COURTS NOT OF RECORD witness is death. A spirit does not have flesh and bones. The book of Luke 24 and 39 reads, "Behold my hands and my feet that it is I and to me and see for a spirit have not flesh and bones as you see me have."

Satan's angels and Satan's agents war against us spiritually the book of Matthew chapter 25 verse 41 states, "Then shall he say unto them on the left-hand depart from me, depart into everlasting fire prepared for the devil and his angels."

Satan and his angels are not after anything in the world because the world belongs to Satan already. Satan's agents and his angels are after those of us that have been taken out of the world if you are in Christ and the spirit of Christ is within you, then you are a new creature so the.
Scriptures read in the book of John chapter 15 verse 19 "if you was of the world the world will love his own but because ye are not.
of the world but I have chosen you out of the world therefore the world hated you." If you are in Christ, you are a new creature.
and you were not of this world.

"WHY AM I HERE?" THE VOLUNTARY TORTURE CALLED LIFE

Satan has been in control of this world since the time that Christ walked the earth in the flesh. Satan has controlled the world
and still does. Let us prove that in the book of Job chapter 9 verse 24. "The earth is given into the hands of the wicked he covered.
the faces of the judges thereof (who painted Christ as a so-called white man, who painted all the Angels as so-called white people, who painted all the prophets as so-called white people?).
That is what the Scripture means he covers the faces of the judges thereof.
So, we see this Scripture coincides with the book of John 14 verse 30 hereafter I will not talk much with you for the prince of this world cometh and have nothing in me. This Scripture is saying that at this current time, the earth is under Satan's authority. U.S.A (UNDER SATAN'S AUTHORITY).

Primarily, I did not say that the earth was given into the hands of the wicked the Bible stated that. Next, who rules the earth? This is rhetorical, you do not have to answer it because both you and I know the answer. The people that rule the world how has it been? Is it just?
Just as he was after Job in the book of Job chapter 1 verse 6, Satan went to Yahuah when the sons of men went to Yahuah and challenged Job's faith in Yahuah Just as he did this with Job, he does this with us day in and day out. Therefore, it is extremely important.
to guard ourselves with the armor of Yahuah. We must be ready spiritually and do all that we can to withstand the evils of this world, resist the devil and he will flee from you.

Ephesians chapter 6 verse 13 says wherefore take into you the whole armor of God that ye may be able to stand (meaning he will be fighting to get you) in these days of evil if you have not done all that you can, you must stand and show thyself to be a man.
Verse 14 says Stand therefore having your loins girt (to girt is to encircle or bring something close to you) about with truth and having on the breastplate of righteousness. What are our loins and

"WHY AM I HERE?" THE VOLUNTARY TORTURE CALLED LIFE

how do we keep them in truth?

Our loins are our restricted areas, but we also must girt our minds which are to be scarce and holy which means set apart in truth. Yahuah says in first Peter chapter 1: verse 16 "For it is written be holy for I am holy". Brothers and sisters, we are not to be committing acts of sex and intimacy or intimate conversations with anyone besides our spouse if we are married. If you have a so-called girlfriend or boyfriend, you are married because in the Bible there is no such thing as a boyfriend or a girlfriend; the act of sex constitutes marriage according to the book of Exodus chapter 22 verse 16. "And if a man entices a maid that is not be throbbed which means engage and lie with her meaning to have sex with her, he shall surely endow her made him promise her to be his wife."

Therefore, we are not supposed to be out in the world talking or committing any acts of affection with anyone other than the person to whom we are espoused. The other intimate relationships or wicked but marriage is honorable. The Book of Hebrews chapter 13
verse 4 reads "Marriage is honorable in all in the bed undefiled both warmongers and adulterers God will judge". Fornication is sexual wickedness or setting up partners with Yahuah. This includes porn movies, dirty music, walking with your private parts exposed on beaches, or any type of wickedness that most deem as being okay because you are just looking or listening. To look at someone
or even think anything that has to do with sex or sexuality is a sin if they are not your spouse. It is lust for a man to look upon a woman in her nakedness who is not his wife, and it is a sin.

There are many women out there that chose to go to male doctors and have the male doctors looking up into their Vagina. There
are many men out there who choose to go to female doctors and have female doctors looking at them in the nude. You cannot say

"WHY AM I HERE?" THE VOLUNTARY TORTURE CALLED LIFE

that you are in a proper mind state if you are doing this intentionally. If you are going to a doctor of the opposite sex, you may be
enticing that man or woman to sin.

A doctor is still a man or a woman and sins like everyone else. Stop placing them on a pedestal. This is not of Yahuah this is of the world this is sin. But many of you do not comprehend the Bible, because you are not spiritual, you would think that I am deranged. But what does the Lord say? The book of James chapter 1 verse 15 says "then when lust has concealed it bringing forth sin and sin when it is finished it bringing forth death".

So, when a man looks upon a woman in lust that is a sin it does not matter if the man's a doctor. When a woman looks upon a man unless it is her husband that is a sin, it does not matter if the woman is a doctor. You are inviting sin into the world, and you will be judged. Let us see what the Lord says regarding this.

The book of Matthew chapter 5 verse 28 "but I say unto you that whosoever look at on a woman to lust after her hath committed adultery with her already in his heart". I have heard of many cases where male doctors have been charged with molesting women in the doctor's office. There have been many cases where male doctors have performed certain procedures on females that was unnecessary.

This is when lust was conceived. Therefore, any woman or man who puts themselves in this position intentionally and thinks little of it gets ready for the judgments of Yahuah. The most high tells us that we are not to associate with those that do not obey the will of Yahuah Second Thessalonians chapter 3 verse 6. "now we command you bretheren in the name of our Lord Yahusha that ye abstain yourselves from every brother that walk disorderly and not after the traditions which he receives of us."

"WHY AM I HERE?" THE VOLUNTARY TORTURE CALLED LIFE

That is clear that people are not following this Bible we are not supposed to be around them, we are not supposed to befriend them we are not supposed to be with them. We are being told to withdraw from such people in the name of our Lord. Second Thessalonians chapter 3 verse 14 says "If any man obeys not our words by this epistle note that man and have no company with him that he may be ashamed."

These worldly people and their positions are Satan's devices of getting to our spirits because everything we see hear, touch, smell, and feel go into our minds. Everything we do and interact with becomes who we are. If we are constantly reading watching listening and associating with evil corrupt worldly things and people, then that is who we will become. Yahuah says we are a temple in which he dwells first Corinthians chapter 3 verse 16 ...... "that that ye are the temple of God and the spirit of God dwells in your if
any man defiles the temple of God himself God destroy for the temple of God is holy which temple ye are."

If we do not put on the armor of Yahuah, we are susceptible to the wiles of the devil and will be defiled and Yahuah will not dwell in us but will destroy us mentally and eventually physically because we will be unholy. Ephesians chapter 6 verse 14 talks about a breastplate of righteousness. The beloved breastplate was a form of protection used to protect soldiers in battle. It protected their middle section. The heart is in the part that the breastplate protects but this scripture is speaking in a spiritual sense meaning to be righteous as a breastplate of honor in truth. Preparing wherever we go with the breastplate of righteousness that will be in front protecting you.
Ephesians chapter 6 verse 15 "Your feet shod with the preparation of the gospel of peace". Sod means to put on foot gear. To
prepare your feet means to put on the protection of foot gear before heading out to battle. Christ ever walked in peace using only the

"WHY AM I HERE?" THE VOLUNTARY TORTURE CALLED LIFE

word of Yahuah to teach, he cashed out evil spirits.

Therefore, we must study and be born in the gospel of the word of the Highest in Christ. Our feet become just as Christ traveling throughout day in and day out with our feet to where Yahuah directs them to take us physically and to not go in the direction which is of the devil and against Yahuah. We must have the word of Yahuah firmly planted within us teaching the Scriptures in our everyday steps. When we go against Yahuah's laws statutes and commandments we are sinning. When we sin, we go against Yahuah himself King David said in the book of Psalms chapter 51 verse 4, "Against the, the only have I said and done this evil in thy sight".

Here we hear from King David that sin is evil, and it is only against the Lord that he sins because he is our ultimate Redeemer. James in the book of James chapter 4 verse 17 "Therefore to him that know what to do good and do a fit not to him it is sin". Here we read that
what we know to be good if we do not do it is sunny. 1st John chapter 5 verse 17 says "All unrighteousness is sin".

Yahuah goes on to say through John in 1st John chapter 3 verse 4 "whosoever sinned transgressive also the law for sin is transgression of the law." We must not go against the Lord we will be put to death not only physically but mentally and will not receive the gift of God's eternal life. Romans 6 verse 23 says "for the wages of sin is death but the gift of God is eternal life through Yahusha our Lord".

Eternal life is something given from Yahuah that we will never receive if we go against his law's statutes and commandments. Yahuah is very
merciful, he forgives but only if our sins are confessed and not hidden. The book of Proverbs chapter 28 verse 13 "he that covers his sins shall not prosper but whoso confess it and forsake it then

"WHY AM I HERE?" THE VOLUNTARY TORTURE CALLED LIFE

shall have mercy."

If we sin, we must admit unto Yahuah what we have done, and we must do our absolute best to never go back to committing those sins again. Yahuah has given us the tools necessary to use to lead by his will but if we cover our wickedness and do not confess Yahuah
will not have mercy on us and we will not inherit the gift of eternal life. We must do the word of Yahuah to stay clean from the wicked devices of Satan and his angels in agents.

The book of Psalms chapter 119 verse 9 "wherewithal shall a young man Clint situates by taking heed thereto according to thy word." The word is the laws statutes and commandments of the highest Yahuah. We must do our absolute best to obey them no matter what! There are no excuses. Yahuah does not play games. Satan and his angels are going all over the earth in every direction trying to take our spirit away from Yahuah.

We need to be sober and ready because Satan deals deceitfully. Once the spirit of Satan is on you will deal deceitfully when one deals deceitfully he conceals the truth knowingly. This is the same as a lie and is of the devil and is also breaking Yahuah's commandments. One of the major tools Satan uses is the lust of the world, such as sex. drugs, cars, jobs, money, a new house, clothes, fame, power, etc. We must withhold ourselves from fleshly lusts because they are in opposition to Yahuah.

First Peter's chapter 2 verse 11 "dearly beloved beseech you as strangers and pilgrims abstain from fleshly lusts which war against the soul." When we complete the act of lust whether it is mental or physical it is a sin and will bring us not only a spiritual death but eventually a physical death. A spiritual death is separation from Yahuah then you eventually die physically. It is okay to lust for your spouse but lust for others leads to sin and wicked practices.

"WHY AM I HERE?" THE VOLUNTARY TORTURE CALLED LIFE

So, the book of James chapter 1 verse 15 says "then when lust hath conceived I bring forth sin and sin when it is finished bring forth death". Satan knows this and is going in many directions to get this to happen, so he can turn you against Yahuah.

First Peter's chapter 5 verses eight through 9 "be sober and diligent (this means keeping careful watch for possible dangers or difficulties) because your adversary the devil is a roaring lion walking about seeking whom he may devour".
Satan is not under the earth with horns and a long tail, or on a hot saucer bottle with a pitchfork. This is just a fable. Satan is real, and his spirit is here throughout the earth. The loin is the king of the jungle, and his roar is fearless so likewise Satan is the king of this world, and he is persistent and fearless and doing all he can to get us to sin not only ourselves, and the ones we love, but against Yahuah. Therefore, Yahuah gave us this armor and his laws, statutes, and commandments.

These were given to us to uphold us in this day and time because this day and time is evil. Most importantly we need to believe in Yahuah himself with his promise that he has sent his Redeemer to deliver us from this wicked devil and all his attempts to take our souls.
The book of Ephesians chapter 6 verse 16 says "above all taking the shield of faith were withal you shall be able to quench all the fiery darts of the wicked."

Darts are used in battle to kill the physical body but here the wicked have darts that they used to kill our spirits. An animal who is shot with a dart in the wilderness not from which it came only suffers from the blow and the affliction that follows. This armor Yahuah has given us will allow us to see the dart before it hits the flush and be able to throw it away and overcome it.

For example, how water quenches a flame of fire or freezing rain on a hot burning mountain top. With faith, we overcome. Now let us ask ourselves, what is faith? The Scriptures are noticeably clear on this. Hebrews chapter 11 verse 1 "Now faith is the substance of things hoped for the evidence of things not seen". This clearly states that faith is something that you long for, and wish for, something you think about having, it is a substance you cannot readily obtain because it has not come yet. In this thing, you hope for evidence meaning it exists even though it is not yet or has not been seen. Just as we have not seen the Father, we have faith in him and what he says.

Though we may not have seen the father or have not seen the son in this life we have faith that he is he was and still lives with the father. It is our very faith that will carry us through challenging times and temptations. Yahuah says in First Corinthians chapter 10 verse 13 "therefore have no temptations taking you but such as common to man but God is faithful who will not suffer you to be tempted above that ye are able but will with the temptation also make a way to escape that ye be able to bear it".

Daily Affirmation: Dear Father Yahuah (God) I forgive all the people who have caused me harm, done me wrong, hurt me, and betrayed me. I forgive myself as well for any illness that I have caused others. I accept your forgiveness and I am placing your freedom of peace and I will walk in your law's statutes and commandments henceforth. The more I let go of the internal hate, discontentment,
and self-loathing, the more I am free thank you, Lord.
Tazadaq's Motivational Quotes for Success.

If you affiliate with losers and naysayers, you will render yourself to be a loser and a naysayer. You will emulate their ways, pick up their habits, and clone their attitude about life. If you are around cynical negative people, most of the time you will end up cynical and negative. It is imperative to align yourself with positive people. The fiercest foe and enemy that you will have to deal with is the Satan of self. If you extract the enemy within the enemy outside

"WHY AM I HERE?" THE VOLUNTARY TORTURE CALLED LIFE

can do you no harm.

How do you define yourself right now? How do you view yourself right now? You are what you think about all day, as a man thinks within his heart so is he. Who are you right now and what must you change to create who you want to be? What must you leave behind to get where you want to go? Whom shall I leave behind to accomplish my goals and your dreams? If you want to keep on getting what you are getting simply keep on doing what you are doing, and you are guaranteed to be average, to be a failure, and to suffer from the disease of normality.

80% of your self-talk is negative you must start concentrating on the positive and live now, life is not about tomorrow is about right. Now is about today. Tomorrow is a great dream but is not real, yesterday may be a great memory but it is not real. Your only reality is right now.
It is When you can envision the invisible you can accomplish the impossible. So, my question is what you are dreaming that you intend to make possible?

You must eliminate self-negativity; you must eliminate all negative thinking and thoughts. If you think something negative, you must not speak it, because the very moment that you speak it is speaking it into existence and you will live it out.

Some people are so negative that even when I attempt to give you a positive statement, or positive energy you take everything that I articulate and transform it into something negative. You are so undetermined to be positive and so determined to be negative that it is astonishing. You have thought your way into extreme depression and being negative, yet you are expecting to produce positive results. The outcome of your life is based on your thinking and the choices that you make. If you choose negative thoughts, you will yield negative results.

"WHY AM I HERE?" THE VOLUNTARY TORTURE CALLED LIFE

Self-Assessment Questions:
1. Why did Yahusha die on the cross?
2. Is there any resentment within my heart that needs to be addressed?
3. Am I in denial or have I rendered true forgiveness?
4. Have I utterly forgiven those people who have hurt me caused me pain, done me wrong or am I just in denial?
5. I am searching deep inside to release and let go.
6. What is the mindset of a person who has truly forgiven?
7. Have I honestly forgiven myself for the wrong things that I have done in the past?

Today's prayer:
I pray to the old Father Yahawah, to reveal to me any unforgiveness within my heart. Help me to address it and completely turn it over to you. Give me the strength to let go of the past and any destructive irrational emotions I cannot carry this burden any longer and gets in the way of our relationships in your name amen.

Daily Prayer: I pray dear Yahawah for you to show me any resentment and unforgiveness that is within my heart. Most High please help me discover it completely and allow you to diminish it. Father provided me with the strength to let go of my dreadful past and destructive emotions. Help me let go of any burden that I have been carrying around that has been a barrier between the relationship of you and others in Yahawashi (Christ's) name I pray amen.

Acting: Now please take out a sheet of paper and write down or type the names of any and everyone that has ever hurt you. Also, anyone who has ever betrayed you. Once you have accomplished this, praying over that list of names will not be easy but pray over that list of names. Ask Yahuah to bless these people who have hurt you and betrayed you in every aspect of their lives. Until you flush all the negative energy away from your mind towards these people completely out of your system you are doomed.

This is the point where everything in your circumference, within your entire life, is about to change for the better. The highest is about to instill in you the knowledge, wisdom understanding and faith to alter your life.

How to set up a Living Trust and file 1041s protect your assets.

Two different trusts by Tazadaq Shah
www.truedisciplesofchrist.org/shop
347-618-1783
tazadaqshah@yahoo.com

What Is a Living Trust?

A living trust is a legal document created by you (the grantor) during your lifetime. Just like a will, a living trust spells out exactly what your desires are regarding your assets, your dependents, and your heirs. The significant difference is that a will becomes effective only after you die, and your will has been entered into probate. A living trust bypasses the costly and time-consuming process of probate, enabling your successor trustee (who fills basically the same role as an executor of a will) to conduct your instructions as documented in your living trust at your death, and if you are unable to manage your financial, healthcare, and legal affairs due to incapacity.

Record a rescission: of signature on all past IRS forms (1040's, W2s, W4s, Form 56).
You can record it in your county and get certified copies back. County record is public so just use the last 4 numbers of your SS number if at all.
Record 2848: To take back the trusteeship of your ALL CAPS

account. [one might ask, do I use my SS # or only the last 4 #'?. I have read that the county recorder will not record anything with one's SS # on it.]

Send to IRS: 4506 Ts for 1099's & W2's [or get the SSA form 7050] Certified copy of recorded rescission of signature on all past IRS forms. Form 2848 (Power of Attorney and Declaration of Representative). W-8CE (Expatriation and Waiver of Treaty Benefits) SS4 (sent to you free via email for attending this webinar).

Record a rescission: of signature on all past IRS forms (1040's, W2s, W4s, Form 56).
You can record it in your county and get certified copies back. County record is public so just use the last 4 numbers of your SS number if at all.
Record a rescission: of signature on all past IRS forms (1040's, W2s, W4s, Form 56).
You can record it in your county and get certified copies back. County record is public so just use the last 4 numbers of your SS number if at all.

Send to SSA: Get the SSA 7050 Form and reconstruct 1041 based on what the SSA said was earned for those years on that annual form they send to everyone telling you what you paid and what the employer paid. SSA-521(Request for Withdrawal of Application.) [It does not make sense to me to send this. If we are canceling the SS# then how can we put it in a trust or make yourself Trustee over a canceled account?
Set up Trust; SS4 (Application for EIN) Fill in the number "98- "so that there is no misunderstanding as to what type of EIN you are creating. Create a simple no-withholding foreign grantor trust with the IRS foreign operations division in Philadelphia.
Take back the trusteeship of your ALL CAPS account by making yourself a Trustee.
Put your SSN and all CAPS names in a non-withholding foreign

"WHY AM I HERE?" THE VOLUNTARY TORTURE CALLED LIFE

grantor trust. If you want true foreign trust, do not use an SSN when setting it up. Name your trust with numbers and/or letters. It is said not to use your name but if you want to be a wise guy, go on. I am merely just an enlightened person.

File 1041's: The Fiduciary/Trustee can charge whatever he wants for fees, which means up to the entire amount of the income of the trust They know we do not owe a tax and that the debt instruments paid to us throughout the year [Federal Reserve Notes] are obligations of United States, Inc. It is a simple means to recoup those funds. Also, line 14 in Part II under Payments asks if any of the tax withheld was from a 1099
.
(Since the mortgage transaction at the closing table was, in fact, an exchange or barter, the 1099 B is the form we use to recoup the promissory note funds for the mortgage.
It appears to me that may be the case. Also, as an afterthought, if anyone had a home foreclosed upon, they might call up the court and get the Cusip number for the court case and do a 1099-A or a 1099-B for that case.

You can then put that amount on line 24 reclaim the sum back and buy a new home. They ARE withholding a tax, so I do not believe this process would be in error. Do not start asking me a deluge of questions about what I just told you.

I went back to the age of 16 when I filed the 1041s and 1041-T's [which must be filed together], but the trust can only be "funded" back 25 years, I do not know if they will reimburse me for all those years. Only time will tell. Also, I purchased a home during those years, and I am going to seek recoupment of all the funds at the maturity dates of the transaction.

I do not know if I will get reimbursement for those sums, but then, again, time will tell. [the original amount of the mortgage's promissory note is certainly a withheld tax because you never received it at closing even though your promissory note says, "for a loan I have received."

The "maturity date amount" after 30 years of payment is what the bank receives, and I do not think we could claim that as a tax withheld. One can certainly also collect back all one's payments because the accrual method of accounting means you owe the bank, and the bank owes you.

Use the SSA annual statement that they send out every year. They provide the amounts you earned for any given year, the total you paid in (not broken down by year), and what your employer paid on your behalf.

Figure out the FICA (.062) and the MEDICAID (.0145), then multiply that amount by 2 [to match the employer's contribution] to get the total tax withheld [shouldn't the employer get that back?] You would also add any IRS tax they withheld as well.

The April 15 filing date does not apply to 1041's. You do not have to rush to get them done. Keep in mind that I never invested, so the schedules did not apply to me. If that is the case for you, as well, just do page one of the 1041 and forget page two, which has the schedules on it. You also MUST file the 1041-T, which is the equivalent of a 1040-V, which tells them to whom the funds are to be paid.

1099-A IS the payment. So, I believe, anyone with an outstanding mortgage can pay off the existing loan with the 1099-A. From what I can see, you could then recoup the original promissory note amount, and all payments made to date on the pooling and servicing agreement (Deed of Trust), which is what 1099-A is paying.

Again, do not call me for coaching on this I am telling you all that I know. You either get it or you do not!

"WHY AM I HERE?" THE VOLUNTARY TORTURE CALLED LIFE

You would use the 1099-B for the original promissory note amount. The 1099-A also might be the preferred form of 1099 for a foreclosure that went through a courtroom (bank). Still, put that on line 24 as Federal tax withheld. Make sure you get the EIN that the court is operating under, and the CUSIP number, if possible, and charge it back to them or the opposing attorney law firm.

Fill in the new trust number as the "payer's identification number." Then, AFTER the form has been filled out, in the spot at the bottom where it asks for account numbers, fill in the SSN / red number on the back of the SS card.
DO NOT PUT THOSE ON ANY CARBON COPIES OF THE 1099 SERIES YOU ARE WORKING ON, AS THAT RED NUMBER IS YOUR ACCOUNT NUMBER THAT THEY ARE WORKING FROM.

Make sure you keep that private so they cannot access that account. Put that ONLY on the original red copy of the 1099 forms. You fill in that red number from the back of the SS card on the 1096 form as well, in the boxed sections that say "for official use only. "

Maybe one can get a quote on a new Mercedes Benz, and "pay" for it with a 1099-A in the trust's name. I do not know how much dissension they will one or if the transaction will be successful, but perhaps you may want to find out.

I am also thinking that this may be "the" method to purchase a new home without a commercial banking institution. Only time will tell if my observations are correct.

Refile the correct form, which is a 1041 and 1041-T form [for a Living Trust] for each year you previously filed, you claim back all the taxes they took out, including IRS, FICA, and MEDICAID, plus recoup the balance as trustee fees, you claim back the entire amount that is on the W-2.

The 1041 also allows recoupment of the mortgage exchange, so you can get that amount back as well. You are making everything so difficult when, in fact, it is as simple as A, B, C [1099 SERIES, 1099 A, 1099 B, 1099 C]. Trusts do not pay taxes, and the IRS knows we are not liable for "income" taxes.

On line 11 of the 1041 form, you fill in all the IRS, FICA, and MEDICAID taxes they have removed for the particular year and claim that back. Then, on line 12, fiduciary fees, you place the difference between what was removed in taxes and the gross amount you received. The Fiduciary/Trustee [you, in a Living Trust] has the right to be paid for the service. You then claim that back as well, which should total the gross amount earned during the year.

Refile the correct form, which is a 1041 and 1041-T form [for a Living Trust] for each year you previously filed, you claim back all the taxes they took out, including IRS, FICA, and MEDICAID, plus recoup the balance as trustee fees, you claim back the entire amount that is on the W-2.

The 1041 also allows recoupment of the mortgage exchange, so you can get that amount back as well. You are making everything so difficult when, in fact, it is as simple as A, B, C [1099 SERIES, 1099 A, 1099 B, 1099 C]. Trusts do not pay taxes, and the IRS knows we are not liable for "income" taxes.

On line 11 of the 1041 form, you fill in all the IRS, FICA, and MEDICAID taxes they have removed for the particular year and claim that back. Then, on line 12, fiduciary fees, you place the difference between what was removed in taxes and the gross amount you received. The Fiduciary/Trustee [you, in a Living Trust] has the right to be paid for the service. You then claim that back as well, which should total the gross amount earned during the year.

"WHY AM I HERE?" THE VOLUNTARY TORTURE CALLED LIFE

You can "fund" a trust as far back as 25 years, and they will ask you to file the 1041s for all those years; however, I would NOT refile in a 1041 form until you have rescinded your signature on all previously filed 1040 forms, for mistake and error [Never say or use error. Errors must be paid for. Mistakes can be corrected].

Even though they requested a 1041 return be filed for the last 25 years, I went back to the year I first began working and reconstructed the 1041 based on what the SSA said I earned for those years on that annual form they send to everyone telling what you paid and what the employer paid.

Also, line 14 in Part II under Payments asks if any of the tax withheld was from 1099. You can search back as far as 10 years for any 1099's filed against the strawman's number on form 4506-T. You can then claim back the amount of the tax withheld on the 1099 on that line. You can do individual searches for a 1099-A or 1099-OID or any other type.

This means you can claim back what was withheld from you by the mortgage company for the promissory note they claimed you abandoned. [or car loans or credit cards.]

You can also use form 4506-T to find out what W-2 forms were filed against the account [the social security account with a name like yours but in all caps], as well, which will enumerate the IRS, FICA, and MEDICAID taxes withheld.

Refile on a 1041 back to the time you started working to reclaim all the taxes they took out plus the difference between the taxes taken and the amount they paid you in debt instruments as fiduciary fees. The IRS in Ogden does not accept Form 56 but will honor 2848.

The banks and mortgage companies take our promissory notes to the Treasury to get the funds to pay the seller then they want us to "pay them back" for accessing our credit. We are the creditors; they are the debtors, but it is taught to us backward.

Which is brainwashing and we ought to be able to bring them up on charges of non-disclosure, except that it is all "explained" in their codes, but it is written in "Legalese" which translates as gibberish. Yet we are still expected to know how to manage commercial paper because we all carry FRNs (Federal Reserve Notes).

Since the instructions state that 1099-A is included in the C, I am only going to order and concern myself with that form and 1096 for future processes. That will cut down a lot of paperwork, at least for me. According to instructions, we include a 1041-T to transfer the assets from our trust account to the STRAWMAN when filing 1041, which is a reasonable deduction; however, after looking at and thinking about that form, and trying to produce some viable method to purchase items without using the Federal Reserve banking system.

other than our trust accounts and the IRS, I was wondering if we might not find some success if we conveyed property to an entity via that 1041-T form, if, in fact, what is paying the beneficiary out of our trust account. What I believe that we might include is to put the entity in the beneficiary spot, along with their EIN where appropriate, the purchase price of the item, and the percentage of 100%.

The title of the document is "Allocation of Estimated Tax Payments to Beneficiaries," and under that, it states: "Under Codes Section 643(g)." When I looked up that section, under definitions, it states that a beneficiary "includes heir, legatee, devisee."

When I looked up those words independent of that code, they all refer to a recipient of land. However, when you think about it, the term "includes" does NOT mean that it is limited to just those words and meanings. Couldn't a beneficiary be a company that we would deal with in getting some form of property, such as a private conveyance or home? Could this be a simple means to convey the value of the property to them for tax purposes, i.e., U.S. funds? Since every commercial transaction is merely a tax, does anyone have any opinion on what this might accomplish?

The Power of Knowing Yahuah's (God's) Will

When they all were telling me I could not, I knew I could I just had to dispatch my thoughts to encourage my spirit to show them otherwise. Once I began to realize that the people who attempt to hurt you in life is doing so because they have not healed, I decided to be oblivious to their insults. I became deaf to third-party insults, doubts, and limitations.

Then I also had to confront the bullies who exerted physical violence to manipulate and bully others. That is why I had to face Jonathan Sample a six-foot-three Goliath in the sixth grade while I was only about four feet eleven. This kid had been in the sixth grade for three years. He came from a home where he learned to abuse and bully others. From the age of seven when those Mexican boys attempted to bully men and I was outnumbered six to one, I decided to study Martial arts. It is where Seni taught me my first art, Samurai Karate Doo. From there I would go on to learn Tang Soo doo Grand Master Brit, Tae Kwon do, Brazilian Jujutsu, Japanese Jujitsu, and Muay Thai.

Currently, I have just one disciple under my belt. The setting was on a school bus, in an area closed which gave this giant more of an advantage to overpower me. To measure up to just his chin I had to stand on the seat. I had been taught to always protect women already men, even as a young boy. This bully was telling my cousin to get up and let him sit down. The entire bus was afraid of this guy. Once he got on the bus, the scene would go from all the students talking like a pep rally to a library.

When he told my cousin to get up I told him to leave her alone. This kind said, "Mother Fucker now I'm going to whip your ass." When he came towards me I knew I had to move swiftly and could not allow this guy to put all his weight on me if I fell or he pinned me down. As he walked toward me, I sprung from my seat and hit him with a straight right hand resulting in his nose pouring with blood, I then got him in a headlock and squeezed so tight that it brought the giant down to his knees on my level. All the students were cheering me on. They all had been bullied by this guy. After we were separated, and he cried I felt sorry for him. Now in life, I have grown to realize that people like him bully others because they have been abused and bullied. This usually started at home with child abuse or neglect.

Love is the only solution for this sick world. Why am I here? I am here to give love to the world. But even when you give love in times of peace and love prepare for war, because love and peace do not last forever. What you have in this world is a superficial love that can deteriorate with disagreement and struggle. A wife claims to love her husband, yet divorce rapes him in a biased court system, strips his children away, and blames him for the destruction of the marriage when 70% of divorces are filed by women. No one wants to discuss this plague that leads to single female parenting which has been detrimental to society and the nation.

Such conversations are labeled hate speech. I then conclude that you can hate me because essentially you hate the truth. This broken system must be fixed. This is why I have created Men Against Feminism (MAF). If you love truth and manhood then I encourage each man and woman reading this book #maf we support Tazadaq.

This book is about transformative thinking to make a better you. There is always the urge to quit once one is focused on change.

"WHY AM I HERE?" THE VOLUNTARY TORTURE CALLED LIFE

Because the human mind likes to delight in taking the path of lesser resistance. We must overpower the urge to quit that arises within us all and push forward into a better you and me. Otherwise, we will die in our current abase states. We all need reconciliation. Begin now.

This entails facing your fears and overcoming any obstacle that you are the Matrix paces in your way. The Matrix uses police and other Alphabet groups for fear-mongering. This sounds ridiculous but think for a moment of the number of people that was innocently killed for reaching for an identification or regular traffic stops where a man simply was going from point A to point B is killed and the police officer gets away simply because he is a police officer. Recently police responded to the address on a domestic violence call, and shot and killed the homeowner.

It was a late-night shooting that killed Robert Dotson. The Police chief suggesting that it was a "justified" use of force by New Mexico police," was a "murderous" act by officers who responded to the wrong house in my opinion.

If we as people continue to allow police to give a dueling narrative of what happens. Around 11:30 p.m. on April 5, when three Farmington police officers responded to the incorrect address for a domestic violence call.

Farmington PD statement GRAB New Mexico police shot and killed a man after they went to the wrong house while responding to a domestic violence call Police bodycam footage shows officers standing outside the front door of Dotson's home, asking a dispatcher to confirm the house number.

After no one answers the door, the police start walking away. Dotson, 52, answers the door with a gun in his hand, and all three officers open fire. Is it not my right to hear someone at my door respond with my weapon in my hand? Police are supposed to be trained to manage situations as such why did Dotson lose his life?

"WHY AM I HERE?" THE VOLUNTARY TORTURE CALLED LIFE

Will you be next because you say," As long as it wasn't me or my loved ones it's none of my business?"

Farmington Police Chief Steve Hebbe said he believes Dotson aimed his weapon at police, but he wants there and in the video, the attorneys representing Dotson's family are disputing claims made by the Farmington Police Department, such as whether Dotson had pointed a gun at officers.

"FPD released a ridiculously false narrative intended and designed to shift focus away from the murderous actions of the officers and to blame Robbie," attorneys Mark Reichel and Shon Northam said in a written statement. "The FPD's false narrative easily is debunked and disproved simply by reviewing the body camera footage and Ring camera footage."

The police bodycam footage shows an officer walking away from the front porch when Dotson, armed with a gun, opens the door.

"There is no announcement of 'POLICE' despite more than ample time. And that is crucial," his family's attorneys said in the statement. "Wrong address. Late at night. The Dotson's never called the police."

According to Dotson's family attorneys, a "freeze frame of the tape shows Robbie holding the gun, and not pointing it at the officers. Rather, the gun is pointed down at the ground."

This world in which we live is at the pinnacle of sin and wickedness. There is a small fraction of men who control the narrative of thought and action. Anyone who dares to speak out as I do will be wisely dealt with. Rather that means finding something to ruin your reputation or just create it. This is the same plan that the new Pharaoh had for the children of Israelites in old Egypt. So, it is in this modern Egypt and Sodom.

"WHY AM I HERE?" THE VOLUNTARY TORTURE CALLED LIFE

Exodus 1: 8]" Now there arose up a new king over Egypt, which knew not Joseph. [9] And he said unto his people, Behold, the people of the children of Israel are more and mightier than we:
[10] Come on, let us deal wisely with them; lest they multiply, and it comes to pass, that, when there falleth out any war, they join also unto our enemies and fight against us, and so get them up out of the land. [11] Therefore they did set over them taskmasters to afflict them with their burdens. And they built for Pharaoh treasure cities, Pithom and Raamses.

[12] But the more they afflicted them, the more they multiplied and grew. And they were grieved because of the children of Israel.
[13] And the Egyptians made the children of Israel to serve with rigour:
[14] And they made their lives bitter with hard bondage, in mortar, and in brick, and in all manner of service in the field: all their service, wherein they made them serve, was with rigour.
[15] And the king of Egypt spake to the Hebrew midwives, of which the name of the one was Shiphrah, and the name of the other Puah:
[16] And he said, When ye do the office of a midwife to the Hebrew women and see them upon the stools; if it be a son, then ye shall kill him: but if it be a daughter, then she shall live.
[17] But the midwives feared God and did not as the king of Egypt commanded them but saved the men children alive.
[18] And the king of Egypt called for the midwives, and said unto them, Why have ye done this thing, and have saved the men children alive?
[19] And the midwives said unto Pharaoh, Because the Hebrew women are not as the Egyptian women; for they are lively and are delivered ere the midwives come in unto them.
[20] Therefore God dealt well with the midwives: and the people multiplied and waxed very mighty.
[21] And it came to pass, because the midwives feared God, that he made them houses."

In order for our women to be strong as were our foremothers and resist the orders of the wicked rulers they must emulate modesty. As it stands currently you are being used as a midwife to destroy your son, and husband with a restraining order, false rape allegation, child custody, and child support, and pharaoh has you parading in public and social media and whore under the proclamation of liberation. Ladies you must wake up and repent or you will regret this when Yahusha judges this earth.

I am sent as a messenger to give you this warning from Yahuah. That is my purpose for being born into this world. Arise and shine because your light has arrived.

Get your Mind Right King/Queen!
Bible Verse: Jeremiah 17: 9 The heart is deceitful above all things, and desperately wicked: who can know it?
Most of the people who would give you advice will tell you to always follow your heart. I contend that this is the most inaccurate advice
one could ever give. Following your heart (mind) can result in quitting during a challenge. If you want to be successful, if you want
to be blessed and unstoppable, it is imperative that you put your trust in the Yahuah wa Yahusha (God and Christ). Once again, everything that I say is rooted in the one of Yahuah.

The book of Proverbs chapter 3 verse five says "Trust in the Lord with all thine heart and lean not unto thine own understanding". This overlays what the Scripture Jeremiah 17 verse 9," he heart is deceitful above all things". The heart spoken of here is not the muscle that is within one's chest, but rather the core of one's thinking and is the brain.
Your brain is a central processing unit akin to a computer. Without that central processing unit, the computer cannot think, nor can it conduct its actions. It requires the brain to call the will of the other units of your body into order.

"WHY AM I HERE?" THE VOLUNTARY TORTURE CALLED LIFE

If your brain is deficient it can be a hindrance or a hold to performance. One cannot anticipate being great if easy and handouts are what they hope for. You must have sound thoughts, a sound mind, and an insatiable will to succeed. One must be driven, and to do so is essential that you exercise the muscles of the brain daily. Just as one goes to the gym, and you push the biceps, the triceps, and the chest muscles beyond the limitations; you must push your brain behind what you anticipate being average, into being exceptional. Remember whatever you think in your mind, this is what you will begin to live out. Because it is our thoughts that is deep within our subconscious that we consciously respond to. You must repeat to yourself daily I can, I will, I must be blessed successful, and unstoppable.

Many of you may have been baffled by that last paragraph because, at the inception of this chapter, we started it by stating that the
heart is deceitful of things. We further explain that the heart spoken here is the brain. So, we first must place our trust in the highest, to direct our thinking in a positive direction to bring forth positive outcomes and results.

What I am suggesting to you is you do not follow your understanding until you have first talked to the Lord in prayer. Do not follow your heart, do not listen to the average people who suggest that you follow your heart. Again, Jeremiah chapter 17 verse nine says the heart is deceitful above all things, and desperately wicked, who can know it? So, you may think that you have an answer, but we should always take our desires first to the Lord in prayer and pray that he gives us the correct answer. Wait for, listen for, he will respond if you are not sinning
.
Daily Affirmation: I like to see any challenge or any possibility of defeat as a temporary barrier that I overcome.
Each minute each second, I shall with supreme divine revelation.

"WHY AM I HERE?" THE VOLUNTARY TORTURE CALLED LIFE

Second by second minute by minute, I will carve my mind into the portion that the creator has destined me to be.

Self–Assessment Question:
In which areas of my life do I most need improvement?
What are my weaknesses that I need more training to strengthen these weaknesses?
What is your mind concerned with that is hindering you from accomplishing success?
Do I currently have the paradigm that it requires to be blessed unstoppable, and successful?
How do those people who are successful respond to a fall or a loss?
Do I overcome struggle with determination or shut down when I am challenged or things do not go my way?
In what ways can I enhance my talents and in what ways can I expand my goals?
What can I do today within this moment that will improve my life?

Today's prayer: I pray to you today Yahuah, for improvement in my mindset. Dear father, please help me overcome the obstacles, setbacks, and losses and see them as a learning process. Lord I submit all my beliefs to you, please assist me in mentally framing each of my experiences properly and constructively for mountain improvements in Yahusha's name I pray amen.

Success Quotes:
"I hated every minute of training, but I said do not quit. Suffer now and live the rest of your life as a champion." Mohammad Ali

"The last three or four reps is what makes the muscle growth. This area of pain drives me to champion someone else who is not a champion. That is what most people live, having the guts to go on and just saying they will go through the pain no matter what happens." Arnold Schwarzenegger

"WHY AM I HERE?" THE VOLUNTARY TORTURE CALLED LIFE

"Life is not about how hard of a hit we can give it's about how many you can take and keep moving forward." Sylvester Stallone

Too many people are falsely proclaiming to possess a warrior mindset but when faced and confronted with a challenge that they consider to be unbearable they tap out to the challenge.
 An obstacle is merely just a challenge however it becomes a barrier once you bow to it. You tap out because of doubt and fear. I see every challenge and barrier as an opportunity to evaluate my determination. I will overcome any challenge or barrier that faces me with my warrior mentality within. By Tazadaq Shah

Action Steps:
To truly conduct the most high's plan for your life you must be Deprogram and reprogram your mind. Most people in the world today, about 99% of the population suffer from cognitive dissonance. To break this mental programming that has been imposed upon you by the global elite, you must be Deprogrammed. Henceforth listen to positive motivational videos, listen to self-help audio, and read the Bible daily. The objective here is to pour so much positivity into your mind that there is no room for anything else.
Inspiration for Victory: Yahuah, who is the mightiest of all, challenges you to trust him with all your dreams and goals. Trust in the
Lord.

Prosperity and Success are on the opposite side of difficulty and struggle., go get it!

1 Kings 2:3 – "And keep the charge of the LORD thy God, to walk in his ways, to keep his statutes and his commandments, and his judgments, and his testimonies, as it is written in the law of Moses, that thou mayest prosper in all that thou doest, and whithersoever thou turnest thyself".

"WHY AM I HERE?" THE VOLUNTARY TORTURE CALLED LIFE

Faith is the four winds that blow the oxygen of life into your lungs for you to be the artist. But with the paintbrush of your mind, you can decide to paint success, or you could paint failure. If you go the way alone, you will see your footprints in the sand, and when you fall, no one will be there to pick you back up, or to assist you in getting back on. But if you traveled this course with Yahusha when you see one set of footprints in the sand, it is not that you are walking alone, it is when Yahuah was carrying you through these challenging times.

But we must first show him that we believe in him and that we obey him. We do this by keeping his laws statutes and commandments and walking how he had ordered us to. Thus, if you want to be successful, if you want to be blessed and unstoppable, keep his laws statutes, and commandments as written in the words of Moses, so that you may have prosperity and all the things that you do.

This is Yahuah's promise to us. The one limitation that Yahuah has it he cannot break his promise. The father chastised those whom he loves and if you have not found chastisement you are bastards and not sons, Hebrews 12:6.
 Do not ever assume that you are going to walk with Yahuah and you do not undergo struggle, difficulties, and pain. You will not be able to properly walk with Yahuah if you attempt to follow him emotionally. You must have a modicum of rules that will prevent you from aborting the path that leads you to success. Yahuah is the greatest, he has no equal. There is no power equal to him. He is omnipotent. The wisdom of this world is in aporia compared to the knowledge of Yahuah.
The naysayers, and your envious family members, may construct a diatribe of attacks to deter you, but do not yield to these negative people. Their lives are desultory, whereas the creator has a perfect plan for you to be successful. However, the greatest enemy
that you will face is your Satan of self, which will attempt to prevent you from pushing yourself beyond what you have been

"WHY AM I HERE?" THE VOLUNTARY TORTURE CALLED LIFE

taught to
believe is a limitation.

You were created in the image and likeness of Yahuah, stop limiting Yahuah. Yahuah is limitless, and you being created in his image and likeness should be limitless as well. Take the limitations off Yahuah. In the book of Psalms chapter 82 verse 6, I have said you are God's and all of you for the children of the highest. If the highest God is my father, and I am his son, then I am a son of God and a God. Stop placing limitations on God.

You must believe, to call it into existence. Doubt is the enemy of success; self-loathing is a dire illness that cripples you from greatness. Excuses are crutches that prevent you from obtaining your goals and dreams. You must run to the challenge and, leap over
the hurdle of hinderance into success. To effectively do so you must have the mind of a champion. A true champion is driven by a warrior's mentality. Success is not going to reach you; you must strive for success. It is a lonely road, a more challenging journey, yet a much more rewarding one. Anyone who is truly in favor of you being successful and great will support you on your mission to greatness. Those that attempt to talk you out of greatness, envy you and secretly yearn to see you fall as they have fallen.

Do not allow the naysayers or the negative people to define you. You must extirpate all negative people and thoughts out of your life! Do it now. Dethatch your emotions and make a rational decision to eliminate all people and things that hurt your life. Such people will drain you mentally and spiritually and thereby destroy what Yahuah has planned for you to be.

They are not a part of what Yahuah has planned for you. They are just a small section of your life, but that chapter is over, and you must move forward to new heights. They are not on your level of vibration. Will you sacrifice your goals and dreams for someone who does not genuinely care for you even though they claim to? Or will you align yourself with Yahuah's divine will and eliminate these unclean spirits that dwell in those people around you?

Your time is now, you will not have a second opportunity. All things are relevant to the time. This is your time. Do it now.

Daily Affirmation: You need to place yourself within a mental state where you can visualize where you want to be five years from now, one year from now, one month, and one minute from now, do it now. You must rapidly develop a sense of urgency for success, you must sweat the perspiration of victory. Success will not come to those sitting around on a sofa dreaming about success. Success comes to those who have the willpower to push beyond their perceived limitations.

Self-Awareness Questions:
Am I allowing outside forces and resources to distract me from accomplishing my mission?
Am I still talking about what I am going to accomplish, or am I speaking my thoughts into existence and making it my reality right now?
Have I done the necessary things to align me with the path that the highest has created for me to follow?

Are you working on a job that you hate going into, but you do it because you need the money for survival, and you fear without that
joy you will be able to make it?
Are you still in a relationship that is causing you a deluge of stress, and worrying, and making you mentally and physically sick?
Why am I still holding on to things and people that are not beneficial to me in accomplishing my goals and what my creator has planned for me?
What is more imperative, is it for me to remain in a relationship with someone that is keeping me on a lower level of vibration; or

"WHY AM I HERE?" THE VOLUNTARY TORTURE CALLED LIFE

to detach that negative person and those negative emotions and accomplish my dreams and goals?

Today's Prayer:
Dear Father Yahuah please keep me focused on the things that I need to be focused upon that will keep me on the straight and narrow path. Please do not let me fall into temptation, and lust. Please instill the mindset in me to have a positive mental attitude to persevere during times of difficulty and struggle when I feel as if I am about to give up. Give me the strength to push forward and keep a positive mental attitude, give me that faith that with Yahuah all things are possible. In Yahusha's name, I pray for amen.

Successful Quotes:
I contend that is the weak that are cruel kindness and gentleness can only be anticipated from the strong.
We all need a target, if there is no target then you have no goal to aim at. If you have no target or any goal then you have no focus. Where there is no focus there are no goals, there are no dreams, and there is no reason for why. What is your why, or reason for being born? Why am I here? Unless you know this, you will always be just average and should never expect to be great.

There is a land of the living and there is a land of the dead. The bridge to cross this great gulf is love. Love me fully or leave me alone fully I am still becoming me, therefore accept me as I embark on this journey, or leave me alone because both Yahuah and Satan are not done with me yet.

We awake and peer into the mirror of our mind's reflection, and witness that there is a war that is going on between the person who we are striving to become and the person that society attempts to program us to be. Some of us give in to the pressures of society and consider that is what is known as adjustment. But there is a selected few, there is 1%, that says I will not be another clone. I will not surrender to the pressures of society. I am becoming, and I will continue to develop into me.

Action Step: from today you're going to commit to being a better you than you were yesterday if you have done 10 repetitions in the gym manage 12 today; if you devoted 30 minutes to reading yesterday to develop your skills, be devoted to 35 today. Your goal from this point forward is to be a better you.

Inspiration for Victory:
If you want to be successful you must find the passion and chase your passion, do not chase money, money will not bring true happiness. When you are doing your passion, it is no longer a job is enjoyment. follow your passion and not a lust for money. Turn off the television, pick up a book, practice, and put in the work towards accomplishing your goals.

"WHY AM I HERE?" THE VOLUNTARY TORTURE CALLED LIFE

It's Grind Season, allow your Grind to Speak for You

Your thought ignites your mind to create dreams, but for this to become your reality it must be constantly nurtured with sweat, blood, and tears. Greatness success and victory come directly off the assembly line of hard work, consistency, and a driven work ethic.

Average or mediocre effort should not be an option for one who wants to live at their highest capacity. Warriors, champions, and winners do not take days off. The competition is so vast that taking a day off may determine either victory or loss. Those with a warrior mentality must go all out every day, or they are never going to be great or successful. To be driven, with consistency and hard work is the membership fee that filters out the weak, feeble, from the strong and driven. The respect and credibility required for the warrior's mindset and high achievers is so costly that only those rich in the wealth called struggle can afford it.

Champions only have one goal they aspire to be great at. They chisel with the hammer and not excuses. They continue with maximum effort until success becomes their reality.
This type of relentless pressure allows those with the warrior's mindset to overcome any talent deficiencies that they may have once possessed. If you want to be a legend, you must refuse to give anything less than 100% because that is the only level of effort the legends know.

Average, and mediocrity are words in a foreign unspoken language that the warrior mindset and champions do not understand. Good is undesirable because they recognize the greatness of the creator. Take the limitations off Yahuah, you are made in Yahuah's image and likeness, and Yahuah breathed the breath of life into you man, and you became a living soul. Therefore, Yahuah is in you. When you place limitations on yourself you place limitations in Yahuah. Those
with a warrior's mindset hold themselves to higher standards, because of the mere fact that they are not just doing it for themselves, they are doing it for the glory and honor of the Yahuah.

Your why, blended with your passion in years of perspiration grants worldwide success. Hustle and grind are universal words respected in every culture in the world.
The work ethic of one with the warrior's mindset and champions will carry them places where 99% of the remainder of the world

"WHY AM I HERE?" THE VOLUNTARY TORTURE CALLED LIFE

will never go or see.

You must discover the most essential factors that determine success in whichever field of endeavor you are in and then put all your time, energy, and devotion into it. We must grind all day doing the right things because grinding all day doing the wrong things
will not only get you nowhere but you will end up a failure. You must be driven to outwork the competition in the areas that decide
who will be the winner. Put 100% towards the things that matter and stay focused.

Most people can give their best for three or four days and perhaps even a week or maybe even a month. But very few can sustain it for a year two years, three years, five years, or a decade. The things worth achieving do not arrive overnight, it takes years of dedication in preparation to bring a dream into reality. A victorious business plan is not constructed around wishing, hoping, or Sherlock. It is constructed on a
silent structure of discipline, commitment, and hard labor.
The one in the arena with his hands held high, this victory belongs to the one who purchased it and sweat.

What you accomplish in life will be equivalent to some level of the effort you exert. No dream, goal, or ambition can deny the person who masters the art of being driven. Success does not have to be complex, just decide what you want and then grind at the level that is required to get it.

Positive affirmation: My grind and driven work ethic becomes my weapon. From today forward no one in my field will ever outwork me again! My dedication, consistency, hard work, and sweat will water my dreams. I will give 100% day in and day out for as long as it takes to accomplish my goals.

Self-assessment questions: How can I increase my work ethic to a level that will ensure success?
How many hours do I need to grind each day to achieve greatness?
Am I willing to pay the price for the things I want in life?
Am I willing to keep up the intensity day in and day out needed to be successful?

Today's prayer: I pray today that Yahuah will instill in me the work ethic required to be successful in life. Provoke me to be driven, and increase my endurance, stamina, and energy so that I can allocate my all to accomplishing the goals and dreams that you put inside me. In Yahushua's name I pray amen

Successful quotes: If people knew how hard I had to work to gain my mastery, it would not seem so wonderful. Michelangelo

If you want to become great. You must pay the price, the price the average is unwilling to pay. Eric Thomas,
I viewed myself as slightly above average in talent. And where I excel is my ridiculous, sickening work ethic. Will Smith

People do not understand that when I grew up, I was never the most talented. I was never the biggest, I was never the fastest. I certainly was never the strongest. The only thing I had was my work ethic, and that is then would have gotten me this far. Tiger Woods

The action steps:
Decide if your dream is worth the time, energy, and effort required to make it a reality. If it is to commit yourself
right now, to get 100% effort every single day from here forward to make it happen. Set the tone for the day by establishing a morning routine of power and purpose. Take ownership of the day by getting into motion. Stay healthy and exercise regularly. Remove and eliminate all distractions from your life and negative people. Figure out the amount of time required each day to

accomplish your goals. Every time someone doubts or debtors criticize you, respond by increasing the number of hours you are putting in towards your dream. Use their negative energy as fuel to grind harder. Stop making excuses, and just do what it takes to get the things you want in life.

Inspirational for victory: the most highs blessing you with power and energy and an incredible work ethic that will make you a thousand times greater.

Explaining Constitutional Torts

Tort

A tort is a civil wrong that causes a claimant to suffer loss or harm, resulting in legal liability for the person who commits the tortious act. Tort law can be contrasted with criminal law, which deals with criminal wrongs that are punishable by the state

A. Definition: Actions brought against governments and their officials and employees seeking damages for the violation of federal constitutional rights, particularly those arising under the 14th Amendment and the Bill of Rights. Note: the only people who can violate your constitutional rights are government employers. The Constitution only limits governmental power, not individuals (the exception is the 13th Amendment prohibiting slavery). Bill of Rights does not apply to the states directly; one must look to the 14th amendment (1st, 4th, 5th, 6th, and 8th) for incorporation. Con torts share main policy goals with/ traditional torts: deterrence and compensation.

B. 42 U.S.C. 1983: "Every person who, under color of any statute, ordinance, regulation, custom, or usage, of any State or Territory or the District of Columbia, subjects, or causes to be subjected, any citizen of the United States or other person within the jurisdiction thereof to the deprivation of any rights, privileges, or immunities secured by the Constitution and laws, shall be liable to the party injured in any action brought against a judicial officer for an act or omission taken in such officer's judicial capacity, injunctive relief shall not be granted unless a declaratory decree was violated or declaratory relief was unavailable. For this section, any Act of Congress applicable exclusively to the District of Columbia shall be a statute of the District of Columbia."

C. 28 U.S.C. 1343(3): (a) The district courts shall have original ax of any civil action authorized by law to be commenced by any person; (3) To redress the deprivation, under color of any State law, statute, or ordinance, regulation, custom or usage, of any right, privilege or immunity, secured by the Constitution of the United States or by any. Act of Congress providing for equal rights of citizens or all persons within the jurisdiction of the United States. (b) For purposes of this section: (1) the District of Columbia shall be a State and (2) any Act of Congress applicable exclusively to the District of   Columbia shall be a statute of the District of   Columbia.

D. Purposes of Section 1983:

1. Supreme Court: Section 1983 opened the federal courts to private citizens, offering a uniquely federal remedy against incursions under the claimed authority of state law upon rights secured by the Constitution and laws of the Nation

2. To interpose the federal courts b/w the states and the people, as guardians of the people's federal rights—to protect the people from unconstitutional action under color of state law, "whether that action be executive, legislative, or judicial".   (Mitcham v. Foster)

3. The Court indicated that section 1983 was designed both to prevent the states from violating the 14th Amendment and   certain federal statutes and to compensate injured plaintiffs for deprivations of their federal rights (Carey v. Piphus)

E. Monroe v. Pape (1961) Established that state officials who abused their positions still acted under the color of law. Do not need to show that there was authority under state law, custom, or usage. Instead, misuse   of power possessed by state law and

"WHY AM I HERE?" THE VOLUNTARY TORTURE CALLED LIFE

only because the individual is clothed with power because of state law means under color of state law

1. 1983 should be read against the backdrop of tort law but there is no intent requirement for 1983 actions
2. Municipalities are not "persons' under 1983—only individuals. Note: this is not altogether still good law. F. Constitutional Torts and Exhaustion of Judicial Remedies
1. Monroe: makes clear that a section 1983 COA for damages need not exhaust or pursue state judicial remedies before filing in a federal forum.
2. Habeas Corpus: Prisoners, like other 1983 plaintiffs, need not exhaust state judicial remedies

a.: A prisoner's 1983 challenge to the fact or duration of his or her confinement is in substance a petition for habeas corpus and must be treated as such by federal courts. Because the federal habeas corpus statute requires the exhaustion of state remedies, the effect would be the dismissal of the claim in federal court. (Presser v. Rodriguez)

b. To recover damages for unconstitutional conviction or imprisonment, or for other harm caused by actions whose unlawfulness would render a conviction or sentence invalid, a 1983 plaintiff must prove that the conviction/sentence has been reversed on direct appeal, expunged by executive order, declared invalid by a state tribunal authorized to make such a determination, or called into question by a federal court's issuance of a writ of

habeas corpus. (Heck v. Humphrey) Due Process: in certain cases, a decision adverse to a plaintiff's DP challenge amounts to a de facto requirement that state judicial remedies be exclusively pursued.

a. A 1983 claim based on DP was not stated where P sought relief from being listed as an active shoplifter by police authorities. The court held that no liberty or property interest was implicated; the plaintiff's sole remedy was an action for defamation in state courts. The court did indicate that an official might be liable for

consequences of defamatory stats if P could demonstrate that he had suffered stigma plus an infringement of some other interest. A P must also show a distinct alteration or extinction of a previously recognized right or status (Paul v. Davis)
b. Procedural DP is not violated when school authorities impose corporal punishment on students b/c students against whom excessive force was used would have a tort COA in the state courts. (Ingraham v. Wright)

c. In certain circumstances, intentional deprivations of property do not violate procedural DP where adequate post-deprivations of remedies are available. (Hudson v. Palmer)
4. Prospective Relief and the Younger Rule a. When state criminal judicial proceedings are already pending, a federal P seeking declaratory or injunctive relief against their continuation will typically be barred from the federal forum. (Younger v. Harris)
b. Younger rule has been expanded to include suitable relief against state judicial proceedings b/w private litigants where important state interests are implicated (Pennzoil Co. Texaco, Inc.) as well as pending state administrative proceedings where important state interests are involved and there is a full and fair opportunity to litigate any constitutional claims upon state judicial review of that proceeding. (Ohio Civil Rights Commission v. Dayton Christian Schools)

G. Constitutional Torts and Exhaustion of Administrative Remedies
1. State administrative remedies, like judicial remedies, need not be exhausted before maintaining a 1983 action in federal court. (McNeese v. Board of Education)
2. The Supreme Court, in 1982, definitively ruled that exhaustion of administrative remedies is not a condition precedent to filing a section 1983 action. (Patsy v. Florida Board of Regents)3. State Prisoners and Exhaustion of Administrative Remedies a. Prisoner's 1983 claims are sometimes treated as federal habeas corpus claims and therefore become subject to exhaustion of state remedy requirement b. Prisoner's 1983 claim attacking prison

conditions and events unrelated to the fact and duration of confinement is not subject to exhaustion of administrative remedies requirement c. Civil Rights of Institutionalized Persons Act (42 USC 1997(e)): Congress legislated an exhaustion of administrative remedies requirement in certain circumstances for persons institutionalized in state or local government correctional facilities.

Secure a Bank Account from Liens and Levy 1

If you allegedly owe an outstanding debt and you are concerned about your wages being garnished, then this section of the book will pay for it 20 times over. A friend Seflon just had a lien placed on his account and child support service overdrew the account. One might ask can they do that? The question is, is it lawful? The issue with too many people is we allow the system to violate our rights and we run and crawl under a rock. In this section, this is how I protect TAZADAQ'S accounts from lien and levies.

The primary objective in securing a bank account from the levy is to obtain the bank's agreement that you, the flesh-and-blood man/woman, are the authorized representative of the account holder, the artificial person TRADE NAME. This reality is spelled out in your security agreement and is echoed in the UCC Financing Statement filed with the secretary of state—but you must also obtain the bank's acknowledgment of this fact. Once documented on the bank signature card as an authorized representative of the account control of the collateral (the funds in the account) is established, thus perfecting your security interest in the account. At that point, your other relationship with the account holder/debtor, i.e., that of the secured party, can be impressed upon bank personnel—and such are obligated to honor the perfected security interest—thus securing account funds from third-party levy.

Pertinent Sections of the Uniform Commercial Code
Here are the sections of the Uniform Commercial Code governing such matters:
§ 9-314. Perfection by Control. (a) Perfection by control. A security interest in…deposit accounts…may be perfected by control of the collateral under Section 9-104…"
§ 9-104. Control of Deposit Account. (a) Requirements for control. A secured party has control of a deposit account if: … (2) the debtor, secured party, and bank have agreed in an authenticated record that the bank will comply with instructions originated by the secured party directing the disposition of the funds in the deposit account without further consent by the debtor…"

The signature card (property of the bank), signed by both account holder (debtor) and authorized representative (secured party), constitutes an agreed-upon, authenticated record "that the bank will comply with instructions originated by the secured party [authorized representative] directing disposition of the funds in the deposit account without further consent by the debtor [account holder]."

Properly Signing the Signature Card

With one exception, the bank signature card should be signed exactly as shown in "How to Sign Your Signature Without Liability" on page 315 of Cracking the Code Third Edition©, "CTC3," with the signature of both the debtor and secured party appearing. Signing in this manner differentiates between the contracting parties, i.e.

True Name and TRADE NAME, corresponds with the documentation you provide and satisfies the requirement of UCC 9-104(a)(2). Select from the sample signatures appearing on page 319 of CTC3 that contain both the debtor's and secured party's signature, but do not place a copyright symbol, i.e., "©," after either of the two names. The copyright symbol, and likewise the copyright notice, is not used here. It is more important to establish the account and be acknowledged as the authorized representative than it is to assert the copyright—which can always be called into play later if necessary, but this is not likely.

1 Levy: n. A seizure. v. To raise; execute; exact; collect; gather; accept; seize. Thus, to levy (raise or collect) a tax.

Secure a Bank Account from Levy 2

For an existing account, a request to examine the signature card for the account will usually be granted, but bank personnel may not be too delighted with your new self-proclaimed status as an authorized representative/agent and the accompanying artwork you render on the card to prove your point. If you can modify the signature card on your account without causing any friction, do so. However, if this is not feasible, the easiest thing to do is simply to close the account and open another. Opening a new bank account is a simple matter, and there is nothing wrong with using the same bank if no undue antagonism is generated in the process. The most hygienic method, however, is to open your new account with another bank and start afresh.

Properly Documenting Your Position

At the time you sign the bank signature card, you should have with you a certified copy of both your UCC Financing Statement and the security agreement referenced within the text of the collateral description of the financing statement (use the "Copy Certification by Document Custodian" form to make a certified copy of the security agreement). These certified copies are to be left with the bank after the signature card is completed.

Upon signing the signature card, inform the bank personnel assisting you that the account holder is also your debtor and that you are the secured party, and then produce the certified copy of your financing statement and security agreement. The identifying number of the security agreement appearing within the collateral-description box (Box 4 on a UCC Financing Statement; Box 8 on a UCC Financing Statement AMENDMENT in the case of a cross-filing MIGHT BE DIFFERENT IN YOUR STATE OR ON UPDATED

FORMS) of the financing statement and the section entitled "Authorized Representative" on page 7 of the security agreement (page 247 of CTC3) should be highlighted for ease of inspection. Bank personnel are only too familiar with such kinds of documents, so there should be no difficulty in understanding what you are presenting. If bank personnel can see that you know what you are doing, there will be no problem.

Guaranteeing Your Success

It is vital that you thoroughly understand that you are not the account holder—and can never be the account holder. The name of all account holders appears in all capital letters in all bank records and documents. All account holders are artificial persons, e.g., your TRADE NAME. This policy is purely of the bank's choosing; all you are doing is respecting the bank's selection/designation of the account holder.

If bank personnel balk at all, have the girl/guy pull out a sample personal check from her/his drawer and point out the name of the account holder printed on the check. The name is set in capital letters. If the secretary of state recognizes the distinction between the two names on your financing statement, it is reasonable to expect that the "New Accounts" officer will too.

In the event there is further resistance, have her/him examine what appears to be the signature line on the sample personal check using the magnifying glass that you produce (bring one with you, if possible). Even though the check is a personal check, and therefore theoretically would have only one signatory, said "line" is for any authorized signatory of the account holder—i.e., an authorized representative—and you are such an authorized signatory/representative.

"WHY AM I HERE?" THE VOLUNTARY TORTURE CALLED LIFE

Secure a Bank Account from Levy 3 These facts should quell any doubts on the part of bank personnel. However, as always, the senior factor is your certainty of what you are doing. The Federal Reserve owns the U.S. Government, and covertly asserts ownership of all property in Banks (Fed instrumentalities) do business only with artificial persons whose names appear in all-capital letters; any party that "volunteers" to function as a surety and give anomalous endorsements and sign as an accommodation party 3 for the account holder, however, is never turned away. It is also wise to familiarize yourself with the section of the security agreement entitled "Event of Default," which can also be highlighted if desired.

This paragraph appears just below "Authorized Representative" at the bottom of page 7 of the security agreement. Any attempt by any third party to remove any of the debtor-account holder's funds (your secured collateral) constitutes an event of default on the part of the debtor and allows you to foreclose on the collateral, i.e., withdraw the funds if necessary. Because you provide the bank with certified documentary evidence of your secured-party status at the time the signature card is signed, no other party can have a prior security interest in those funds, and all bank personnel must acknowledge this fact and honor your perfected security interest or risk both civil and criminal charges.

As a final note on securing your position, a certified copy of your UCC Financing Statement and security agreement left with bank personnel could conceivably be misplaced/lost, although this is unlikely based on the potential liability attendant with such oversight. However, it is nevertheless a clever idea to send the manager of the bank an additional certified copy of both the financing statement and security agreement by Registered Mail (Restricted Delivery), with an Affidavit of Mailing. A cover letter confirming your perfected security interest in the collateral in the account and the bank's responsibility in protecting this secured collateral should also be enclosed. If you can prove that the manager received the above cover letter and the certified copies of the documents (evidence), the bank is liable for any pilferage of the account

2 Senate Document No. 43, 73rd Congress, 1st Session. (March 9 – June 16, 1933) "…The ownership of all property is in the State; individual so-called ownership is only by government, i.e., law amounting to mere user; and use must be by law and subordinate to the necessities of the State."

3 If these terms are not readily understood, it is vital that you re-read "How to Sign Your Signature Without Liability," beginning on page 315 of CTC3, and get them cleared up.

Open a bank account without having to provide an SSN

USING THE SUBSTITUTE FORM W-8 or FORM 1099 The form is filled out, signed, notarized, and filed with the County Recorder. It can then be used to open a bank account without having to provide an SSN. If the people in the bank say they absolutely must have a number, suggest that they use "999999999." CONSTRUCTIVE NOTICE To:

____   (Person being served)   Of:

____ (Name and address of Institution) You are being made aware by this Constructive Notice that it is a violation of Federal Law to refuse to: (a) Open a non-interest-bearing bank account if the party wanting to open the account does not provide a social security account number or a taxpayer identification number; or (b) To provide your services to a client or potential client because the client or potential client does not provide a social security account number or a taxpayer identification number. You personally, and the Institution you represent, may be liable for damages and attorney's fees. By Section 1 of Pub. L. 93-579, also known as the "Privacy Act of 1974," and Title 5 of the United States Code Annotated 552 (a), also known as the "Privacy Act," you are being informed of the following:

"The right to privacy is a personal and fundamental right protected by the Constitution of the United States. You may maintain in your records only such information about an individual as is relevant and necessary to accomplish a purpose required by statute or by executive order of the President of the United States."

Section 7 of the Privacy Act of 1974 specifically provides that it shall be unlawful for any Federal State or local government agency to deny to any individual any right, benefit, or privilege provided by law because such individual refuses to disclose his social security account number.

"Right of privacy is a personal right designed to protect persons from unwanted disclosure of personal information..." CNA Financial Corp. v. Local 743 515 F. Supp. 942. "In enacting Section 7 (Privacy Act of 1974), Congress sought to curtail the expanding use of social security numbers by federal and local agencies and, by so doing, to eliminate the threat to individual privacy and confidentiality of information posed by common numerical identifiers." Doyle v. Wilson; 529 F. Supp. 1343. "It shall be unlawful for any Federal, State or local government agency to deny to any individual any right, benefit, or privilege provided by law because such individual refuses to disclose his social security number."

Doyle v. Wilson; 529 F. Supp. 1343. An "agency is a relation created by express or implied contract or by law, whereby one party delegates the transaction of some lawful business with a more or less discretionary power to another." State Ex-Real. Cities Service Gas v. Public Service Commission; 85 S W. 2d 890. If the Institution you represent is a Bank, you are advised that if such Bank routinely collects information and provides such information to Federal, State, or local government agencies, then such Bank is an agency of government. The 1976 amendment to the Social Security Act, codified at 42 U.S.C.A., Sec 301 et seq., 405(c)(2) (i, iii), states that there are only four instances where social security account numbers may be demanded.

These are: 1. For tax matters; 2. To receive public assistance; 3. To obtain and use a driver's license; 4. To register a motor vehicle. You are advised that a non-interest-bearing account does not pertain to any of the above. Because the account pays no interest, there is no "need-to-know" on the part of the government. In accordance with the Privacy Act of 1974, whenever an agency fails to comply with the law, the party wronged may bring a civil action in the district court of the United States against such agency.

Should the court determine that the agency acted in a manner that was intentional or willful, the agency shall be liable to the wronged party in an amount equal to the sum of: 1. Actual damages sustained, but in no case less than $1,000; and 2. The costs of the action together with reasonable attorney's fees. Constructive Notice issued by:
_____
Representing:
_____
_____   Witness:
_____   Date:
_____

Revocation/ Withdrawal From Social Security/ Social Insurance Numbers and I.R.S. jurisdiction
If you do not have an SSN there is no obligation to pay income

taxes. With this in mind if there is a way to a revocation of SSN which is a withdrawal then we can be free. The Social Security number is an important weapon in the hands of territorial gangsters (people who use deception, fraud, coercion, and terror to claim "jurisdiction" (so-called) over people who happen to be in a certain geographic territory). Territorial gangsters (TGs) love to create systems that enable them to dominate and control their victims so they can live off the fruit of their labor like parasites or cannibals. They use the Social Security number to keep track of their victims. Other agencies, such as Credit Bureaus and Banks, also use the Social Security number (SS#) to identify people. Watch this series of videos then judge for yourself.

AFFIDAVIT

RESCISSION OF SIGNATURE SOCIAL SECURITY

COMES NOW John-Q; Public, the affiant, who is of lawful age and sound mind, who is a competent witness and is telling the truth, voluntarily relating the following firsthand knowledge of the facts, and stating that these facts are true and represent the best of my knowledge.

I hereby revoke my signature, for good cause, off of the "Form SS-5, Application for a Social Security Card," which was signed in the year of our Lord nineteen hundred eighty-one when I applied for benefits provided by the Social Security Administration located at 1800 Chicago Ave s Minneapolis, Minnesota [and off of the Form SS-5, Application for a Social Security Card signed in the year of our Lord nineteen hundred ninety-seven in Orlando, Florida or any other replacement card FormSS-5, Applications.Because the application for a replacement card depends on the validity of the first application and was signed under mistake and economic duress, the application for a replacement card/cards is also null and void.]

"WHY AM I HERE?" THE VOLUNTARY TORTURE CALLED LIFE

The original "Form SS-5" contract/ instrument was entered into when I was fifteen years of age, which means the contract/instrument is null and void by Minnesota statute 502.66 which says, any donee, **except a "MINOR"** who would be capable of conveying the property covered by the power may exercise a power of appointment.

Because a contract/instrument is only valid if entered into knowingly and voluntarily, all contracts/instruments are null and void because of coercion through misinformation, disinformation, misdirection, and threats of economic duress.

Because fraud vitiates contracts/instruments and even judgments, these contracts are null and void through various elements of fraud

This document is the preparation of the undersigned.

Before the Almighty God and under His statutes, I declare that the foregoing is the truth in accord with the best of my knowledge on this second day of September in the year of our Lord two thousand two.

_____

John-Q; Public, Sui Juris

ACKNOWLEDGMENT

Signed this day, _____, at _____, _____

_____
NOTARY PUBLIC
My commission expires on: _____

"WHY AM I HERE?" THE VOLUNTARY TORTURE CALLED LIFE

Legal Notice for Checking Account

TO

_____

_____

_____

REGARDING ACCOUNT

\# _____

LEGAL NOTICE: I, _____, a checking deposit account holder in
_____
(hereinafter "bank"), account # _____, hereby certify, warrant, and give Legal Notice to the bank that I was not, at any time, and by any legal or lawful process, made aware by bank, inasmuch as each alleged money instrument containing the words "Federal Reserve Note" thereon or any credit transaction which shall be consummated at any time with the Federal Reserve Bank represents and is a debt instrument, that any money deposited by me into said checking account was going to be used in such a way as to increase the national debt of the United States by ANY system, no matter what such a system might be called.

Whatever proposed method of calculations such system might have professed or claimed as its basis for being so justified, by which said national debt would ultimately come back to harm either me or anyone else that I might know or have caring or concern about or for, in violation of my rights against a conflict of interest being applied against me, accordingly.

Therefore, since the rights of any such decision to so establish any such checking account denied me the rights that I have in contract law and constitutional law since the making of a decision on any basis whatsoever would have been, was, and is, my right alone, no matter what the reason that I have or might have for so making any decision, constituting thereby a fraud, both a legal fraud as well as a constitutional fraud upon me.

Creating at the least the rights, on my part, of voiding of the fraudulent action taken against me by the bank, then I, as a checking account depositor in the bank, being such a checking account depositor since ___/___/___, and having therefore been a checking account depositor at any time when any such loan was made, hereby VOID the rights, if any, of bank to use or to have used any checking account deposits of mine to make ANY loan whatsoever.

ANY party in conjunction with the use of any so-called "fractional reserve banking system" or any "capital net worth" of the bank upon which any form of said "fractional reserve banking" might rely, even if as a zero percent ratio, whether or not proclaimed for such use by either any Federal Reserve Bank, the government of the United States, or its Congress and/or President and/or Supreme Court, MY checking account deposit(s).

In whatever form they may have been provided to the bank, for such use are declared, warranted, and given Legal Notice Nunc Pro Tunc (now as then) irrevocably and irreversibly to be, and are, permanently VOID ab initio ([from the beginning] of the opening of said account).

LEGAL NOTICE.   ALL PARTIES DEMANDED; MUST TAKE LEGAL NOTICE. The Federal Reserve Act, even if believed to be binding upon any government of or within the United States, was not and is not binding upon the rights of a private citizen. I, the undersigned, am a private citizen, being so established at not less than Article I, Section 2, Clause 1 and the Fifth, Ninth, Tenth, and Fourteenth Amendments of the Constitution.

"WHY AM I HERE?" THE VOLUNTARY TORTURE CALLED LIFE

Additionally, I have undeniable rights under Article I, Section 8, Clauses 5 and 1, laid procedurally in that order. ALL PARTIES who have been or may be recipients of any loan generated by the bank when utilizing any so-called fractional reserve banking system including any reliance upon the bank's capital net worth as a basis for utilizing a zero percent for said fractional reserve banking system purposes, whether or not supported by either the United States, any branches thereof.

Also by any Federal Reserve Bank itself, and whether or not in (or irrespective of any) pursuance to any Federal Reserve Act that might have been thought to pertain thereto, are PUT ON NOTICE by this action that NO part of any checking account deposit which was derived by use of any application for a checking deposit account that I have caused or allowed to come into existence in association with the said bank, may be used or relied upon for any fractional reserve system loan for any purpose whatsoever.

LEGAL NOTICE: Bank is given further Legal Notice that it may not – except bank by so doing shall give and gives forthwith its tacit and binding confession that its activities engaged in heretofore as it relates to these matters, conditions, and charges, forementioned, have been those exhibiting and executing utmost fraud of myself as a checking account depositor. This also includes other checking account depositors in the bank, as _any_ result of this Notice – in any manner reduce or terminate any interest paid in my checking account.

If any, nor may the bank close my checking account for the same reasons except that it by so doing gives its tacit consent by tacit confession that it be obligated to pay court costs, attorney fees, and treble damages or $10,000 in Civil Rights damages, whichever is the greater.

_____/_____/_____

_____ NOTARY PUBLIC

"WHY AM I HERE?" THE VOLUNTARY TORTURE CALLED LIFE

"WHY AM I HERE?" THE VOLUNTARY TORTURE CALLED LIFE

"WHY AM I HERE?" THE VOLUNTARY TORTURE CALLED LIFE

"WHY AM I HERE?" THE VOLUNTARY TORTURE CALLED LIFE

"WHY AM I HERE?" THE VOLUNTARY TORTURE CALLED LIFE

"WHY AM I HERE?" THE VOLUNTARY TORTURE CALLED LIFE

"WHY AM I HERE?" THE VOLUNTARY TORTURE CALLED LIFE

I have made myself completely vulnerable in this book to guide you into admitting your shortcomings and overcoming them with growth. You must start within this moment. Just talking and not doing it is nonproductive. This is an instructional manual to be read at least ten times. It has been stated that we only retain seven to ten percent of what we read. To retain it all we must read it at least ten times. If you have learning disabilities, which I do not agree with we all learn at different rates, then you must read it more.

No longer will you allow others to define you, nor will you give into the urge that we all have, which is to quit when things become difficult or uncomfortable.

Two days before the completion of this book I had to deal with the unexpected death of a close friend Barak Shar Qadar, and I had just gotten off the phone with him because he told us that he was going to the bank to converse with them because Child Support Services had overdrawn his account by Four thousand dollars. He only had nine hundred in the bank account. When he attempted to withdraw a few dollars to get something to eat and to go to work his account was frozen. He was facing an Incarceration hearing on May 15, 2023 which was less than eleven days away.

Add to this while he was fighting for fifty custody of his daughter the state of New York enforced an order to give him less time with his daughter. This had a tremendous impact on him emotionally and mentally.

On top of that earlier this week when his daughter was supposed to spend time with him she decided to stay with her stepdad because her mother Monique had been telling their daughter what a horrible father he is. This was a devastating lie. He was a great father and man. This is why I speak out as a spokesman 4 men and women who love them. This made it abundantly clear that the system does not care about men. This is not an isolated incident of a man taking his own life because of child support, custody orders that deprived them of their child, and a wicked woman working to destroy him resulting in him taking his own life. This is an epidemic. Are you set silently on your loved one or you could be next? Please join #maf # by emailing kahantazadaq7@gmail.com.

Once he got off the phone with us he felt that h we just couldn't take anymore. He went into his backyard, Slit his wrist, and started bleeding out. The neighbor discovered it and tried to stop him. He told the neighbor stand back or I will shoot you. He went into his car and shot himself in the head.. this was a man who was fighting for his daughter and loved her more than anything. The mother was moving to destroy him by trying to have him Incarcerated for only two thousand dollars owed on child support. This is Appalling. This is a perfect example of how children and the system can be used to bring a man to his knees. If you are a bitch you will get fucked each time.

I surmise he had reached the zenith of his tolerance. They drove him to snap. Now you have a daughter that may be scared for her life because of a wicked woman, a broken system that continues to divorce rape men and deprive them of an ability to live. They broke his will. Anyway, that is dealing with depression please get help do not take your own life it is no coming back from that. I have stared Men Against Feminism and Women Against Feminism #maf, #waf. Join today by emailing kahantazadaqy@gmail.com.

"WHY AM I HERE?" THE VOLUNTARY TORTURE CALLED LIFE

Barak Shar   April 1975 to May 4, 2023

I liked You before they licked me, so their likes are extra. I didn't need them to like me. No matter what they say of me or think of me because I know who I am.

Their likes are good but are not required. No one else can jump for me or experience my fall, and if I fall I must stand back up again and again. Those who say they are on your team; must examine how they contribute to your life. If it is not positive maybe you need new teammates.   Let me tell you like I told Barak Shar;

"WHY AM I HERE?" THE VOLUNTARY TORTURE CALLED LIFE

everything you need to get back up is on you already.

People want to say I am extremely gifted because this enables them to create excuses for their failures. The beauty in my success is I came to the bottom.

It is time to stop leasing your brilliance and own it. If you did not sign up for failure then make it work! Play the hand that you were dealt with, if it is what you like then play this game called life until you change it. Rise king, rise. You have to overcome, advance, not retreat push forward its Grind Season.

In times of peace prepare for war because peace does not last forever. The most difficult battle you will ever fight is your number one foe which is the Satan of self. Your inner me is your enemy.

If you do not overcome this Satan of self it could lead to suicidal thoughts.

Allow your Grind to Speak for You. But for this to become your reality it must be constantly nurtured with sweat, blood, and tears. Greatness success and victory come directly off the assembly line of hard work, consistency, and a driven work ethic.

Average or mediocre effort should not be an option for one who wants to live at their highest capacity. Warriors, champions, and winners do not take days off. The competition is so vast that taking a day off may determine either victory or loss. Those with a warrior mentality must go all out every day, or they are never going to be great or successful. To be driven, with consistency and hard work is the membership fee that filters out the weak, from the strong and driven. The respect and credibility required for the warrior's mindset are high achievers, it is so costly that only those rich in the wealth called struggle can afford it. Do you want it bad enough? If so go and get it!

Jason one Wes in Texas," I stand by my brother I love my brother I wish my brother would have called me, I wish I would have called my brother. I will never stop this journey for our seeds □. May the most hi bless his family and bless us all."

"Barak Shar was a genuine brother who embraced me from the start, and I will never forget that he will truly be missed, Shalom."
Justice Raheem

"To my brother Barak Shah,
"If you go to the doctor with a broken leg and tell them your stomach hurts you'll never get the remedy you desired."

Aphorisms and idioms akin to these would often be said by the brother Barak Shah, and they stand true to the test of time. Being honest with yourself is one of the most necessary things to make a change in your life. Barak Shah was being filled with Ruach Ha'Qodesh and in turn, began to be honest with himself, and his life began to change. Although we were not able to see the fulfillment of that change, the time spent learning from his life experiences and trials is something I will not ever forget. I lost a good brother and pray that Yahuah has mercy on your spirit.
All love My G"!
Banayah Israel

The following message was handwritten by Nick Carefoot.

Common Sense Conversation Barak Sharr 13 days ago said to me on YouTube: "My g...you already family" - @ManoftheMostHigh (167 videos on YouTube) All of this is for entertainment purposes only. I can neither disprove nor prove the veracity of any of the conversations I am about to share about Barak Sha. While I have little doubt in my mind that he was telling the truth for this publication all I can say is that a lot was going through the mind of Barak Sharr even past the point of the cut-off bell for many stream yard broadcasts often we would talk about 'do the 14 eyes be listening to even this conversation after its not live?'

"WHY AM I HERE?" THE VOLUNTARY TORTURE CALLED LIFE

He had purported to me since last summer that he was being spied on by surveillance operations drones in New York from conversations he had had about the redeeming of his soul that he had over his jack as he put it. I told him for the most part, you will not find consumer-level drones that have all these surveillance capabilities. I explained to him this is, however, illegal since no American in their debtor capacity is allowed to infringe on the privacy of others, especially in a no-fly zone.

We talked about the various levels of Surveillance drones which are extensively used by military and intelligence agencies, but I tried to figure out what or rather who at the local levels, including by state and city public safety agencies would want to use such devices on him at the federal level by organizations such as the, and the Public safety agencies routinely use drones for surveillance missions, investigating crime scenes, search, and rescue operations, finding stolen goods, and disaster relief management. So, to answer Barak Shar's question, yes! Drones can be used for surveillance if they are equipped with the appropriate technology. It should, however, be noted that using drones to spy on fellow Americans is a felony.

This conversation went on all last year with Barak Sharr. He did not take any drugs, and did not drink, but this year after I left a political running man's campaign I mentioned that I had stayed past the cut-off, so the regulars were showing up to the venue armed to the teeth. Barak had opened up to me after the broadcast was cut off that he had seen the same type of activity in his hay day and how he would routinely risk his life to be in that type of environment. Barak Sharr was a veteran of the type of life seen in movies and, did not glorify it he let you know openly that he did not approve of it, but it was what it was that he had learned it was dehumanizing what street life does to you.

The level of paranoia that he had experienced did not appear to be a mental illness and, while some may have thought he was depressed I never got that vibe off Barak Sharr.

He always struck me as a hard worker, often on calls at job sites, and he was a cool cat. I did not have the foresight to guess he would allegedly end his own life. I think that neither Marty Marr nor Barak Sharr killed themselves of their own volition. Let me take this opportunity to say that under no circumstances would I take my own life nor am I suicidal. I can say the same for all members of TDOC, none of them are in a circumstance that would evidence some brooding depression or give me the impression someone here would do such a thing. Perhaps Barak Sharr did, and perhaps Marty did, however, I would like to note that my conversations with both these men give me no indication that such behavior was possible out of them. I keep skepticism of what I am told until the very end without a shadow of a doubt until the truth reveals itself.

Barak Sharr was ice cold, very laid back, and opinionated, but he was also a councilor to many women who hired him to clean their houses or men who would have him cut his hair. He was not the type to shy away from the fact he was a believer in the most high with any of his clients, his daughter, or his ex who seemingly drove him to this very reality we live in now.

I still do not believe Barak Sharr is gone, and that if he is not with us then who is? I think he could have done the paperwork to make everything good again, but I think for him it was more about sending a message that OK you do not want me to see my Daughter then here this is what you get exactly what you wanted never again can Eve blame Sharr for what he did in any capacity

"WHY AM I HERE?" THE VOLUNTARY TORTURE CALLED LIFE

because this is what she drove him to.

Love the man, he was walking testament to how to be a G from the East Coast, and, never asked for help he simply just checked out he was done with this club. Hope the most high has him waiting for TDOC with Marty right now. I am sure Marty needed someone to talk to anyway.

All the best, if your Barak Sharr's daughter reading this right now knows that your father was a very cool man who was Avant grade in the way he spoke, thought, and acted he was far ahead of his time as far as his attitude which was very much so in the pocket. He loves you very much and has extremely lofty expectations of you so should you make your way to TDOC then most highly willing I know he would approve.

Peace be with you, Shalom

Barak Shar meaning blessed prince we woke up 5 am for the past 6 months to study and put in too much work to give up no matter what never break never fall down and never give up the day we decide to quit the next day is your success so we must always push through the tribulations to obtain remarkable success we must endure struggle. Much Love and respect MY G.

Qadar

Shalom King,

I hate to see you go out this way, but I am grateful for Yahuah for granting me the opportunity to know you as a brother. You always spoke wisdom and looked out for what may be in my best interest. You held me accountable without hesitation, and that is invaluable love I will cherish forever.

You encouraged me to be a better man. You are one of the men who inspired me to be a good father to my son. Yahuah willing, I will reach out to your daughter when she has reached the age of maturity, so that she may know that her father was fighting for her. I pray Yahuah has mercy on your soul, and I pray that I may see you again in the spirit realm and that our spirits may rejoice on what we as brothers have accomplished through His grace and strength here in this world. Your death will not be in vain. We will continue to fight this world as Yahuah's warriors and fulfill His will. Until next time good brother. Yours truly, Jadier. My G.

Jadier

Despair and suicide are the result of certain fatal situations for those who have no faith in immortality, its joys, and sorrows. NEVER GIVE UP ON YOU. Napthali ISRAEL

"Barak Shar wanted for others that he did not have for himself, strength, and hope. I checked up on Marty often and not as often with Barak and yet their end result was the same. There is a lesson and I also pray that all of us in connection to these men take to the scriptures even more, especially me. He has always told me that "I will be my brother's keeper until I die" He heard some adverse things about me and still sought to reach out to say that he believed in me and my good heart.

"I pray you call me so we can help fix your situation. I know you have a good spirit, King. Shalom."

Though he was not specific on the alleged offenses I appreciate that he comprehended that I may be misunderstood. I have in return sought to continue on my path and prove him and the brothers right in strength and hope and to give back what Tazadaq has given. I pray he is at peace and rest in the love of the Heavenly father."

Yahshobeam

"WHY AM I HERE?" THE VOLUNTARY TORTURE CALLED LIFE

11 HOW THE COURT SYSTEM WORKS UNDERSTAND CONTRACTS AND YOU WILL

I am about to share some information with you that no one has ever shared in your life. Those who have attempted to do it only contained a glimpse of the right knowledge that they took from my seminars, books, and livestreams. This is how the Court System works and how I have been winning.

You are embarking upon a mental journey that is about to hurt what you have been taught in the Matrix which only teaches you common Parlance. Each time that you enter a colorable courtroom henceforth I encourage you to pay attention to every word therein. Each word that I write here is specific because each one is didactic. Therefore, you need to ride my wave of this Right Knowledge like a stocking cap. You are in a sea of commerce, either you swim as a creditor or drown as a debtor.

An aphorism worth repeating. Living in a world of Commerce you must learn to swim or drown. If you attempt to save some of the drowning debtors they will pull you down with them. You must save yourself. In this sea, you cannot be a lifeguard until Kahan Tazadaq has taught you to swim. The judge and attorney will cast waves at you. Do not go under the waves of deceit. Commerce here is composed of the sea and the sea is water, the water has a current. The current is from where the government gets its currency, created from our energy. Currency is also referred to as funds or money.

The entire purpose of Commerce is to extract as much money as possible from you as the system can. Since 1933 there has been no money of intrinsic value such as gold and silver. Money was deprived by way of Franklin Dela nor Roosevelt, who was imposed upon by the Federal Reserve Banks. Since that time, you could not be able to own anything thing because of these federal reserve notes that replaced real money with a tax attached. There is an interest in the debt of the United States corporation.

These debts started with World War I and continued into World War 2. I encourage each one of you to go and check out everything that I am saying. I dare you to prove me wrong about anything that you read in this book. The people are in a sea of Commerce and if you have not learned how to swim as a creditor with the necessity of comprehending contracts in Commerce, you will drown.

The harsh fact of the matter is most people are drowning within a sea of Commerce; most of you are going down for a third time. Yahuah, the one that you call God the YHWH, has raised me to be your savior currently. I am not the Christ, but I am sent in the spirit of Yahusha to liberate your thinking. I liberate the oppressed.

You could therefore consider me as a lifeguard. I am a star seed sent here solely to prevent you from drowning in the sea of Commerce. I will teach you how to swim. You must learn to swim against the current of Public Policy, which is the currency. You must flow with the current which will save your life, improve your life, and transform you from the debtor that you are right now into a creditor. A secured party creditor. A secured party creditor holds the Paramount interest and title. The SPC holds the superior claim. This is who we all should be.

We all should be creditors. The book of Romans 13 and 8 tells us to owe no one anything but love. Therefore, we were never born to be debtors or employees. The employer is the master the employee is the slave. A debtor is also a slave to whom he owes a debt until that debt is utterly paid. An employee goes in and works for an employer who is a master because he orders the employee what to do and what not to do. If you are not content being a nine-to-five slave and want true liberty visit www.truedisciples.org/shop and order all of my books now.

This is not legal advice. I do not offer legal advice. If you need legal advice seek a competent counselor and then please be advised everything written in these texts is strictly for educational, informational, and entertainment purposes only.   I can promise you one day if you want to be great if you find a great man and you emulate his lifestyle, then you can be great.

We can use Napoleon Hill. He emulated the lifestyles of many men such as Carnegie and Henry Ford. Now Napoleon Hill's book Thank And Grow Rich is one of the best sellers ever about success written until I authored this book. This book that you are holding in your hands or that you have on your lap reading will change your life if you study correctly and if you read it at least ten times at a minimum.

This book will make you rich you are already rich, but this book will teach you how to tap into that richness and realize it now. This book teaches you how to operate in a colorable world. Colorable is something that resembles the truth, but it is not the truth it is colorable. It looks like the truth, it sounds like the truth, but it is not the truth it has the resemblance of the truth it is colorable. Such it is with our courts today; the courts are colorable. So, inside such courts, they do not want to hear the truth.

 They only want a portion of the truth because they want what is colorable, they are not interested in the entire truth As Jack Nicholas said in A Few Good Men "You cannot handle the truth." One does not check the truth or facts in colorable court you simply trust that which is colorable.

so, I am going to suggest right now that you stop listening to other YouTubers and only listen to me because I have listened to some of the YouTubers, and their knowledge is at least 10 years behind mine. I am not bragging but I am the best that has ever done this Secure Party Creditor Redemption process.

I am he that that the most high has sent to free your mind, to liberate your thinking, to make you great. Before you is an open door. Keep in mind it is colorable, the courts are colorable the statues are colorable they resemble law, but they are not law they sound like law, but they are not law they are colorable. Colorable lawyers, you have colorable people, they call them Black people.

If it is colorable, it is not black it is not white because something is missing. So how do you learn the truth? The scripture tells us how to learn the truth in the book of Isaiah 28 verse 10 it tells you how to understand the Bible. precept up upon precept, line upon line, here a little there a little. That is how the truth is learned The truth is also learned through stammering lips through the mouth of a foreigner, I am a foreigner because I exist outside of your world because I am an idiot. One may say, "You should not insult yourself like that: that is not an insult look at the etymology of the word idiot it means a private person an outsider and I am an outsider from the system.

I therefore reiterate that I am an idiot because I exist outside of your society, I am not stupid, but I am an idiot. Doesn't that describe a legal lease? It is outside of the regular English language some of the language that you will learn in the processes will take you outside of the system and make you a foreigner and you will begin to learn not only how to swim in the sea of Commerce but to

"WHY AM I HERE?" THE VOLUNTARY TORTURE CALLED LIFE

go with the currency which is a flow of the money. I know you want to go with the flow. We are foreign to their flow, lawyers, and judges. By the way, throughout this book, I often replace the word lawyer with a briefcase. And I replace the word judge with a robe. So that you can comprehend while I am using those terms. It has been a legal language that I have been teaching you. It is from a stammering mouth that I am establishing truth because they only use a little here and a little there. You are going to be required not to just get this book but to go to my website www.truedisciplesofchrist.org/shop and order all my books to learn this legal lease and learn how to properly swim in the sea of Commerce.

When the robe asks you do you promise to tell the truth, the whole truth, and nothing but the truth? If you say yes, then you will lose because they will not be interested in the whole truth they are interested in that which is colorable, this is how you win in their court. if any of you are beginning to doubt anything that I'm saying here this is why you've been losing. You tried your way. You have tried it by what these other YouTubers say; now try it the correct way because I am the truth.

 I have been sent with the truth through the spirit of the Ruach ha Qadash. If it is colorable, essentially, you are saying I am going to tell you the truth but not the whole truth. I am going to give you part of the truth. So colorable in Black's Law Dictionary is described as similar or resemble in appearance. You are just getting a portion of the story. Is it not a fact that you cannot properly judge a thing if you only have a portion of the story? That is Rhetorical If you have children and you have 1 that is 15 and you told him, Anthony, I need you in the home by 11 PM tonight and Anthony shows up at 3 AM and you hear Anthony coming in at 3

"WHY AM I HERE?" THE VOLUNTARY TORTURE CALLED LIFE

AM, he gets in his bed, and you ask him in the morning where were you last night Anthony?

Anthony is going to give you a colorable truth. Anthony is going to say I was with my homies Because Anthony knows if he told you the truth and nothing but the truth then it would incriminate Anthony. So, Anthony Gives you a colorable truth because the entire truth would incriminate Anthony. So, it is with colorable courts.

The problem is most debtors do not separate private from public. A creditor does everything in private. His documentation is set in the judge's chambers. It is sent through the officer of the court, not the clerk. A debtor does everything in public, he goes to court, and he starts talking and it overrides everything that he submitted into the record. The briefcase is there to get him to argue, and he gets him to argue by asking him questions. Creditors ask the questions; debtors make statements and either pay the bill Or get locked up and thrown in jail or both. "He that is asking is as king." When you go into a court it is a military tribunal. Every tribunal is a battleground, you are going against the military, I reiterate court is a battleground.

And within that arena called court, the robe represents the military which conceals all truth. In his court you are playing by different rules in a common law court, you want the whole truth and nothing but the truth. But in this military tribunal that these modern robes are running you want colorable truth. The military tribunals do not want to hear the truth they do not care about the truth; the facts are on the moon they are going to cover up their wrongs. And bring things against you by charging you and seeing how you will respond. Because it is an Inquisition the reason that you are going into these military courts it is to determine whether you are a good guy or a bad guy.

They do not care about your issues because again they are like the military the rule represents the military. They are just there to control and if you comply or create harmony. The facts are on Mars. So, what I am telling you right now is counterintuitive to all of you who go out and get briefcases the briefcase would tell you. "This guy Tazadaq doesn't know what he's talking about, that's not the law." When it is just the opposite. You see I know the law most briefcases only have no procedure unless they are high-level judges.

They do not care about the facts. Look at today's court settings. It is not set how the original courts were set up. In the original court everyone was operating on the same level, everyone was actually on the same floor. Today's court they are separated by boxes. In the original court, the robe was sitting on the floor where everyone else was. Today the robe is in a Box on a raised platform. The jury is in a box. The witness is in a witness box. They are not there. This is the four corners rule, anything in a box Is not there.

The bailiff is a Carrier he is carrying a document from one party to another, so he is like the postal service. If I am outside the Box then I am not on the vessel. The bailiff will come to the edge of the vessel and receive anything that I am attempting to put into the vessel. The bailiff would then carry that to the captain of the vessel which is the robe that you call the judge. The courtroom is behind the bar. Everything is separated into boxes. A court is a Box in a Box and what is outside the Box is not in the Box. And therefore, it is not part of it. So, when you approach the courtroom from outside the courtroom the court building is a Box. When you go inside of the court building you have different courtrooms therefore you have boxes inside of boxes in each of

"WHY AM I HERE?" THE VOLUNTARY TORTURE CALLED LIFE

these courtrooms.

The judge's courtroom is a Box within the building. Every robe's particular courtroom is only in that Box and has nothing to do with the remainder of the building. Now within the judge's courtroom, it is divided into two areas outside of the bar and inside the bar. So, the bar separates the Box making it two boxes. Now we have a public box and a private box.

I said that creditors operate in the private, So the bar is akin to a wall separating the public side of this judge's courtroom from the private side of the judge's courtroom. "Kahan Tazadaq, how can you say what about traffic court that does not have a bar?" That means you are all within a private area. So, when you walk through the door you come through the private area of the court because we know these courts are corporations that are contracting, and contracts take place in these courts. So, when you go into these public courts, and you go in front of the robe you are contracting with them privately in front of him.

They usually trick you in traffic court because someone is receiving the guest and they will have you sign in. So, you are signing a contract with the court. When you sign in you have done an appearance, not a special appearance, but you have done an appearance by signing in so now you are contracted with them. It is clear that most do not know this you want to argue, but you gave up jurisdiction when you contracted with them and so the robe sees you as double-minded and finds you in contempt. So, how do I avoid contracting? Well, you are not contracting when they ask if are you John Doe and you say that I am here today As John Doe. When were you born? My response is well "John Doe was born December 10th 1975".

"WHY AM I HERE?" THE VOLUNTARY TORTURE CALLED LIFE

The robe asks where were you born? I say, " John Doe was born in New York City." The robe says where do you live? I say John Doe lives and New York City. Did you notice that I am creating a distinction? I am speaking in the third person. Everything that I am saying is colorable because I am in a colorable court not once have, I admitted to being the defendant which is John Doe. I am here as John Doe I am not John Doe. I am here as John Doe. Once again in the colorable, they do not care about your testimony the facts are on Mars on Jupiter it is colorable.

The courtroom behind the bar is really the ship, the vessel. Again, what is outside the Box is not inside the Box and not part of it. The bar is separated. It is making two boxes. so now we have a private box and a public box. The bar is a way of separating the public side from the private side. Even though they tell you that there is a public court when you are in front of the robe, you are privately contracting in front of him. Do you think you could listen to these YouTuber's and be able to separate public from private? No, you cannot. I am the only one who has this Right Knowledge because the most high has given this to me.

When the robe asks me is TAZADAQ in court today? My response is that I am here as Tazadaq. They will not sign me in the book if I say I am here today as TAZADAQ because I am not contracting with them. When they ask me when was born? I say well TAZADAQ was born December 9, 1975. If they ask, where do you live? I say well TAZADAQ was born at 3400 church Avenue Brooklyn New York 11204. I always create a distinction between me and fiction. I, man am the living soul. I will go into that more later. What is occurring here folks is I am technically not signing in. I am not creating a joinder that they want me to because I am not contracting. I am not the DEBTOR I am the living soul. When they ask what your

"WHY AM I HERE?" THE VOLUNTARY TORTURE CALLED LIFE

birthday is my response is, I am not a party to this matter so you must want TAZADAQ'S birthday. Well, TAZADAQ'S birthday is December 9th, 1975.

I am rebutting the presumption that I the living soul am the name TAZADAQ. I am making this distinction that I am not a debtor to TAZADAQ.

Those of you that are actually in prison or have been in prison will say when you come to the door I want your name and the inmate's number. The proper way that one should answer that is that the inmate's name is John Doe the inmate's number is 123456789. Do you see the distinction? Do you see what I am saying here? See brothers and sisters when you make those distinctions, you are rebutting the presumptions Identification of being the same as the corporate construct. Remember as I have told you previously identification means to make the same. Again, identification means to make the same.

So, if you give them any information, you are going to make yourself the same as the legal fiction. When you are in the bar, You're inside a Box. There is a jury box, there is a witness box, there is a Box the judge is sitting on a raised platform, which is a box. Once you are inside the bar the bar excludes everything that is outside of the bar. Since the jury box is a Box, it is outside the court. so is the witness box. The judge is sitting on a raised platform on a Box outside the court. The only entities inside the court are the defendant and the plaintiff, the prosecution, and the stenographer.

What goes on in the witness box stays in that box. What happens in the jury box stays in that box; it has no relevance to the witness or the defendant. When you are doing a private process the notary's relationship to you is a witness. The notary is your court on the private side memorializing what goes on in the court when you are on the side of the defendant, and you receive something from the plaintiff what are you receiving? You are receiving a complaint or a claim and what is the court? The court is the witness so when you do your private administrative procedures your notary is your witness.

The robe plays two roles in such courts, he is paying an administrative role or a judicial role. If the defendant and the plaintiff cannot agree on their contract, then the judge has the power to order whoever is in dishonor to pay. The robe will enforce some sort of penalty.

The witness, jury, and robe are not in your court unless you go in dishonor then the robe intervenes. What occurs in the witness box does not leave that box, it is the same for what occurs in the jury box. What goes on in Las Vegas stays in Las Vegas. What is going on in the witness box and the jury box has no relevance to what is going on in the court. A court is a legal relationship between the parties.

The court has nothing to do with your relationship with the defendant and plaintiff. When a complaint is filed or a claim in court, the only thing that the court is doing is to be a witness. The judge is determining if the two parties are not settling their own contract. If the parties fail to settle their contract the judge has to act judicially and find one of the parties in contempt for not being able to reach an agreement in their contract, So, the judge orders a decision unless they agree to the terms of their contract. But if the two parties are negotiating in good faith, then the judge does a continuance to allow them to leave the court and settle it in the private then come back in thirty for a ruling.

"WHY AM I HERE?" THE VOLUNTARY TORTURE CALLED LIFE

The robe is saying, "I am A facilitator and I'm just monitoring the situation." If the plaintiff and defendant go on back and forth the judge will not tell you what he is doing, but what he does is he schedules a recess and he says we will come back in 30 days. So, what the judge is doing is allowing the defendant and the plaintiff to settle this in private between each other and come back in 30 days.

If you fail to reach an agreement the judge will step in to issue or enforce an order that is how the court works. So, who are the court brothers and sisters? The court is the parties of the defendant, the prosecution the stenographer, and plaintiff are part of the court. The judge is not part of the court. Read Black Law's 4th Court of Record. The stenographer is on level ground. It has been up to you to settle your problem all along. It has never been the judge's duty; The judge only gets on board because you people cannot settle your problems on your contracts.

You go out and you settle your problems and then you put in your agreement and the robe will say is that what you agree to, is that what you agree to? Then it is settled. You settle your problems. So, what the robe is doing in a public forum is to rule on what you agree to in a private setting and in its public form.

That is following Genesis chapter 23 how you bring your private settlements into the public for verifications. If you have been reading my books, you should be familiar with the administrative process, and you can get remedy on the private side. But what I am teaching you here is how I have gotten remedy in the Public. In the law, you have two categories you have substantive, and you have procedure damage. Yahuah is the same today yesterday and tomorrow. The law never changes.

"WHY AM I HERE?" THE VOLUNTARY TORTURE CALLED LIFE

In their colorable proceedings, they deal with substantive. It does not damage you. The robe will call you names, stupid he may call you an idiot but that's not real damage. Sticks and stones may break my bones, but words will never hurt me. The police officer pulls you over and says you are driving without a license. You cannot drive without a license! That is not a damage. He is making you an offer to get you to argue. You must rebut it, or you agree to the contract. Do you understand? Negotiations do not constitute damages Substance constitutes damage.

The substantive law never changes. In 1933 they dropped law courts, and they gave us maritime admiralty equity courts. They changed the law; they changed that portion of the law dealing with remedy, not substance. Remedy or remedial law is a process in which you must cover the damage. The remedy is not substantive for the law; the remedy is just a process so you can obtain some actual compensation for some damage you may have sustained.

The substantive law can never change the remediable law can change any time they want to if there is a remedy provided and that remedy gives due process of law and equal protection to both parties. So, they have never changed the substantive law. All they change is the procedures by the way which you could get a remedy. So, they went from procedures in a common law court to procedures in a maritime court. If you have a remedy in these new court proceedings it does not violate you or. anyone else's rights. Stop saying it is a fraud and stop listening to these bozo Youtubers.

YouTube's who do not have any clue how the court works. A lot of patriots and Freeman are yelling, "I want a common law court." You can argue until you are red as a tomato. They have given you a remedy, so shut up! If it continues to provide you with a remedy where it does not discriminate against you, it is OK. There is a difference between common law and equity and what I am talking about is not common law procedures because it changed in 1933.

What is required to get the remedy? See when you change your money from gold and silver to money of account you also change your remedy as well. So, you went from a remedy on the land to a remedy on the vessel on the sea. Federal reserve notes are for money of the sea not money of intrinsic value. So much of what I am discussing is about procedures in their courts. Maritime law because we are dealing with money of the sea. we are dealing with the public. What I am talking about is not common law procedures because the remedy Changed in 1933. We Went on a Maritime adventure going to sea. When you are dealing with the DTC if you use your assets funds you have both legal title and equitable title which is as good as gold.

Why are you debtors complaining If you have both legal and equitable title out of those electronic funds coming out of your TDA from the DTC? Because you are debtors, and you do not comprehend this process. Isn't that as good as the gold that you had when you had gold and silver of intrinsic value?

I contend that it is. I am Kahn Tazadaq and I approve of this message. That TDA account is as good as gold. I would say that it is better than gold. In the banking system future, everything will be electronic. so why are you folks complaining? Learn to swim in the sea of Commerce. They are right now trying to do away with paper money and checks to try to make everything electronic. You get on board, or you get left behind. You will not be able to determine who is operating on assets accounts or who is operating on liability accounts. Everyone will look the same because now you have people going to a grocery store with an EBT that looks like a credit card paying for groceries that you and I are funding. The people that had the assets accounts had legal titles but the slaves who operated on the liability accounts had no rights. They have some privileges, and they have some benefits that is it. The context of this information of I am bringing is the procedural remedy. In England, they said that after 2018 there will be no paper money, everything will be electronic. They are still headed towards that.

We have reached the end of another book; you need to read this one nine more times. Order my other books at www.truedisciplesofchrist.org/shop. Become a Secured Party Creditor now by visiting the website above or email tazadaqshah@yahoo.com for the cost. Send your donations to cash.me/$tazadaqshah or on Zelle tazadoctrine@gmail.com. I am say shalom and leave love in the air.

CONDITIONAL ACCEPTANCE

Kahan Tazadaq will cover 3 sections within this course:
1. Creating the Contract
2. Enacting the Contract
3. Enforcing the Contract

Kahan Tazadaq requires that you make a donation of $30 US dollars to cash.me/$tazadaqshah or on Zelle @ tazadoctrine@gmail.com or PayPal.me/tazadaq

Let us begin by defining some very key words to understand Acceptance.

Contract. An agreement between two or more people which creates an obligation to do or not to do a particular thing. Its essentials are competent parties, subject matter, legal consideration, mutuality of agreement, and mutuality of obligation. Offer. v. To bring to or before; to present for acceptance or rejection; to hold out or proffer; to make a proposal to; to exhibit something that may be taken or received or not. n. A proposal to do a thing or pay an amount is usually accompanied by an expected acceptance, counter-offer, return promise, or act.

"WHY AM I HERE?" THE VOLUNTARY TORTURE CALLED LIFE

A manifestation of willingness to enter into a bargain, so made as to justify another person in understanding that his assent to that bargain is invited and will conclude it. Offer and acceptance. In a bilateral contract, the two elements which constitute mutual assent, are a requirement of the contract.

In a unilateral contract, the acceptance is generally the act or performance of the offeree, though, in most jurisdictions, a promise to perform is inferred if the offeree commences the undertaking and the offeror attempts to revoke before the offeree has had an opportunity to complete the act. Offeree. In contracts, the person to whom an offer is made by the offeror. Accept. To receive with approval or satisfaction; to receive with intent to retain. Admit and agree to; accede to or consent to; receive with approval; adopt; agree to. Accept. [L. accept are, from ad, to capio, to take.]

To take or receive, as something offered; received with approbation or favour; take as it comes; accede or assent to (a treaty, a proposal); to acknowledge, especially by signature, and thus to promise to pay (a bill of exchange). The Consolidated Webster's Encyclopedic Dictionary 1933 Acceptance. The taking and receiving of anything in good part, and as if it were a tacit agreement to a preceding act, which might have been defeated or avoided if such acceptance had not been made. Tacit.

Existing, inferred, or understood without being openly expressed or stated; implied by silence or silent acquiescence, as a tacit agreement or a tacit understanding. Done or made in silence, implied, or indicated, but not expressed. Manifested by the refraining from contradiction or objection; inferred from the situation and circumstances, in the absence of express matter. Tacit acceptance. A tacit acceptance of inheritance takes place when some act is done by the heir which necessarily supposes his intention to accept and which he would have no right to do but in his capacity as heir.

Tacit law. A law which derives its authority from the common consent of the people without any legislative enactment. As you know by now, UNITED STATES is a trust with our forefathers as the Grantors, the government agents as the Trustees, and we as the beneficiaries or "heirs." All property and "energy" (in the CAFRs) that the government has in its "apparent" possession is our inheritance. But, we have never ACCEPTED it! We have never claimed it back….. until now. Power. [LL potere, to be able, from L. posse, from potis, able + esse, to be.]

Ability to act; the faculty of doing or performing something; capability; the right of governing or actual government; dominion; rule; authority; a sovereign; a spirit or superhuman agent having a certain sway (celestial powers); the moving force applied to produce the required effect; Power of Acceptance. The capacity of the offeree, upon acceptance of terms of the offer, to create a binding contract. When you get an offer, THE OFFEROR JUST PUT YOU IN A POSITION OF POWER!

What an honor! Why not accept that gift? Since the strawman is a corporation created by the State to account for the credit that they are using in your name, it stands to reason that the strawman represents UNITED STATES and THEIR debt – not you and your debt. You are the Creditor, and the State or UNITED STATES is the debtor.

They owe you an exemption for using your credit, but since they are bankrupt, there is no "substance money," so you, as the creditor, will have to get paid by taking equity, such as your house and your car as a setoff. As one can see from the above definitions, you are a "banker" that can "issue BILLS OF EXCHANGE (BOE) intended to be circulated as money." Since that is what ALL currency is today – your credit – it should not be a stretch for the imagination to think that you can USE YOUR OWN CREDIT!

However, you are not going to use your credit which creates more debt – you are going to by using your EXEMPTION. Exemption. Freedom from a general duty or service; immunity from a general burden, tax, or charge, Immunity from service of process or from certain legal obligations, as jury duty, military service, or the payment of taxes Property exempt in bankruptcy proceedings is provided for under Bankruptcy Code sec. 522.

"WHY AM I HERE?" THE VOLUNTARY TORTURE CALLED LIFE

Exempt. [L. exemptum, to take out, to remove, from ex, out + emo, to buy, to take.] To free or permit to be free from any charge, burden, restraint, duty to which others are subject; to grant immunity. Accept. [L. acceptare, from ad, to + capio, to take.] To take or receive, as something offered; to acknowledge with a signature and thus promise to pay a Bill of Exchange.

All municipalities and corporations are bankrupt because they have no substance to back up their currency. We, as sovereigns, bailed them out by letting them use OUR PROPERTY as collateral, then they mortgaged it, and – Voilà! – there was currency. However, we are EXEMPT because they are using our credit to make trillions of dollars a year, and therefore, we are entitled "to take" a portion of their equity in return. You are going TO TAKE what is already yours and in your possession. Since there is no money, you can only "take" equity – goods and services – from the corporations using your credit as they are BANKRUPT! You will be sending a copy of the BOE to Paul O'Neill in a "private" capacity as the trustee for the US Bankruptcy. This is done privately because you cannot deal with fiction. You are "foreign" to UNITED STATES and all other corporations, so you can use your EXEMPTION as a FOREIGN BILL OF EXCHANGE to pay the balance due in another country (or should we say "corporation" such as UNITED STATES). The "balance" represents the interest that a person owes you when they are using YOUR credit. Since the strawman is a corporate/juristic entity created by the State to account for the credit that they are using in your name, it stands to reason that the strawman represents UNITED STATES and THEIR debt – not you. You are the Creditor, and the state or UNITED STATES is the debtor.

They owe you interest for using your credit, but since they are bankrupt, there is no "substance money," so you, as the creditor, will have to get paid by taking equity, such as your house and your car as a setoff. Power of acceptance. The capacity of offeree, upon acceptance of the terms of the offer, to create a binding contract. House Joint Resolution 192, June 5, 1933, states that one cannot demand a certain form of currency that they want to receive if it is dollar for dollar as ALL CURRENCY IS YOUR CREDIT!! If they do, they are in breach of the contract of HJR 192.

"WHY AM I HERE?" THE VOLUNTARY TORTURE CALLED LIFE

You have already accepted this contract and now they must perform. Pursuant to the contract with the corporation that you are discharging the debt of HJR 192, they must give you a Letter of Release or Payment in Full. If you have not received the release in 14 days then send them a DEFAULT and contact a notary to do a process that will give you a CERTIFICATE OF DISHONOR, because they are in breach of the contract at this time Remember in the Bible who offers? Sinners "offer" offerings to Yahuah.

That is why you never, never make an offer, because you are admitting that you are the sinner – the debtor, one who is obligated. So, when an agent of a fictitious entity (your creation) gives you an offer, they are acknowledging that you are their creator, their "god" and that they are honoring you and returning their appreciation and energy back to you that you have created them. There is another type of acceptance called a "conditional acceptance." Acceptance, Conditional. An engagement to pay the draft or accept the offer on the happening of a condition.

A "conditional acceptance" is in effect a statement that the offeree is willing to enter into a bargain differing in some respects from that proposed in the original offer. The conditional acceptance is, therefore, itself a counteroffer. Counteroffer.

A statement by the offeree that has the legal effect of rejecting the offer and of proposing a new offer to the offeror As one can see if you have a condition, it is not complete acceptance. One is actually "rejecting" and making a "new offer." Now you have just turned the power to them. I have seen particularly good "conditional acceptances" which shift the burden of proof to the one making the offer, and this appears to be effective.

Conditional acceptances are a particularly good gradient to the full acceptance or "absolute acceptance." Absolute. [L absoluts to set free, from ab from + solve to loose.] Freed from limitation or condition; unconditional; unlimited by extraneous power or control; complete in itself; finished; perfect; positive; decided; self-existing; without restriction. Since you are the creator or the "god" of this

"WHY AM I HERE?" THE VOLUNTARY TORTURE CALLED LIFE

system and everything in it, then you can accept all the offers they give you - ABSOLUTELY!

Remember what "duplication" means and that no 2 objects can be in the same space at the same time? Well, when you DUPLICATE an offer, you make the entire matter disappear! Which acceptance do you think has more power, "Conditional Acceptance" where you are depending on THEM to provide the condition, or "Absolute Acceptance" where it does not matter what offer is made, you are able or have the power to accept it and it becomes "perfect" and "finished."

It "sets you free" from the obligation completely! However, some may be saying "I would never accept what the government is trying to get me to do!" You must first do what is called "Finding it." You must first "look" at the document or "hear" what they are actually saying. Who are they talking to, you or the strawman?

Who does the strawman represent – you or the one who created that "account" to keep the accounting of how much they owe you as the Creditor? This is one of the biggest misconceptions of the "strawman" – that it represents you. No, it represents UNITED STATES. It is a subcorporation of UNITED STATES, a transmitting utility, to deal with you, to interface with the Creditor and to get the Creditor to "think" he is the debtor.

So, how do you "find" it? You just read and define the words, take the viewpoint of the Creditor, and listen to what they want the DEBTOR to do – not you. They cannot even see you or hear you because you are real, not fiction like them. Can a fiction see or hear ANYTHING? Can you see or hear a fiction? Nope! So why do you insist that you are the one they are dealing with? Find it and do an "ABSOLUTE ACCEPTANCE!" As far as the truth goes, I do not care WHAT they do with the fictional debtor, in their fictional courts with fictional statutes. In the Matrix, while waiting to see the Oracle (the word or thought), Neo observed a gifted child "bend a spoon." The child said, "try not to think that you can bend the spoon, which is impossible. The truth is there is no spoon." Remember when Neo got shot in the chest and thought he was dead? Through unconditional love, Trinity called him back and "woke him up." He "thought" he was dead, but he was not. When he got up and looked again at the "agents" what did he see? He saw them as they really were – digital images with no significance. What was there to be afraid of? He then realized that he was the ONE and that he had no limitations, and they did.

He saw through the Matrix, behind the curtain of the Wizard of OZ, through the corporate veil. They were created so they had limitations. He was not the creation but the creator and therefore had no limitations. Look at what this system REALLY is – not what it "appears" to be. Let us go into a specific demonstration of a Contract. Let us assume you have just received an offer from someone, it could be a traffic ticket, a demand from an insurance company, a demand to stop crossing someone else's property, or a Notice of Foreclosure, etc.

CREATING THE CONTRACT

PURPOSE: As a Creditor of UNITED STATES and all other sub-corporations private and public, you are owed equity and interest for the gold and all property that your forefathers and you "loaned" them starting March 9, 1933, to date.

There is NO MONEY, so in order to start getting integrity and ethics back into society, you must NOTICE your debtors what you expect them to do and the consequences if they do not comply, but first you must ESTABLISH THE LAW. Your acceptance of any and all offers is a binding contract to the Offeror and tells them what you want and how things are going to be done in this CREDITOR/DEBTOR relationship.

This file contains all the documents you will need to PERFECT YOUR CLAIM, TAKE BACK YOUR EQUITY and most of all, ENSURE JUSTICE IS DONE; 1. Notice of Acceptance to Contract 2. Notice of Default 3. Notice of Dishonor – from Notary Public 4. Notice of Protest and Opportunity to Cure – from Notary Public 5. Certificate of Dishonor - from Notary Public 6. Notice of Default and Entry for Default Judgment

7. Default Judgment - from 3 Creditors 8. Notice of Acceptance - to be file at the Secretary of State The following steps are sequence of events that must occur to get your Contract established and enacted as the supreme law of the land.

1. NOTICE OF ACCEPTANCE TO CONTRACT Word process the Notice of Acceptance to Contract for all of the correct information Print the Notice of Acceptance to Contract out, read it several times for correctness, and MAKE SURE YOU DESIGNATE A THIRD-PARTY RECEIVER WITH NAME AND ADDRESS, Stamp the OFFER with your Acceptance for Value stamp and sign it and send the ORIGINAL OFFER to Respondent, then get the Notice notarized. Send the Notice of Acceptance to Contract by registered mail, and return receipt so you have proof that they received your Contract you are in the process of creating. Send the copies of the above documents to the Respondent(s) and keep the originals 2. NOTICE OF DEFAULT After the 10 days send them a Notice of Default. This means total failure. This notice completes your court procedure as a sovereign in your nation that is foreign to the public venue. Now you will need to pursue this matter in the "public venue" in their legal proceedings, however, it will not go into the courts you are familiar with.

You must take this matter up with the SECRETARY OF STATE of the state you are in. Secretary of State. In American law. The title of the chief of the executive bureau of the United States called the "Department of State." He is a member of the cabinet and is in charge with the general administration of the international and diplomatic affairs of the government. In many of the state governments, there is an executive officer bearing the same title and exercising important functions. In English law.

The secretaries of state are cabinet ministers attending the Sovereign for the receipt and dispatch of letters, grants, petitions, and many of the most important affairs of the kingdom, both foreign and domestic. Black's 4th edition You are a Foreign Nation in their eyes, so you must go through the proper channels so that you can utilize the functions and duties of the Secretary of State – "general administration of the international affairs" and "attending the sovereign."

There are many "designees" of the Secretary of the state in the area you live, normally called Notary Publics. Find a private Notary Public that you can work with; OR create one by getting a friend to become a Notary who understands this procedure.

3. NOTICE OF DISHONOR – Notary Public
Now we will go through the process called a Notarial Protest, an immensely powerful process that will create a witness against the debtor through a Public Official. Following is the definition of a Notary Public according to Black's Law Dictionary, 6th edition. It is important to know why you need to use a Notary Public. Notary Public:

A public officer whose function it is to administer oaths; to attest and certify, by her or his hand and official seal, certain classes of documents, in order to give them credit and authenticity in foreign jurisdictions; to take acknowledgements of deeds and other conveyances and certify the same; and to perform certain official acts, chiefly in commercial matters such as the protesting of notes and bills, the noting of foreign drafts, and marine protests in cases of loss or damage.

One who is authorized by the State or Federal Government to administer oaths, and to attest to the authenticity of signatures. Black's 6th edition NOTARY PUBLIC. A legal practitioner, usually a solicitor, who attests or certifies deeds and other documents and notes or protests dishonored bills of exchange. Dictionary of Business, Oxford University Press, © Market House Books Ltd 1996 Pursuant to Arizona Revised Statutes (ARS) Title 41-332; Secretary of the State; deputy county clerk; county clerk functions "…each clerk of the superior court shall deputize the secretary of state and the secretary's designees as deputy county clerks of the superior court solely for the performance of the superior court clerk's functions…"

All notary publics are assigned a "commission" by the secretary of the state and deputized by the notary public of the Superior Court. Commission: An authority or writ issuing from a court, in relation to

"WHY AM I HERE?" THE VOLUNTARY TORTURE CALLED LIFE

a cause before it, directing and authorizing a person or persons named to do some act or exercise some special function; usually to take the depositions of witnesses.

NOTE A BILL. When a foreign bill has been dishonored, it is usual for a notary public to present it again on the same day and if it be not then paid, to make a minute, consisting of his initials, the day, month, and year, and reason, if assigned, of non-acceptance. The making of this minute is called "noting the bill."

UCC 3 § 505. Protest: Noting for Protest * * * (b) A protest is a certificate of dishonor made by a United States consul or vice consul, or a notary public or other person authorized to administer oaths by the law of the place where dishonor occurs. It may be made upon information satisfactory to that person. The protest shall identify the instrument and certify either that presentment has been made or, if not made, the reason why it was not made, and that the instrument has been dishonored by nonacceptance or nonpayment. The protest may also certify that notice of dishonor has been given to some or all parties.

NOTING. 1. The procedure adopted if a bill of exchange has been dishonored by nonacceptance or by non-payment. Not later than the next business day after the day on which it was dishonored, the holder has to hand it to a notary public to be noted. The notary represents the bill; if it is still unaccepted or unpaid, the circumstances are noted in a register and also on a notarial ticket, which is attached to the bill. The noting can then, if necessary, be extended to a protest. Dictionary of Business, Oxford University Press, © Market House Books Ltd 1996

NOTING. The act of a notary in minuting on a bill of exchange, after it has been presented for acceptance or payment, the initials of his name, the date of the day, month, and year when such presentment was made, and the reason, if any has been assigned, for non-acceptance or non-payment, together with his charge. Black's 4th

MINUTES. Practice. A memorandum of what takes place in court, made by authority of the court. Black's 4th edition CHARGE. In Equity practice. A written statement presented to a master in chancery (notary public) by a party (you) of the items with which the opposite party should be debited or should account for, or of the claim of the party making it. A charge may embrace the whole liabilities of the accounting party.

TICKET. In contracts. A slip of paper containing a certificate that the person to whom it is issued, or the holder, is entitled to some right or privilege therein mentioned or described, Black's 4th edition

JUDGMENT NOTE. A promissory note (contract), embodying an authorization to...a clerk of the court (or a notary public), to enter an appearance for the maker of the note and confess a judgment against him for a sum therein named, upon default of payment of the note. Black's 4th edition

PROTEST. A notarial act, being a formal statement in writing made by a notary under his seal of office, at the request of the holder of a bill or note, in which it is declared that the bill or note described was on a certain day presented for payment or acceptance and that such payment or acceptance was refused, and stating the reasons, if any, given for such refusal, whereupon the notary protests against all parties to such instrument, and declares that they will be held responsible for all loss or damage arising from its dishonor. It denotes also all the steps or acts accompanying dishonor necessary to charge an indorser. Black's 4th edition

PROTEST. 2. A procedure by which a notary provides formal evidence of the dishonor of a bill of exchange. When a foreign bill has been dishonored by non-acceptance or nonpayment it is handed to the notary, who usually presents it again.

If it is still dishonored, the notary attaches a slip showing the answer received and other particulars - a process called noting. The protest, in the form of a formal document, may then be drawn up at a later time. Dictionary of Business, Oxford University Press, © Market House Books Ltd 1996

Locate a Notary Public that is knowledgeable and willing to do your Notarial Protest. There are 3 documents needed for this process: Notice of Dishonor, Notice of Protest and Opportunity to Cure, and a Certificate of Dishonor. The first document is a Notice of Dishonor, which the Notary issues to the Offeror to allow them a second opportunity to provide evidence to substantiate their claim.

Basically, the Notary Public is acting in the capacity of taking a deposition from witnesses. The Notary Public has been shown your affidavit (sworn statement) and now the Notary is asking for the Offeror's affidavit (sworn statement).

4. NOTICE OF PROTEST AND OPPORTUNITY TO CURE – Notary Public This notice will allow an additional 10 days to give the debtor another chance to bring the evidence forth to support any claim that they may be professing. 5. CERTIFICATE OF DISHONOR – Notary Public If in 10 days the Notary Public does not receive a response point for point by affidavit with documented evidence, the debtor has defaulted and therefore dishonored your acceptance. Then the Notary prepares a Notarial Protest which the Notary keeps for her/his own records and issues you a Certificate of Dishonor. The Certificate of Dishonor is actually just as valid as a Default Judgment in a Superior Court.
6. NOTICE OF DEFAULT AND ENTRY OF DEFAULT JUDGMENT Now that you have a Default in your private venue and a Default in the public venue and the Debtor is still not responding, you will go to an international venue to finalize this matter. This will be done by an INTERNATIONAL TRIBUNAL consisting of 3 other, disinterested parties that are Creditors (anyone who has filed a UCC-1 in the state you are doing business in).

International agreements. Treaties and other agreements of a contractual character between different countries or organizations of states (foreign) create legal rights and obligations between the parties

Tribunal. The seat of a judge; a court of law; the place where he administers justice. The whole body of judges who compose a jurisdiction; a judicial court; Blacks 6th edition Tribunal. [L. tribunus, a magistrate or officer, from tribus, tribe.] Tribune. An officer in ancient Rome who represented a tribe for certain purposes; an offer or magistrate chosen by the common people of Rome to protect them from the oppression of the patricians; also, a military officer commanding a division or legion; a raised seat or stand; the throne of a bishop; a sort of pulpit or rostrum where a speaker stands to address an assembly. Tribe. [L. tribus, one of the three bodies into

"WHY AM I HERE?" THE VOLUNTARY TORTURE CALLED LIFE

which the Romans were originally divided, from tres three.] A division, class, or distinct portion of a people or nation. The reason we call this court an INTERNATIONAL TRIBUNAL is that it is an action where an "organization of a state" has not performed according to the original agreement (such a HJR 192, Public Policy 73-10, etc.) they have with the initial Creditor who is foreign to said organization's venue.

The "magistrates" who judge this matter "represent" their own "nations." Therefore, this matter is an "international "matter, which must be decided in an international venue. You will present the 3 Creditors with a package consisting of all of your notices and actions that you have done up to this point.

The 3 Creditors will review what you have done for correctness with specific attention on continuity of what you have claimed throughout your contract. Any contradictory statements or facts will be pointed out and will need to be corrected or amended as necessary. It may even require sending a correction statement to the Debtor to handle the error or out point in the paperwork.

You will write the NOTICE OF DEFAULT AND ENTRY OF DEFAULT JUDGMENT in affidavit form summarizing the actions of what you have done to this point. The purpose for this document is to enter this matter into the international venue where 3 Creditors will review the matter and witness a response, if any, from the Debtor.

7. DEFAULT JUDGMENT BY 3 CREDITORS After ten (10) days have elapsed with no response from Debtor, and after inspecting that all documents are in alignment and correct, and upon finding no evidence of a proper response to the contract, the 3 Creditors will sign a DEFAULT JUDGMENT in front of a Notary Public stating what they have found is true and correct. UCC 9-601. Rights After Default; (a) [Rights or secured party after default.] After default, a secured party has the rights provided in this part and except as otherwise provided in Section 9-602, those provided by agreement of the parties. A secured party: 1. may reduce a claim to judgment, foreclose, or otherwise enforce the claim, security interest, or

agricultural lien by any available judicial procedure; and UCC 9-607.

Collection and Enforcement by Secured Party. (b) [Nonjudicial enforcement of mortgage.] If necessary to enable a secured party to exercise under subsection (a)(3) the right of a debtor to enforce a mortgage non-judicially, the secured party may record in the office in which a record of the mortgage is recorded:

1. a copy of the security agreement that creates or provides for a security interest in the obligation secured by the mortgage; and 2. the secured party's sworn affidavit in recordable form stating that: a. a default has occurred, and b. the secured party is entitled to enforce the mortgage non-judicially.
Your contract is the "security agreement." The affidavit, entitled NOTICE OF DEFAULT, is the "affidavit in recordable form stating that a default has occurred." UCC 9-609. Secured Party's Right to Take Possession After Default.

(a) [Possession; rendering equipment unusable; disposition on debtor's premises.] After default, a secured party: 1. may take possession of the collateral; (b) [Judicial and nonjudicial process.] A secured party may proceed under subsection (a): (2) without judicial process if it proceeds without breach of the peace. Now that you have completed your "nonjudicial process," you can collect the collateral and take possession of it. This completes the Dishonor process. The next process will be covered in a separate set of instructions. The next process is the INVOLUNTARY BANKRUPTCY PROCEDURE.

John Henry Doe
c/o 6880 S. Broadway
Tucson, AZ 85746
Secured Party
Contract No 101101-JHD-US
UNITED STATES OF AMERICA
Virginia Mathis, d.b.a. Magistrate Morton Sitver, d.b.a. Magistrate Dick Mesh, d.b.a. Assistant U.S. Attorney Roland Mendoza, d.b.a.

"WHY AM I HERE?" THE VOLUNTARY TORTURE CALLED LIFE

Secret Service Agent Chuck Jones, d.b.a. Secret Service Agent Mr. Metelski, d.b.a Police Officer #5794 Mr. Moore, d.b.a. Police Officer #6803 Raymond Garcia, d.b.a. U.S. Pretrial Services Officer Donna Long, d.b.a. Finance Manager, BELL LEXUS Respondents

NOTICE OF ACCEPTANCE TO CONTRACT Arizona) NOTICE TO AGENT IS NOTICE TO PRINCIPAL) ss NOTICE TO PRINCIPAL IS NOTICE TO AGENT Pima

County) I, John Henry Doe, hereinafter "Secured Party", am competent to state the matters included in this contract which are true, correct, and complete, and not meant to mislead. PARTIES AND CAPACITY OF 1. Secured Party I, John Henry Doe, am a Sovereign, without subjects. I am a Foreign Nation (not a person) who rules autonomously and is not subject to any entity or jurisdiction anywhere. My authority for this contract is the age-old, timeless, and universal respect for the intrinsic power, property, and responsibilities of the sovereign individual.

I choose to comply with mutual respect, which serves to bring harmony to society. All national and state "constitutions, laws, statutes, ordinances, regulations, rules, codes and public policy" in all nations and states are private copyrighted material. I do not possess a license or have authority to use such copyrighted material and consequently, this material does not have any authority over me, my property, or my personal affairs. I have complete sovereign immunity and therefore, my power to contract is unlimited. 2. Respondents

The UNITED STATES OF AMERICA is a legal person and a corporation, and the following persons in their private capacities: Paul O'Neill, d.b.a. Secretary of the Treasury; Virginia Mathis, d.b.a. Magistrate; Morton Sitver, d.b.a. Magistrate; Dick Mesh, d.b.a. Assistant U.S. Attorney; Roland Mendoza, d.b.a. Secret Service Agent; Chuck Jones, d.b.a. Secret Service Agent; Mr. Moore, d.b.a. Police Officer #6803; Mr. Metelski, d.b.a.

Police Officer #5794, Raymond Garcia, d.b.a. U.S. Pretrial Services Officer; Donna Long, d.b.a. Finance Manager, Bell Lexus; Bell Lexus; and John Doe, 1-10; are agents of the private corporations, BELL

"WHY AM I HERE?" THE VOLUNTARY TORTURE CALLED LIFE

LEXUS, COUNTY OF MARICOPA, STATE OF ARIZONA, UNITED STATES and UNITED NATIONS. STATEMENT OF FACTS 3.

In 1871, the UNITED STATES incorporated in England, which in turn made it an English corporation. Due to impending bankruptcy in 1933, the UNITED STATES made a "New Deal" (a contract) with the UNITED STATES citizens (not the American Sovereigns) in March 9, 1933, entitled, Senate Document No. 43, 73rd Congress, 1st Session. The contract stated that "It (the new money) will represent a mortgage on all the homes and other property of all the people in the Nation." As a result, title of property was turned over to the State as evidenced by the statement in the contract, "The ownership of all property is in the State". In order to account for the increase gained by the use of the people's property, the UNITED STATES created artificial entities for each of the people using their own names, however, spelled in all capital letters. For example, John Doe the man would have an entity entitled JOHN DOE.

4. On or about October 31, 1954, The UNITED STATES under contract with the creditor of the bankruptcy created an artificial entity entitled JOHN HENRY DOE. The application for the birth certificate created by the state when John Henry Doe was born was the instrument upon which the Artificial Entity was created.

Thus, the application for the birth certificate, hereinafter "title," was registered in the commercial registry through a constructive contract created by the state and through this title made John Henry Doe the fiduciary for the artificial entity. 5. All contracts i.e., application for driver's license, application for Social Security, and any other adhesion, constructive, gratuitous, onerous, quasi, and any other invisible contracts were made with the artificial entity created by the state –
NOT with the Secured Party, John Henry Doe as the Secured Party, I hereby accept for value all of the above contracts. 6. On August 23, 2000, I, John Henry Doe filed UCC-1 Financing Statement #2000-236-0017 with the Secretary of State in the State of Washington which included the Security Agreement between the Debtor, JOHN HENRY DOE (the fictitious entity created by the state) and the

superior claimant of right, John Henry Doe. This act secured title to the artificial entity created by the state and secured to John Henry Doe all property attached to the artificial entity under the Henry Doe is Secured Party, Holder In Due Course and Creditor of JOHN HENRY DOE. 7.

On October 1, A.D. 2001, Secured Party was arrested by Phoenix Police Officers Metelski and Moore in the office of Donna Long, at Bell Lexus and was handcuffed and detained against his will. Secret Service Agents Jones and Mendoza arrived, and Agent Mendoza proceeded to interview the Secured Party. Secured Party immediately gave the above-mentioned parties testimony of the Secretary of State of the State of Washington that stated John Henry Doe is in fact the Secured Party and superior claimant to all matters involving the person charged.

Officer Metelski, Officer Moore and Secret Service Agents Jones and Mendoza knew or should have known that Secured Party is not in the UNITED STATES or any of their agent's jurisdiction. Officer Metelski threatened Secured Party with physical violence if Secured Party did not comply with their demands. 8. Secured Party was then asked for consent to search his house, which Secured Party shares with the owner of the house, Darren Starwynn. Secured Party initially declined said consent and then was advised by Agent Mendoza that if he did not give consent that they would get a search warrant and violate Mr. Starwynns privacy as well.

Only under this threat, duress, and coercion, did Secured Party agree to allow the agents to search only his own possessions in residence. Agents Jones and Mendoza then took Secured Party's two computer systems, along with several boxes of files and folders of legal documents, as well as checks and other documentation against Secured Party's will. 9. Secured Party was then incarcerated, arraigned before Virginia Mathis on 10/2/01, and was taken before Morton Sitver on 10/3/01 on a detainment hearing.

Secured Party conditionally accepted a public defender to represent the debtor under the condition that the interests of the Secured Party be put first before the interests of the court and the interests of the

"WHY AM I HERE?" THE VOLUNTARY TORTURE CALLED LIFE

UNITED STATES.

On 10/3/01 Secured Party was released on personal recognizance and was advised that the Debtor would be placed in third party custody of Darren Starwynn, with various restrictions and requirements of reporting. 10. Secured Party has accepted for value all offers to contract made by the above-named respondents with a qualified acceptance of Secured Party's additional terms and conditions. 11. Secured Party, on behalf of the artificial entity, JOHN HENRY DOE, hereby accepts the offer to contract with a qualified acceptance and herein states the new terms and conditions TERMS AND CONDITIONS OF CONTRACT 12. Each Respondent agrees to compensate Secured Party for the following: A. $10,000,000.00 for each arrest @1 arrest $10,000.000. B. $1,000,000.00 for each day of involuntary servitude @ 2 days $2,000,000. C. $1,000,000.00 for each court appearance, warrant or ticket @ 1 arrest warrant, and 2 court appearances $3,000,000. D. $100,000.00 per day that the warrant is in effect @ 8 days $800,000.

E. $100,000.00 per day that Secured Party's possessions are retained.@ 8 days $800,000. TOTAL as of October 9, 2021, $16,600,000. 13. Each Respondent has 10 days from the time of this notice to deliver funds to Secured Party. 14.

In the event each Respondent does not deliver $16,600,000. plus, daily fines to the Secured Party as agreed to in the contract, Respondent hereby agrees to be subject to involuntary bankruptcy proceedings on each party in their private and public capacity. 15. In the event Respondents withdraw their offer to contract entitled, CRIMINAL COMPLAINT, Case Number 01-0313M, within 10 days then this contract will become void and Secured Party will not proceed with the enforcement of the above terms and conditions. 16.

Notice is hereby given that Secured Party does not consent to Respondents judging him on any matter in any instance, at any location, at any time now or in the future. 17. Secured Party does not consent to incarceration, detainment, or punishment in any manner. 18. Secured Party hereby demands that all personal property that was taken from him without his free will consent from the Secret Service agents and Jones be returned to him immediately.

19. All terms and conditions of this agreement are approved by both parties. 20. If Respondent wishes to respond to this contract, it must be in form of Affidavit, point for point, with supporting documentation and mailed to Secured Party's agent, Notary Public William Smith at 41 S. Mesa Drive, #A, Mesa, Arizona 85210. So, it has been written, so let it be done. Signed and Sealed this 9 th Day of October 2021.

John Henry Doe, Secured Party Arizona)) ss ACKNOWLEDGEMENT Maricopa county) As a Notary Public for said County and State, I do hereby certify that on this _____ day of _____ A.D. 2022 the above mentioned appeared before me and executed the foregoing. Witness my hand and seal: _____ Notary Public

John Henry Doe
c/o 6880 S. Broadway
Tucson, AZ 85746
Secured Party Contract No 101101-JHD-US
To: UNITED STATES OF AMERICA Virginia Mathis, d.b.a. Magistrate Morton Sitver, d.b.a. Magistrate Dick Mesh, d.b.a. Assistant U.S. Attorney Roland Mendoza, d.b.a. Secret Service Agent Chuck Jones, d.b.a. Secret Service Agent Mr. Metelski, d.b.a Police Officer #5794 Mr. Moore, d.b.a. Police Officer #6803 Raymond Garcia, d.b.a. U.S. Pretrial Services Officer Donna Long, d.b.a. Finance Manager, BELL LEXUS
NOTICE OF DEFAULT AND ENTRY FOR NOTARIAL PROTEST Arizona)
 NOTICE TO AGENT IS NOTICE TO PRINCIPAL) ss NOTICE TO PRINCIPAL IS NOTICE TO AGENT

Pima County) Notice is hereby given, that the above-named respondents are in Default upon the contract, entitled Notice of

"WHY AM I HERE?" THE VOLUNTARY TORTURE CALLED LIFE

Acceptance to Contract presented to you on 7 November 2021, and therefore a Notarial Protest has been entered upon them. By the terms and conditions of the agreement contained in the Secured Party's affidavit, you were under obligation to timely and in good faith protest and make proper presentment with proof of your claim or interest. Your failure to do so is a dishonor and places you at Default. By your default, you are deemed to be under the new terms and conditions of our original contract #101101-JSC-US and have therefore waived all of your rights to your original presentment and terms. Any attempt to collect on your original presentment places you personally at risk for any damages incurred per this contract and may subject you to criminal sanctions and involuntary bankruptcy.

In order to exhaust all administrative remedies, it is required that a Notarial Protest be executed to obtain any evidence and/or testimony from Respondent that could aid in his defense. In the event no response is received by the Public Official (Notary), this will act as a witness against Respondent. Upon default, a CERTIFICATE OF DISHONOR will be issued which will act as a Default Judgment against Respondent who will then be taken into bankruptcy liquidation whereby all the equity in the name of Respondent will be disposed of in a foreign proceeding.
_____ 11/27/21 John
Henry Doe

July 13, 2022
John Henry Doe
c/o 6880 S. Broadway
Tucson, AZ 85746
William Smith, Notary Public
P. O. Box 86182
Tucson. Arizona 85754
Request for Notarial Protest

This is a request for you to enter a Notarial Protest to the attached list of Respondents at their respective addresses. I have included Contract #101101-JHD-US beginning with the first Notice mailed, with proof of service, dated August 19, 2021; The Second Notice dated September 6, 2001; and Default Judgment, dated October 7, 2022, Would you please follow up on this private negotiation under your notary seal and send along the accompanying acceptance of each of their acts and actions of which I have enclosed herewith. Thank you for your prompt attention in this matter. Sincerely, _____ John Henry Doe

NOTICE OF DISHONOR 1/3/2021
Roland Mendoza, d.b.a.
Secret Service Agent
105 E Speedway
Phoenix, Arizona 85684

Dear Mr. Mendoza,
I received a request by affidavit for a protest pursuant to Arizona Revised Statues at Sections 47- 3505(a), from John Henry Doe, who informed me you dishonored his presentments consisting of the NOTICE OF ACCEPTANCE TO CONTRACT and NOTICE OF DEFAULT dated 1/2/2021 and sent to you at 105 E Speedway NW, Washington D. C. 20220 on 1/2/2021, as evidenced by U.S. Postal Service CERTIFICATE OF MAILING verifying the contents of the Mail package.

In the event your dishonor through non-acceptance or non-performance was unintentional or due to reasonable neglect or impossibility, I am attaching a copy of the same presentment to this Notice. You may respond to me, and I will forward your response to John Henry Doe. Your response is expected no later than ten (10) days from the postmark of this Notice of Dishonor. Thank you for your prompt attention to this matter. Sincerely,
_____ Notary Public
(name) Address: _____
_____
_____ (Stamp) (Seal

"WHY AM I HERE?" THE VOLUNTARY TORTURE CALLED LIFE

NOTICE OF PROTEST AND OPPORTUNITY TO CURE

1/4/2021
Roland Mendoza, d.b.a. Secret Service Agent
105 E Speedway
Phoenix, Arizona 85684
Dear Mr. Mendoza,

On 1/3/2021, I sent you a Notice of Dishonor regarding the presentments of a NOTICE OF ACCEPTANCE TO CONTRACT and a NOTICE OF DEFAULT sent to you on 1/2/2021.

You failed to accept or perform after receiving these presentments from John Henry Doe, and you failed to accept or perform after receiving the same presentment from me. You are now in default and have stipulated to the terms of John Henry Doe's 1/2/2021 dated presentment through your dishonor. You have the right to cure this default and perform according to said terms within ten (10) days from the postmark of this Notice. Should you fail to cure the default, I will issue a CERTIFICATE OF DISHONOR pursuant to Arizona Revised Statutes 47- 3535. Thank you for your prompt attention to this matter. Sincerely,

_____ Notary Public

_____ Address of Notary (Stamp)
(Seal

CERTIFICATE OF DISHONOR

I, William Smith, am the notary to whom all communications are to be mailed regarding the contract entitled CONDITIONAL ACCEPTANCE and Contract #101101-JHD-US in response to Public Account # 01-0313M, herein "presentment." Pursuant to Arizona Revised Statutes 47-3505(b), and Uniform Commercial Code 3- 505(b) and 1-202, a Notice of Protest is hereby given with a Certificate of Dishonor regarding the following:

On September 22, 2001, I sent a Notice of Dishonor of John Henry

Doe's presentment to Respondent Roland Mendoza, d.b.a. Secret Service Agent, herein "Respondent," located at 1500 Pennsylvania Ave, Phoenix, Arizona 85684, who was given 10 days to respond. On October 22, 2001, Proof of Service shows a Notice of Protest and Opportunity to Cure was mailed to Respondent who was given 10 days to respond. As of this date, no response had been delivered to me, the designated receiver.

I interviewed John Henry Doe, whose affidavit is attached to this Notarial Protest. John Henry Doe has stated to me by affidavit that Petitioner has received no response to said Contract at any other mailing location. Based on the foregoing information, Respondent has dishonored John Henry Doe's presentments by non-acceptance and/or nonperformance and have therefore assented to the terms and conditions in said Contract.

_____
William Smith, Third Party Witness
Arizona)) ss ACKNOWLEDGEMENT Pima County)
As a Notary Public for said County and State, I do hereby certify that on this _____ day of _____ 2022 the above-mentioned appeared before me and executed the foregoing. Witness my hand and seal:
_____ Notary Public

INTERNATIONAL TRIBUNAL
Contract No 101101-JHD-US John Henry Doe
c/o 6880 S. Broadway
Tucson, AZ 85746
Affiant UNITED STATES OF AMERICA
Virginia Mathis, d.b.a. Magistrate
Morton Sitver, d.b.a. Magistrate
Dick Mesh, d.b.a. Assistant U.S. Attorney
Roland Mendoza, d.b.a. Secret Service Agent
Chuck Jones, d.b.a. Secret Service Agent
Mr. Metelski, d.b.a. Police Officer #5794
Mr. Moore, d.b.a. Police Officer #6803

"WHY AM I HERE?" THE VOLUNTARY TORTURE CALLED LIFE

Raymond Garcia, d.b.a. U.S. Pretrial Services Officer Donna Long, d.b.a. Finance Manager,
BELL LEXUS Respondents
NOTICE OF DEFAULT AND ENTRY FOR DEFAULT JUDGMENT
Arizona)
NOTICE TO AGENT IS NOTICE TO PRINCIPAL) ss NOTICE TO PRINCIPAL IS NOTICE TO AGENT

Pima county) I, John Henry Doe, herein "Affiant," having been duly sworn, declares that affidavit and response of the parties to the contract entitled, Notice of NOTICE OF ACCEPTANCE TO CONTRACT, hereinafter "Contract," are in full agreement regarding the following: 1.

Affiant is competent to state the matters included in his/her declaration, has knowledge of the facts, and declares that to the best of his/her knowledge, the statements made in his/her affidavit are true, correct, and not meant to mislead.
2. Affiant is the secured party, superior claimant, holder in due course, and principal creditor having a registered priority lien hold interest to all property held in the name of JOHN HENRY DOE organization # 520-80-6307, evidenced by UCC-1 Financing Statement #0565988 filed with the Secretary of State of the State of West Virginia.
3. On October 9, 2001, Affiant sent Respondents a Notice of Acceptance to Contract, each by registered mail, stating that he had exercised his power of acceptance and accepted all offers and actions made by Respondents with qualified terms as detailed in the Contract. 4. Affiant or the designated Notary has received no response to date, so Respondents are in Default and have therefore fully agreed to all of the terms and conditions of the contract 5. Respondents have fully assented to all the actions as described in the contract and therefore have confessed to the following felonies: aggravated kidnapping, terrorism, terroristic threats, trespassing, grand theft, impeding the commerce of the Secured Party, and involuntary servitude 6. All administrative remedies have been exhausted including the execution of a Notarial Protest to obtain any evidence and/or testimony from Respondent that could aid in his

defense.

No response has been received by the Public Official (Notary), and therefore this acquiescence will act as a witness against Respondent as evidenced by the attached CERTIFICATE OF DISHONOR which will act as a Default Judgment against Respondent who will then be taken into bankruptcy liquidation whereby all the equity in the name of Respondent will be disposed of in a foreign proceeding. It has been said, so it is done.

Dated this day of , 2022. _____ John Henry Doe, Affiant Arizona)) ss ACKNOWLEDGEMENT Pima county) As a Notary Public for said County and State, I do hereby certify that on this _____ day of _____2022 the above mentioned appeared before me and executed the foregoing.

Witness my hand and seal: _____
Notary Public

INTERNATIONAL TRIBUNAL
Contract No 101101-JHD-US
John Henry Doe
c/o 6880 S. Broadway
Tucson, AZ 85746
Affiant
UNITED STATES OF AMERICA
Virginia Mathis, d.b.a. Magistrate
Morton Sitver, d.b.a. Magistrate
Dick Mesh, d.b.a. Assistant U.S. Attorney
Roland Mendoza, d.b.a. Secret Service Agent
Chuck Jones, d.b.a. Secret Service Agent
Mr. Metelski, d.b.a Police Officer #5794

"WHY AM I HERE?" THE VOLUNTARY TORTURE CALLED LIFE

Mr. Moore, d.b.a. Police Officer #6803
Raymond Garcia, d.b.a. U.S. Pretrial Services Officer
Donna Long, d.b.a. Finance Manager, BELL LEXUS
Respondents

DEFAULT JUDGMENT - DECISION
having the same effect as Res Judicata and Stare Decisis
Arizona) NOTICE TO AGENT IS NOTICE TO PRINCIPAL
) ss NOTICE TO PRINCIPAL IS NOTICE TO AGENT
Pima county)
Based on the attached affidavit entitled "Notice of Default, RE: Private Contract entitled,
Notice of Acceptance to Contract, hereinafter "Contract", and the evidence attached to said affidavit, all of which has been presented to this panel,
JUDGMENT

IT IS THE JUDGMENT OF THIS PANEL that: 1. Petitioner is a Secured Party/Creditor over the property of JOHN HENRY DOE. 2. On three occasions Petitioner properly noticed Respondents, in their private capacity and in his public capacity as an agent for the UNITED STATES, of the Contract and Respondents' corresponding duty to respond, and that he properly commenced, continued, and concluded said Contract. 3. Respondent failed to answer or otherwise respond and therefore stands in
agreement with Petitioner.
4. Maxims of law in support of Petitioner's request to this panel are: An unrebutted affidavit is a judgment in commerce. In commerce, truth is sovereign. Truth is expressed in the form of an affidavit. A lien or claim can be satisfied only through rebuttal by counter-affidavit point-for-point, resolution by jury, or payment. The proof lies on him who affirms, not on him who denies.
The agreement of the parties makes the law of the contract.

A man's word is his bond. For truth to be established, it must be expressed. Silence is agreement. He who leaves the battlefield first loses by default. When a party has a duty to speak, his silence equates with fraud. An accessory follows the nature of his principal. A contract founded on a base or unlawful consideration, or against good morals, is null. Sacrifice is the measure of credibility. One who has not been damaged by, given to, lost on account of, or put at risk by another has no basis to make claims or charges against him.

DECISION

 THEREFORE, IT IS THE DECISION OF THIS PANEL that the parties have reached the following agreement: 1. Petitioner has exercised his power of acceptance and has accepted all offers made by Respondents to contract and therefore has undisputed ownership of the Contract.
 2. Respondent has agreed that John Henry Doe is in fact the Secured Party in this matter and has agreed to all of the terms and conditions set forth in the Contract.
3. Respondent, in their private and public capacities as agent for UNITED STATES, failed to state a claim upon which relief can be granted, against the property of JOHN HENRY DOE which is currently pledged as security to the Petitioner.
 4. Respondents have agreed to be subject to Involuntary Bankruptcy in their private and   public capacities.

 5. Respondent's claims are unenforceable ab initio. Done this day of , Two Thousand Two. L.S. (SEAL) disinterested third party, as private administrative judge L.S. (SEAL) disinterested third party, as private administrative judge L.S. (SEAL) disinterested third party, as private administrative judge

 Arizona)) ss ACKNOWLEDGEMENT Pima county) For the purpose of verification of signatures and for public notice,

"WHY AM I HERE?" THE VOLUNTARY TORTURE CALLED LIFE

I the undersigned Notary Public, being commissioned in the county noted above, do declare on the day of , 2021, the ones known to me to be, or who proved to me to be did execute this document before me. Notary Public My Commission expires.

EDIFICATION ON ENACTING THE CONTRACT

PURPOSE: The purpose of this procedure is to file and PERFECT the claim that you have against a debtor if they have dishonored you or your acceptance of their offer AND ENACT IT AS LAW. Before starting this process, one must have accepted all offers given to them, completed the administrative procedure, including the Notarial Protest, and now have a secured claim against the debtor. This procedure starts once you have a CERTIFICATE OF DISHONOR from the notary, which is as valid as a Default Judgment in a Superior Court. Bankrupt [L bank a bench + ruptus broken, literally one whose bench has been broken, the bench or table which a merchant or banker formerly used in the exchange having been broken on his bankruptcy.] The Consolidated WEBSTER'S Encyclopedic Dictionary 1939 edition. Bankrupt. Originally and strictly, a trader who secretes himself or does certain other acts tending to defraud his creditors. In a looser sense, an insolvent person.

In English law there were two characteristics which distinguished bankrupts from insolvents; the former must have been a trader and the object of the proceedings against, not by him. As used in American law, the distinction between a bankrupt and an insolvent is not generally regarded. Do you find it interesting that a "bankrupt" acts to "defraud his creditors?" Who fits the description of a trader and who is the creditor? Trader. One who makes it his business to buy merchandise, goods, or chattels to sell the same at a profit. One who sells goods substantially in the form in which they are bought; one who has not converted them into another form of property by his skill and labor.

The above definitions for "bankrupt" or "trader" could not be found in the Black's 6th edition and here is probably why. What institution do you know of "sells chattels substantially in the form in which they are bought?" Here is a hint – what does the bank do when they deposit your promissory note as an asset instead of a liability, then write a check off of the deposit to give to the seller of the property? First of all, bankers do not "buy" your credit with "money.

" After you GIVE your credit to them, they sell your credit to the seller of the property without "converting it into another form." It goes in and comes out the same – your credit! Or as they would say "money." Could this be considered of the bank to be an "act to defraud his creditor?" Bankrupt Law.

The leading distinction between a bankrupt law and an insolvent law, in the proper technical sense, consists in the character of the persons upon whom it is designed to operate, - the former contemplating as its objects bankrupt only, that is traders of a certain description; the latter insolvents in general, or persons unable to pay their debts. This has led to a marked separation between the two systems, in principle, and in practice, which in England has always been carefully maintained, although in the United States, it has of late been disregarded. The only substantial difference between a strictly bankrupt law and an insolvent law lies in the circumstance that the former affords relief upon the application of the creditor, and the latter upon the application of the debtor. Why do you think that the United States has failed to maintain the difference between bankruptcy and insolvency? I have a theory.
Since they call you "bankrupt," they are "assuming" that you are acting to defraud your creditors and therefore you are in dishonor before walking into the courtroom, and that you are considered a "criminal" by the mere fact that you filed your bankruptcy petition.

"WHY AM I HERE?" THE VOLUNTARY TORTURE CALLED LIFE

Following is a step-by-step set of instructions that will assist you in your taking the equity from your debtors.

Note, this is only an example that has been used to take property – one will still have to continue processes to KEEP IT! This procedure will, of course, be improved from time to time, but it is a good place to start.

Steps in Sequence 1. Notice of Substitution of Trustee 2. Notice of Bankruptcy Petition in a Foreign Proceeding 3. Collateral Found 4. Substitution of Trustee 5. UCC-1 assigned 6. Notice of Disposition 7. Disposition – Real Property 8. Disposition — Personal Property 9. Disposition — Vehicle 10. Confirmation of Receipt of Recordings and Filings .

1. Notice of Substitution of Trustee Information. An accusation exhibited against a person for some criminal offense, without an indictment. An accusation in the nature of an indictment, from which it differs only in being presented by a competent public officer on his oath of office, instead of a grand jury on their oath. The function of "information" is to inform the defendant of the nature of the charge made against him and the act constituting such charge so that he can prepare for trial and to prevent him from being tried again for the same offense. Black's Law Dictionary 6th edition Notary Public. A public officer whose function it is to administer oaths; to attest and certify, by his hand and official seal, certain classes of documents, in order to give them credit and authenticity in foreign jurisdictions; the noting of foreign drafts. Operating outside a bankruptcy proceeding is considered to be a crime according to 11 USCA. Any public official who is aware of an activity evidencing "unlawful operations" must report such activity to the "proper authorities" such as a US Attorney or the US Bankruptcy Trustee (Paul H. O'Neill).

An information is an accusation exhibited by a "public official." Since a notary is a "public official" and has firsthand knowledge of the crime by doing a Notarial Protest on that person, the notary must report such activities by "information." The information will be in the form of a "Certificate of Dishonor" issued by the notary that will include all previous notices and evidence of noticing that you have done since the beginning of the matter. The information will be written by you and will contain all details and specifics on such activities and must be in affidavit form in order for a criminal complaint to be initiated and the matter investigated by the US Attorney or any other agency with a duty to handle the matter.

ACCEPTANCE SUPRA PROTEST (Acceptance for Honor). The acceptance or payment of a bill of exchange, after it has been dishonored, by a person wishing to save the honor of the drawer or an endorser of the bill. Dictionary of Business, Oxford University Press, © Market House Books Ltd. 1996 Supra Protest. In mercantile law. A term applied to an acceptance of a bill by a third person, after a protest for nonacceptance by the drawee.

Black's 4th edition The second purpose for sending this document is to allow all of the notified parties an opportunity to "accept for honor" this matter. This package is to be sent to the Trustee of the UNITED STATES Bankruptcy, Paul H. O'Neill, so they can investigate why the debtor is unlawfully using your exemption and operating outside the US Bankruptcy. If this third party (who represents you, the Creditor) does not wish to save the honor of the debtor (a sub-corporation or the U.S.), you will put the debtor into Involuntary Bankruptcy.

You will give a ten (10) day notice to the "proper authorities" in order to accept for honor or handle the situation. If they fail to respond, their silence is their consent for you to administrate and conclude the involuntary bankruptcy in a foreign proceeding – your court, as a foreign nation.

This is pursuant to 11 U.S.C.A. 303(b)(4). At this point, the State, United States, or all of their agents cannot come back to you and bring up the fact that you "did not have the authority" to liquidate the debtor's property. The third purpose of this document is to give Paul H. O'Neill, the Chapter 11 – Re-organization Bankruptcy Trustee, a notice of substitution. Being a Chapter 11 trustee, he is not qualified to commence with any Chapter 7 – Liquidation proceedings so he must be "substituted" by another who is qualified to do so.

11 USCA 703 Successor trustee (a) If a trustee dies or resigns during a case, fails to qualify under section 322 of this title or is removed under section 324 of this title, creditors may elect, in the manner specified in section 702 of this title, a person to fill the vacancy in the office of trustee.

Since the proceeding is foreign, you would not need a "person to fill the vacancy in the office of trustee," you would elect or assign a "private" trustee yourself. Substitution. Putting in one person in the place of another; particularly, the act of a testator in naming a second devisee who is to take the bequest on failure of the original devisee after him. Black's 4th edition Testator. One who makes a will. Devisee. A person to whom lands or other real property are devised or given by will. In the case of a devise to an existing trust or trustee, or to a trustee on trust described by will, the trust or trustee is the devisee, and the beneficiaries are not devisees. Devise.

A testamentary disposition of land or realty by the last will and testament of the donor; to dispose of real or personal property by will. You may be asking "What does a will have to do with bankruptcy or trusts?" or "Who died leaving you in charge anyway?" One must remember that the debtor is a cestui que "trust" created by the State in order to keep an accounting of all the credit they are using in the creditor's name.

It is just an account with the debtor showing how much the state or United States is liable to the Creditor – the real Man or Woman. The debtor is actually an unincorporated corporate entity (pursuant to 15 USCA 44) that has been operating in the public venue as a sub-corporation of UNITED STATES in chapter 11 – Reorganization Bankruptcy. You as its creditor have allowed UNITED STATES and all its sub-corporations to operate in the bankruptcy on the condition that they must honor your method of payment per HJR 192.

As creditor, your method of payment is a "set-off," or a cancellation of mutual debt. Their debt being interest due for the use of your credit that is backed by your Property and your Production. However, once the debtor dishonors your method of payment, then you may choose to "liquidate" the debtor by disposing all the property in the debtor's name. In other words, "game over." When the debtor is liquidated, that corporate entity "dies." Now the trust becomes a will, and you have the superior claim to the property - unless the state wanted to bring their claim against the debtor! I would love to see them do that – they would have to admit to creating the strawman and consequently blow the lid off this whole scam. After ten days with no response received regarding this matter, you will file a petition with the US Bankruptcy Court.

2. Notice of Bankruptcy Petition in a Foreign Proceeding

11 USCA 303. Involuntary cases (b) An involuntary case against a person is commenced by the filing with the bankruptcy court of a petition under chapter 7 or 11 of this title – (4) by a foreign representative of the estate in a foreign proceeding concerning such person. An involuntary bankruptcy proceeding is commenced "by filing with the bankruptcy court of a petition under chapter 7..."

Chapter 7 is the "liquidation" of all the assets under the debtor's name. You prepare a NOTICE OF BANKRUPTCY PETITION IN A FOREIGN PROCEEDING. Then you will take it to the US bankruptcy clerk and pay them with a private check. The clerk will then stamp the original and keep it, then stamp your copy. It does not really matter what they do with this petition as it is serving as a "notice" to the court that a foreign proceeding will be commencing on the debtor.

2. Collateral Found and Listed There are a number of ways to find collateral. The fastest and easiest way is to call an online private detective, the website is www.americafind.com. The phone number is 713-271-9518. For $99 the detective searches 22 databases to find the address, social security number, real property, and other information of the Offeror. One can also go down to the Department of Motor Vehicles and tell them that you are going to place a lien on the Offeror's vehicle and that you need the Vehicle Identification Number (V.I.N. number) for the lien.

There are other detective services that are being tested and you can find your own methods by trial and error (one is Windsor Judicial Services). However, the main object of finding collateral is to find their social security number, address, real property, and vehicle. List all the collateral as a separate attachment. An example of the specific descriptions is provided with these instructions. The goal is to attach this list of collateral to a UCC-3 with the Offeror as the Debtor and claim it as your own property by filing it with the Secretary of State.

3. Substitution of Trustee This document substitutes Paul H. O'Neill, chapter 11 – Re-organization Trustee, with the Chapter 7 – Liquidation Trustee. The substitution trustee will be named, and an address given where to contact the trustee. This is a straightforward simple summary which will be attached to your UCC-1 when you file it along with the list of collateral. 5. UCC-1 assigned When you get the list of collateral done you are now ready to fill out a UCC-1. Fillin the Debtors information and your information as the Secure Party in the appropriate boxes.

The assignee, in section 5, who will receive the "Assignment for the benefit of Creditors" (you as the creditor), will be someone you know and trust. You will assign the collateral to the assignee, with the intent to dispose of it. The assignee is actually listed as an unincorporated foreign corporation, which is the straw-man corporation of the flesh and blood Man or Woman. This is a method of separating and using the strawman as an interface to the public venue, while remaining in the private side. This assignment is described more fully in Black's Dictionary, 6th Edition. Assignment for benefit of creditors:

A general assignment for benefit of creditors is transfer of all or substantially all of debtors property to another person in trust to collect any money owing to debtor, to sell property, to distribute the proceeds to his creditors and to return the surplus, if any, to debtor.

Under the Bankruptcy Act of 1898, such assignment was an "act of bankruptcy" if made within four months of bankruptcy. Now that the UCC-1 has been filled out, attach the NOTICE OF SUBSTITUTION OF TRUSTEE, SUBSTITUTION OF TRUSTEE, LIST OF COLLATERAL, CERTIFICATE OF DISHONOR and your NOTICE OF ACCEPTANCE TO CONTRACT with the DEFAULT. File these documents in the office of the secretary of the state, then when you get your copy back from them, send a copy to the Debtor

6. Notice of Disposition You must give the debtor at least a 10-day notification before you dispose of the property. Less is not considered a reasonable period of time. "Authenticated" in the definition below means notarized by a Notary Public and recorded at the County Recorder's Office of the county the property is in. UCC-9-611(b) [Notification of disposition required.] Except as otherwise provided in subsection (d), a secure party that disposes of collateral under Section 9- 610 shall send to the persons specified in subsection (c) a reasonable authenticated notice of disposition. UCC-9-612(b) [10-day period sufficient in a non-consumer transaction.] In a transaction other than a consumer transaction, a notification of disposition sent after default and 10 days or more before the earliest time of disposition set forth in the notification is sent within a reasonable time before the disposition. Make a copy of the Notice of Disposition before you record it and send it to the Debtor giving him at least 10 days (21 to 30 days is better) notice to allow him a last chance

remedy. Send this Notice by Certified Mail or any other proof of service.

7. Disposition – Real Property The assignee you assigned in your UCC-1 has the duty to dispose of all the collateral that you find under the debtors name or is associated with the debtor. Bill of Sale. In contracts, a written agreement, formerly limited to one under seal, by which one person assigns or transfers his right or interest in goods and personal chattels to another. Legal document which conveys title from seller to buyer When one transfers title using a bill of sale it is actually the only real title that exists on the private side.

This means that once you pay your property taxes with a closed checking account (substance) it takes the property out of the public side and a bill of sale is the only way it can be transferred privately. Any and every other form of title, i.e., deed of trust, warranty deed, etc. is a fiction and will transfer the private property back to the public side. The description of the real property should be in metes and bounds and township, section, and range if at all possible. Include the address and former property identification (tax I. D.) with a note that this is a fictional description.

8. Disposition — Personal Property All other personal property will be transferred with a bill of sale or a UCC-3. Personal property may include BAR Licenses, business licenses, tradenames, trademarks, copy-righted materials, bank accounts, computers, and any other equipment. 9. Disposition — Vehicle Vehicles will be transferred with a bill of sale and a transfer statement. Transfer statements are normally provided by the Department of Motor Vehicles. Request a transfer statement when you go to your DMV to register the vehicle and fill it out with the appropriate information. Present the transfer statement with the bill of

sale at the DMV window and you will receive your new registration and plates.

10. Confirmation of Receipt of Recordings and Filings This final step is to verify that all collateral is properly disposed of, and titles transferred to their new owners.

John Henry Doe
c/o 6880 S. Broadway Tucson, AZ 85746
Creditor Contract No 101101-JHD-US
UNITED STATES OF AMERICA Virginia Mathis, d.b.a. Magistrate Morton Sitver, d.b.a. Magistrate Dick Mesh, d.b.a. Assistant U.S. Attorney Roland Mendoza, d.b.a. Secret Service Agent Chuck Jones, d.b.a. Secret Service Agent Mr. Metelski, d.b.a Police Officer #5794 Mr. Moore, d.b.a. Police Officer #6803 Raymond Garcia, d.b.a. U.S. Pretrial Services Officer Donna Long, d.b.a. Finance Manager, BELL LEXUS
Debtors

NOTICE OF SUBSTITUTION OF TRUSTEE Arizona) NOTICE TO AGENT IS NOTICE TO PRINCIPAL) ss NOTICE TO PRINCIPAL IS NOTICE TO AGENT

Pima County) I, John Henry Doe, herein "Creditor," hereby state that I am competent to make the following statements, have knowledge of the facts stated herein, that they are true, correct, complete, and not meant to mislead and are presented in good faith: 1. The corporations, entitled UNITED STATES OF AMERICA, UNITED STATES, STATE OF ARIZONA, and above named, herein "Debtors," are Bankrupt and must operate pursuant to House Joint Resolution 192, June 5, 1933.

The above corporations have been using the credit of

Creditor since his Birth, January 22, A.D. 1958, without remuneration to Creditor; 2. Creditor has accepted all offers and returned them to the above-named Debtors thereby discharging all controversy and all charges. Debtors then claimed the charge still exists and therefore they are liable for the debt.

3. Creditor has accepted all offers and claims issued by Debtors and returned them to Debtors for proper processing. Debtors have failed to provide a remedy and is operating outside the UNITED STATES Bankruptcy – a criminal offense

4. Debtors are holding the discharging instrument but has failed to provide Creditor with a copy of the 1099 Original Issue Discount, therefore Debtors are TAX DELINQUENT since the claim is considered to be Creditor's exemption; 5. Creditor has timely noticed Debtors and has properly commenced and concluded a perfected security interest against Debtors.

The perfected security interest, Contract No. 101101-JHD-US herein "Contract," includes all notices including a Certificate of Dishonor, herein "Information," issued by a Public Official. TERMS AND CONDITIONS 6. Paul O'Neill, the Chapter 11 bankruptcy trustee for the UNITED STATES, is hereby given a final opportunity to execute an Acceptance for Honor if he wishes to save the honor of the Debtors by giving the Creditor a remedy. In the event Paul O'Neill does not wish to save the honor of Debtors, it will constitute Paul O'Neill's consent for substitution of trustee, whereas the Creditor will designate an assignee of his choice to liquidate all of Debtor's property in a foreign proceeding pursuant to Contract #101101- JHD-US; 7. The debtor has ten (10) days from the date of the postmark on this mailing to provide a remedy regarding this matter.

In the event the Debtor fails to provide a remedy, the Creditor will accept evidence of Debtors' dishonor as a refusal to volunteer into the bankruptcy remedy, whereby Debtors will be stripped of all immunity that UNITED STATES public policy may have otherwise afforded him. Upon dishonor, Debtors agree in the alternative to Involuntary Bankruptcy that will be initiated on Debtors in a private capacity; 8. In the event Debtors dishonors, Debtors agrees to provide a BANKRUPTCY FORM 5 in accordance with 11 U.S.C.A. 303 which is a property description list of all the property held in Debtors' names.

The creditor will take the equity place it for sale and proceed to liquidate the personal property for settlement of this account. Debtors additionally agree to be placed on a UCC-1 Financing Statement as DEBTOR attaching it to a Declaration of Involuntary Bankruptcy and a list of Debtors' collateral. Upon filing the UCC-1 form with the Secretary of State of Arizona, the liquidation and disposition of property will be executed immediately. Dated this _____ of _____, 2022.
_____ John Henry Doe Arizona)) ss ACKNOWLEDGEMENT Pima county) As a Notary Public for said County and State, I do hereby certify that on this _____day of_____ _____ the above mentioned appeared before me and executed the foregoing. Witness my hand and seal:
_____ Notary Public

ABOUT THE AUTHOR

Kahan Tazadaq Shah is an internationally successful Author, hip-hop Artist, Dating Coach, influencer, writer, and entrepreneur. He rose to from the bottom with an determine, champion warrior mindset to overcome the hand he was dealt. Order all of his books @ www.truedisciplesofchrist.org/shop
347-618-1783

Made in the USA
Columbia, SC
06 July 2024